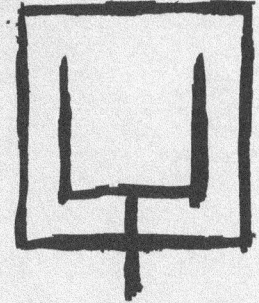

2016

Foreign Direct Investment
in Latin America and the Caribbean

UNITED NATIONS

ECLAC

Alicia Bárcena
Executive Secretary

Antonio Prado
Deputy Executive Secretary

Mario Cimoli
Chief, Division of Production, Productivity and Management

Ricardo Pérez
Chief, Publications and Web Services Division

The 2016 version of *Foreign Direct Investment in Latin America and the Caribbean* is the most recent edition of an annual series published by the Unit on Investment and Corporate Strategies of the Division of Production, Productivity and Management of the Economic Commission for Latin America and the Caribbean (ECLAC). This year's edition was prepared Álvaro Calderón, Olaf de Groot, Nicolo Gligo, Georgina Núñez, Wilson Peres and Cecilia Plottier, under the coordination of Giovanni Stumpo. The databases were prepared by Leandro Cabello.

Comments and suggestions were received from Mario Cimoli, Hugo Beteta, Daniel Titelman, Verónica Amarante, Martín Abeles, Juan Carlos Ramírez, Ricardo Sánchez, José Luis Lewinsohn, Jorge Mario Martínez, Ramón Padilla, Cecilia Vera, Olga Lucía Acosta and Felipe Correa.

Thanks are due to the government authorities and executives of companies consulted, for their inputs for the preparation of this document.

Any comments or suggestions concerning the contents of this document should be addressed to Giovanni Stumpo (giovanni.stumpo@cepal.org) and Álvaro Calderón (alvaro.calderon@cepal.org).

The boundaries and names shown on the maps included in this publication do not imply official acceptance or endorsement by the United Nations.

Explanatory notes

- Three dots (…) indicate that data are missing, are not available or are not separately reported.
- A dash (-) indicates that the amount is nil or negligible.
- A full stop (.) is used to indicate decimals.
- The word "dollars" refers to United States dollars unless otherwise specified.
- A slash (/) between years (e.g., 2013/2014) indicates a 12-month period falling between the two years.
- Individual figures and percentages in tables may not always add up to the corresponding total due to rounding.

United Nations publication

ISBN: 978-92-1-121914-2 (print)

ISBN: 978-92-1-057538-6 (pdf)

ISBN: 978-92-1-358035-6 (ePub)

Sales No.: E.16.II.G.4

LC/G.2680-P

Copyright © United Nations, 2016

All rights reserved

Printed at United Nations, Santiago

S.16-00662

This publication should be cited as: Economic Commission for Latin America and the Caribbean (ECLAC), *Foreign Direct Investment in Latin America and the Caribbean, 2016* (LC/G.2680-P), Santiago, 2016.

CONTENTS

Tables

Figures

Executive summary

Inflows of foreign direction investment (FDI) into Latin America and the Caribbean declined by 9.1% between 2014 and 2015, dropping to US$ 179.1 billion, the lowest level since 2010. This performance reflected the drop in investment in natural resource sectors, especially mining and hydrocarbons, and the slowing of economic growth, particularly in Brazil.

Inflows of foreign direction investment (FDI) into Latin America and the Caribbean declined by 9.1% between 2014 and 2015, dropping to US$ 179.1 billion.

A. Foreign direction investment in Latin America and the Caribbean

In 2015, global FDI flows jumped by 36%, reaching almost US$ 1.73 billion, the highest level since 2007. Most of this growth was accounted for by an intense wave of cross-border mergers and acquisitions mainly in developed countries, especially the United States. While FDI flows to developed countries grew by 90% in 2015, developing countries recorded an increase of only 5.3%, and economies in transition saw a sharp contraction of 55%. The increase in flows to developing countries is accounted for mainly by higher inflows to developing Asia (15%), while FDI flows to Africa and Latin America and the Caribbean fell by 31% and 9.1%, respectively.

In this scenario, the Latin American and Caribbean region is losing ground as a recipient of FDI, although FDI inflows to the region have stabilized at around 3.5% of GDP as a long-run average (see figure 1). This percentage varies from one country to another and is associated with the size of the respective economies: in larger economies, FDI has a smaller weight in output; for example, in 2015 FDI represented 2.5% of GDP in Mexico, but almost 10% in Chile and Panama.

The performance of FDI inflows was uneven among the countries of the region. Flows into Brazil dropped by 23%, although the country maintained its lead as the region's main recipient of FDI, accounting for 42% of total flows into the region. Brazil was followed, some distance behind, by Mexico, Chile, Colombia and Argentina. FDI into Mexico was up by 18% in 2015 to reach US$ 30.285 billion, one of the highest levels for seven years, with the largest investments going to the manufacturing sector, mainly the automotive industry, and telecommunications.

Falling prices for metals affected FDI inflows to Chile and Colombia, which were down by 8% and 26%, respectively in 2015. In Argentina FDI inflows stood at US$ 11.655 billion, representing a rise of 130% over the figure for 2014, although this great difference reflected the fact that the nationalization of 51% of YPF, which took place in 2012, was accounted for in 2014, thus representing a major divestment that year. Had this transaction not been included, the 2015 figure would have been similar to that of 2014. In Central America, FDI inflows rose by 6%, totalling US$ 11.808 billion. Within the subregion, Panama was the largest recipient, with 43% of the total, followed by Costa Rica (26%), Honduras (10%) and Guatemala (10%). FDI in the Caribbean was down by 17%, to US$ 5.975 billion.

The downward phase of the commodity price cycle affected the sectoral composition of FDI in 2015, with flows into the natural resources sectors losing ground. In Colombia, for example, FDI in the primary sectors came down from 51% of total flows in 2010-2014 to 31% in 2015. In Central America, the natural resource share of FDI dropped from 13% to 8% between the same two periods. On the other hand, the importance of the services sectors appears to be rising, especially telecommunications, renewable energies and retail trade. FDI in renewable energies is substantial in Chile and in Central America, where this category of investment seems to be driving a shift in the energy mix.

Figure 1
Latin America and the Caribbean: foreign direct investment inflows, 1990-2015
(Billions of dollars and percentages of GDP)

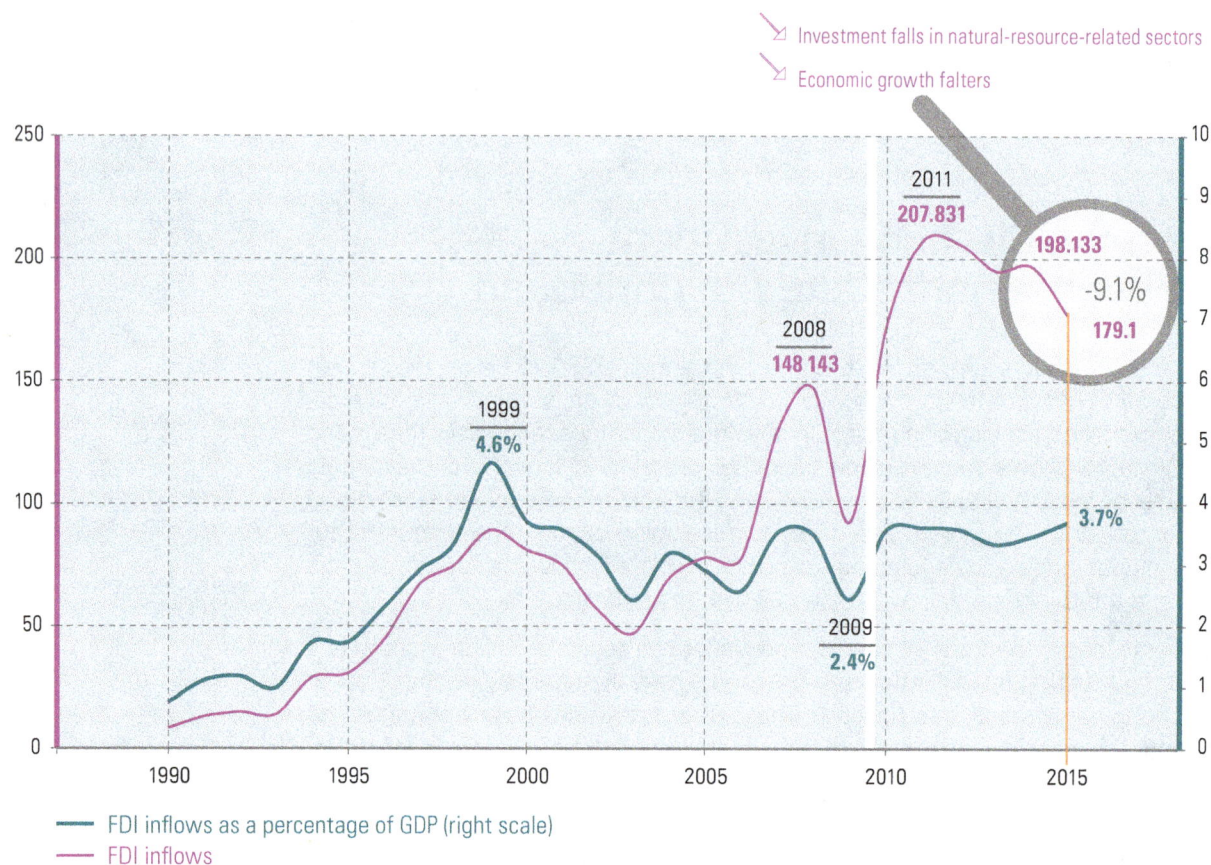

↘ Investment falls in natural-resource-related sectors
↘ Economic growth falters

2011
207.831

198.133
-9.1%
179.1

2008
148 143

1999
4.6%

3.7%

2009
2.4%

— FDI inflows as a percentage of GDP (right scale)
— FDI inflows

Source: Economic Commission for Latin America and the Caribbean (ECLAC), on the basis of official figures as of 27 May 2016.
Note: The FDI figures do not include flows into the main financial centres of the Caribbean. FDI figures indicate inflows of foreign direct investment, minus divestment (repatriation of capital) by foreign investors. These figures differ from those set out in the 2015 edition of the *Economic Survey of Latin America and the Caribbean* and the *Preliminary Overview of the Economies of Latin America and the Caribbean,* because they show the net balance of foreign investment, that is, direct investment in the reporting economy (FDI) minus outward FDI. Flows as a percentage of GDP exclude the Bolivarian Republic of Venezuela. From 2010 on, the figures for Brazil include reinvested earnings; as a result, these figures are not directly comparable with those from before 2010. This is represented by a white line on the graph.

In 2015, the United States again became the main source of FDI flows into the region. For those flows that have a clearly identified origin, the United States accounts for 25.9%, followed by the Netherlands (15.9%) and Spain (11.8%). The significance of the Netherlands in the statistics does not necessarily reflect a presence by Dutch companies in Latin American economies, since many transnational firms establish subsidiaries in the Netherlands, attracted by its tax advantages, and then go on to invest in third countries. In Mexico, as in many Central American and Caribbean countries, the United States is by far the largest source of FDI inflows, accounting for 52%. In the case of Brazil, 23% of flows come from the Netherlands, although the ultimate origin of many of these investments is unknown.

Outward FDI flows from Latin American and Caribbean countries declined substantially to US$ 47.362 billion, down by 15% from the previous year, as the expansion undertaken by the trans-Latin firms between 2007 and 2012 slowed. By stock of investment abroad, Brazil and Mexico are the countries that invest the most beyond their borders. In 2015, however, direct investment abroad by Brazilian firms fell more sharply than investments by other countries, and Chile became the largest source of direct investment within the region, reflecting the rapid growth of the Chilean trans-Latins. Chilean firms' direct investment abroad rose by 22% in 2015, to US$ 15.794 billion. Outward direct investment by Mexican firms climbed sharply, to US$ 12.126 billion, representing a jump of 62% from the previous year. Colombian firms have shown a noteworthy capacity to exploit external markets in recent years, with a growing presence in Central America.

In 2015 the stock of FDI in the region shrank, and FDI earnings dropped yet more sharply. As a percentage of the FDI stock, profits reached their most recent peak in 2011, and then began to drop. In 2015, they stood at 5.0%, the lowest level in 13 years. By country, the steepest falls in returns occurred in the mining economies (Chile, Colombia, Peru and the Plurinational State of Bolivia), although these downtrend is not confined to these. In conditions of shrinking FDI earnings, transnational firms have at least two options: to reinvest a smaller proportion of profits or to remit fewer profits. In Latin America and the Caribbean, the reinvestment rate is declining, and this can be a negative factor for the host economies.

In nominal terms, FDI inflows to Latin America and the Caribbean are showing signs of stagnation. In 2015, FDI inflows posted no significant growth for the fourth year running. FDI has been crucial in Latin America and the Caribbean to support the region's model of integration into the international economy, with investments in natural resources, exports and modern services. It has had, however, a moderate and somewhat limited impact in terms of technology content, innovation and research and development. By adopting strategies to combine FDI attraction with policies to drive economic modernization and production diversification, the region would not only encourage transnational firms to establish in sectors with greater prospects for development and capacity-building, but would also facilitate these firms' integration into local economies. It would also enhance economic growth of a type that fosters social inclusion and environmental sustainability. When FDI attraction and development policies are coordinated with each other, FDI can contribute to achieving the strategies the country has defined. In this way, policymaking aims not only to attract FDI, but to create the conditions to absorb its benefits.

In the current global conditions, FDI flows into Latin America and the Caribbean will likely shrink again in 2016. The Economic Commission for Latin America and the Caribbean (ECLAC) has estimated a 0.6% contraction in output, which will continue to dampen investment in supplying domestic demand at the regional level. The South American economies will be the hardest hit, owing to their specialization in primary goods, especially oil and minerals, and their strong trade integration with China. In fact, signs of a slowdown in China and low raw material prices have already paralysed investment in areas relating to natural resources exports. Conversely, prospects are brighter for Mexico and Central America, with average GDP growth estimated at 2.6% in 2016, just below the previous year's rate. The upturn in the United States economy has led to new investment announcements, particularly in export manufacturing. Overall, therefore, ECLAC estimates that FDI flows into the region could drop by as much as 8% in 2016.

ECLAC estimates that FDI flows into the region could drop by as much as 8% in 2016.

B. Foreign investment in metal mining

The metal mining sector presents certain characteristics that are key to understanding its dynamics and its close relationship with FDI. On the one hand, it is highly concentrated, both in terms of international demand and production; on the other, the specific nature of the investment and production process, notably long project durations, extremely high capital requirements and high risk, mean that the vast majority of leading firms are transnational.

In the past 15 years, global markets for the main metallic minerals have experienced profound changes, with huge swings in demand, prices and output. International demand has seen strong shifts, with China's rise to prominence a key factor.

China's exceptional growth and its industrialization strategy caused a substantial increase in its consumption of metallic minerals. Between the mid-2000s and 2015, China transformed itself into the world's leading importer of iron, copper concentrates and bauxite, overtaking countries that traditionally had carried most weight in these markets, such as Germany, Japan and the United States. China's growth and industrialization strategy had further consequences. Not only did the country import metallic minerals to supply its domestic market, but these imports also allowed it to satisfy international demand for metals and metal manufactures.

Changes in demand, together with China's new position in the world economy, created a cycle of extremely high prices, before the onset of a downtrend that commenced in 2012 and which continues today. This marked trend shift is chiefly due to slower growth in China and weak demand from developed countries, combined with increased global production capacity for minerals and mineral products.

Rising prices fuelled a steady increase in global metallic mineral production from 2003 onwards. The countries of Latin America and the Caribbean played an important role in this process, especially Brazil in iron ore production; Chile and Peru in copper; the Bolivarian Republic of Venezuela, Brazil, Guyana, Jamaica and Suriname in bauxite, and Mexico and Peru in gold and silver. A high percentage of the world's metallic mineral reserves is concentrated in Latin America and the Caribbean: 66% of its lithium, 47% of its copper, 45% of its silver, 25% of its tin, 23% of its bauxite, 23% of its nickel and 14% of its iron, among others.

Increased production coincided with a process of strong FDI inflows to metal mining in the region and the consolidation of some leading trans-Latin corporations such as Brazil's Vale, Chile's National Copper Corporation (CODELCO) and Grupo México.

The largest mergers and acquisitions in the history of the global metal mining sector took place between 2000 and 2015. In value terms, approximately 16% of these transactions targeted Latin American and Caribbean firms, amounting to US$ 78.0 billion during the period. Target companies in eight countries accounted for 92% of this total, with Brazil, Chile, Peru and Mexico clearly leading destinations for mergers and acquisitions.

Acquiring firms were more sparsely concentrated, with the main purchasers, in value terms, originating in Canada, China, the United Kingdom and the United States, while Australia also figured among the countries with the largest number of transactions. China was remarkable for the completion of a large transaction: in 2014, MMG Ltd and partners acquired the Las Bambas copper deposit from Switzerland's Glencore for US$ 7.005 billion. Another important operation took place in 2011, when Norway's Norsk Hydro purchased a number of bauxite extraction and alumina production assets from Brazil's Vale for US$ 5.27 billion.

A new scenario of heightened uncertainty took shape with the onset of the downward phase of the commodity price cycle in 2012. In a sector in which the minimum required rates of return have topped 15%, the average return on capital employed among the world's 40 leading mining companies fell to 9% in 2014, a 10-year low. This decline in profitability, both in the world and in Latin America, had repercussions for investment announcements in the metal mining sector, which in 2015 marked a low for the period 2003-2015. Just eight projects were announced, amounting to US$ 674 million or 1.1% of total announced investment for the region, compared with 12.2% on average for the period.

> A new scenario of heightened uncertainty took shape with the onset of the downward phase of the commodity price cycle in 2012.

In this new scenario, Latin American and Caribbean countries have fallen behind somewhat in the mining value chain. During the mining boom, Chinese companies stepped up mineral extraction and demanded more minerals on the international market, as well as investing in refining and smelting and thus moving up the mining and metallurgy value chain. By contrast, refining and smelting capacity in Latin American and Caribbean countries did not keep pace with rising mineral production, which helped create a pattern of growth in exports of mined minerals rather than refined metals.

The exploitation of natural resources for inclusive economic development entails huge challenges: from the essential requirement that the sector's development is compatible with safeguarding the environment and the rights of peoples and communities, and the creation of production linkages and synergies with other sectors, to fiscal and monetary issues and infrastructure investment.

The favourable price cycle benefited the expansion of mining in Latin American and Caribbean countries, which in turn improved the availability of resources. However, a quantitative analysis of linkages shows that mining is generally a sector with low spillovers in terms of demand for other economic activities. Consequently, the main effects of mining in the region are apparent in the greater availability of fiscal revenues, and in exports. However, a qualitative overview of metal mining suppliers in the region revealed that some domestic firms have found niches in which to export to third markets, which suggests that these enterprises have attained a greater degree of competitiveness. If the expansion of metal mining in the region is conducive to the growth of highly productive and competitive domestic firms, then it would also be contributing to greater economic diversification and would be an example of how FDI can drive local business development.

Such impacts are of limited magnitude in the countries of the region, but progress has been achieved in some areas. Chile is emerging as the Latin America country that has made most progress in developing sophisticated mining suppliers with the capability to export, albeit only a fraction of them do so.

In the current context, company strategies aim to reduce costs and minimize environmental impacts, and technological progress offers solutions to these problems. The energy and water requirements of mining mean that technological development is fundamental for the growth of the sector, which needs cheaper, more sustainable sources of energy and water. Attracting FDI to provide solutions in these areas may create an opportunity for growth that contributes to the creation of intangible capital.

The benefits of foreign direct investment in the mining industry are far from being automatically accrued. International market dynamics dictate that investment is attracted to locations that combine the availability of mineral resources with stable regulatory conditions for their exploitation and an adequate infrastructure for exports. The development of externalities, from the basic exploitation of natural resources to greater complexity and diversification, will depend to a large extent on local capacity (in terms of institutions, technology and access to energy, human capital and financing, among others). In this context, a policy space is emerging for countries to promote the accumulation of local capacities linked to the development of a sustainable mining sector that drives production diversification.

The region enjoys comparative advantages in the exploitation of metallic minerals, and most countries have directly or indirectly encouraged FDI in the sector. How to keep step with the expansion of mining activity through policies in support of the production sector, while securing the maximum possible benefit for inclusive and sustainable development, remains a major challenge for Latin American and Caribbean countries.

C. Foreign direct investment as a driver of intangible capital accumulation

The positive effects of foreign direct investment can foster development in recipient economies; in particular, they can supplement national saving through new capital contributions and stimulate transfers of technology and improve management systems to enable productive modernization. These effects are not automatic, however, and the results obtained may not meet expectations.

Foreign direct investment flows have a variety of destinations that do not always entail the creation of new fixed capital; in other words, they do not translate directly into the formation of physical capital in the receiving country. The dynamic of FDI flows and the trend of fixed capital investment follow different but related paths. One simple estimate is that each additional dollar of FDI increases gross fixed capital formation by 34 cents. This means that around one third of FDI flows actually contribute to fixed capital formation in the receiving economy.

Although FDI makes only a small contribution to gross fixed capital formation, transnational enterprises can play an important role in economic development by helping to transform economies through the creation of intangible capital. The positive effects of FDI can be transmitted through technology transfer and skill development, while also encouraging local firms to enter value chains that increase their exposure to the international economy.

The amount of FDI flows is a limited measurement of its potential benefit in the receiving country. The benefits cannot be taken for granted through spillover effects, nor do aggregate statistics adequately reflect certain characteristics of FDI.

> There is consensus on the potential benefits of FDI, but harnessing them is not an automatic process.

This scenario again highlights the need to focus on the quality of FDI, particularly its capacity to contribute to the formation of intangible capital in the local economy. There is consensus on the potential benefits of FDI, but harnessing them is not an automatic process. The transfer and absorption of FDI benefits depends on the characteristics of the investment and the specific features of the recipient country.

The possibility of harnessing these benefits depends on the skill level of the labour force, the competitiveness of the local industry and its capacity to supply foreign firms, and the existence of an associated cluster. Host countries must meet the challenge of capturing these benefits because, in the absence of the necessary conditions, foreign firms could become enclaves within those countries, and only a fraction of their benefits will be transferred to local economies.

Overview of foreign direct investment in Latin America and the Caribbean

A. FDI in the global economy is growing despite a recessionary bias

In a context of low growth and great uncertainty in the world economy, foreign direct investment (FDI) has been remarkably robust. In 2015, global flows of FDI jumped by 36%, reaching an estimated US$ 1.73 trillion, the highest level since 2007 (UNCTAD, 2016a) (see figure I.1). Underlying this outcome was an intense wave of mergers and acquisitions, especially cross-border transactions, and heavily focused on developed countries, especially the United States (Deloitte, 2015). In 2015, cross-border operations represented 31% of all mergers and acquisitions worldwide (JP Morgan, 2016) (see figure I.2).

Foreign direct investment is up worldwide, driven by the developed economies

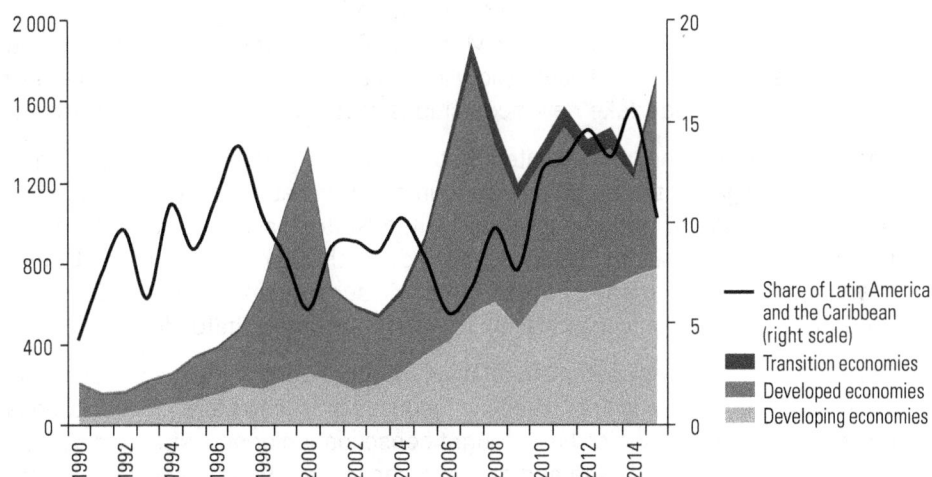

Figure I.1
Global direct foreign investment flows by groups of economies, and proportion corresponding to Latin America and the Caribbean, 1990-2015
(Billions of dollars and percentages)

- Share of Latin America and the Caribbean (right scale)
- Transition economies
- Developed economies
- Developing economies

Source: Economic Commission for Latin America and the Caribbean (ECLAC), on the basis of United Nations Conference on Trade and Development (UNCTAD), *Global Investment Trends Monitor*, No. 22, Geneva, January 2016; and *World Investment Report, 2015* (UNCTAD/WIR/2015), Geneva, 2015.

The value of global cross-border mergers and acquisitions has doubled in two years

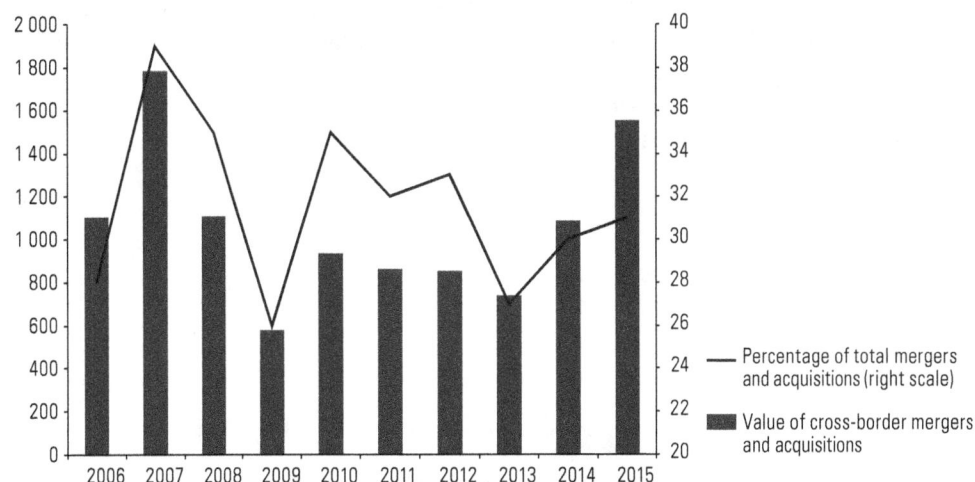

Figure I.2
Global cross-border mergers and acquisitions, 2006-2015
(Billions of dollars and percentages)

- Percentage of total mergers and acquisitions (right scale)
- Value of cross-border mergers and acquisitions

Source: Economic Commission for Latin America and the Caribbean (ECLAC), on the basis of JP Morgan, *2016 M&A Global Outlook. Higher deal count drives continued strength*, New York, February 2016 [online] https://www.jpmorgan.com/country/US/EN/insights/maglobaloutlook.

This strong growth was also determined by the levels of the previous year, which reflected a large divestment (in the amount of US$ 130 billion) in the United States.[1] Excluding that transaction, FDI growth in 2015 would drop to 21%, which is still high but less spectacular.

At the same time, new announcements of greenfield investment projects suggested an upturn in this sector, although to a much lesser extent than in mergers and acquisitions.[2] In 2015, there was an overall increase of 9% in the value of announced FDI projects, to US$ 713 billion (fDi Intelligence, 2016). As with mergers and acquisitions, the rise in project announcements in developed countries offset a downtrend in investments by transnational firms in developing economies.

The new cycle of cross-border mergers and acquisitions has resulted from a combination of various factors that have given businesses the confidence needed to seek acquisitions that will allow them to cope with slow organic growth and limited improvements in operating margins. Those factors include:

> New announcements of greenfield investment projects suggested an upturn in this sector, although to a much lesser extent than in mergers and acquisitions.

- A high level of private-sector liquidity, estimated at more than US$ 6 trillion in cash reserves available globally (JP Morgan, 2016),[3] combined with favourable credit access conditions marked by low interest rates, has placed firms in a very good position to undertake new acquisitions that will help them create value.

- The sustained recovery of the United States economy and the sharp depreciation of the dollar against the euro have encouraged purchases on both sides of the Atlantic. As well, FDI inflows into the United States have also been driven by mergers and acquisitions designed to reduce the tax obligations of United States firms. In fact, many of these firms will subsequently relocate abroad in order to avoid the high corporate tax rates in the United States (OECD, 2016).

- Certain sectoral dynamics that are relatively independent of the macroeconomic cycle, especially on the part of "defensive" industries,[4] such as telecommunications and pharmaceuticals, which have sought consolidation or new strategic assets. In the first sector, the strong and growing consolidation of different segments has continued in an industry that is converging rapidly towards common platforms. The pharmaceuticals industry, in addition to consolidation, is also attempting to replace patents that are beginning to expire and is placing new faith in segments such as biotechnology (JP Morgan, 2015). These dynamics have offset the slowdown in certain more cyclical sectors, such as those related to commodities, which have been affected by the sharp fall in prices.

Recently, developing economies have seen their importance as FDI recipients increase, and in 2014 they accounted for 55% of worldwide flows (UNCTAD, 2015). However, the sharp increase in FDI flows to developed countries in 2015 has shifted the regional distribution of these capital flows. At present, developed countries once again represent more than half of worldwide FDI flows (see table I.1).

---

[1] In that transaction, United States-based Verizon Communications repurchased the 45% share in Verizon Wireless previously held by the United Kingdom's Vodafone, thus giving itself full control of the mobile telephone operator (ECLAC, 2015a).
[2] The figures on newly announced investment projects are not strictly comparable with statistics on FDI inflows. The first reveal only an intention to invest, one that may materialize over a fairly long period of time extending to several years. The second, by contrast, represent actual inflows of foreign currency to finance transnational business activities during the course of a year, in a specific host economy.
[3] Liquidity is calculated as the aggregate cash balance (cash and short-term investments) of firms listed on the stock exchange with a market capitalization of more than US$ 1 billion worldwide.
[4] Generally speaking, it is the cyclical industries that drive the rally in mergers and acquisitions, as they rise and fall in tandem with macroeconomic trends. On the other hand, the defensive sectors, such as public services, have a low correlation with economic cycles.

Table I.1
Global foreign direct investment inflows, rates of change and distribution by region, 2006-2015
(Billions of dollars and percentages)

FDI inflows to developing economies are still growing, but their share in the world total declined in 2015

Regions	Amount (billions of dollars)						Variation (percentages)						Distribution by region (percentages of global total)					
	2006-2010	2011	2012	2013	2014	2015	2006-2010	2011	2012	2013	2014	2015	2006-2010	2011	2012	2013	2014	2015
Global total	1 521	1 610	1 432	1 479	1 274	1 727	12	14	-10	4	-14	36	100	100	100	100	100	100
Developed economies	860	828	679	697	493	936	10	23	-18	3	-29	90	57	51	47	47	39	54
European Union	475	444	364	332	254	426	5	24	-18	-9	-24	68	31	28	25	22	20	25
North America	278	269	209	301	146	429	26	19	-22	44	-52	194	18	17	15	20	11	25
Transition economies	82	97	85	100	49	22	27	30	-13	17	-51	-55	5	6	6	7	4	1
Developing economies	579	685	668	682	732	769	15	3	0	4	8	5	38	43	47	46	57	45
Latin America and the Caribbean	173	208	207	196	198	179	26	20	-1	-5	0	-9	11	13	14	13	16	10
Africa	48	48	56	54	55	38	11	8	18	-4	2	-31	3	3	4	4	4	2
Developing Asia	354	425	401	428	475	548	14	6	-6	7	11	15	23	26	28	29	37	32

Source: Economic Commission for Latin America and the Caribbean (ECLAC), on the basis of United Nations Conference on Trade and Development (UNCTAD), *Global Investment Trends Monitor*, No. 22, Geneva, 2015; *World Investment Report, 2015* (UNCTAD/WIR/2015), Geneva, 2015; and official figures and estimates as of 27 May 2016.

While FDI flows to developed countries grew by 90% in 2015, developing countries recorded an increase of only 5.3%, and economies in transition saw a sharp contraction of 55% (see figure I.1 and table I.1). Between 2013 and 2015, this last group of countries experienced a sustained decline in its share of global FDI flows, as a result of political and economic uncertainty in Ukraine and the Russian Federation, as well as the fall in oil and natural gas prices, especially in the Russian Federation, among other factors (UNCTAD, 2016b).

By region, the developing countries of Asia have received the greatest FDI flows, ahead of the European Union and North America. In 2015, developing Asia recorded a 15% increase, setting a new historic record, led by Hong Kong Special Administrative Region (SAR) of China, China, Singapore and India. However, in Hong Kong SAR an important part of this growth was accounted for by the merger and restructuring of Cheung Kong Holdings and Hutchison Whampoa into CK Hutchison Holdings, which did not represent any investment in new production capacity. By contrast, Africa recorded the greatest decline —31%— among developing regions in 2015, concentrated primarily in the sub-Saharan region. Lastly, Latin America and the Caribbean recorded the worst performance since 2010, with FDI inflows falling by 9% in 2015. In both regions, the end of the commodities supercycle had an especially heavy impact on FDI inflows.

Despite these shifts and the effects of a few large-scale transactions, developing countries still accounted for one half of the leading recipients of FDI (see figure I.3). In 2015, the United States and the Hong Kong SAR were the main recipients. However, the increase in FDI inflows into both economies was due, at least in part, to corporate restructurings that involved great volumes of resources on the financial account of the balance of payments, but little movement in terms of real resources.

Figure I.3
Ten leading host economies for foreign direct investment, 2013-2015
(Billions of dollars)

The United States has regained its position as the largest destination of FDI

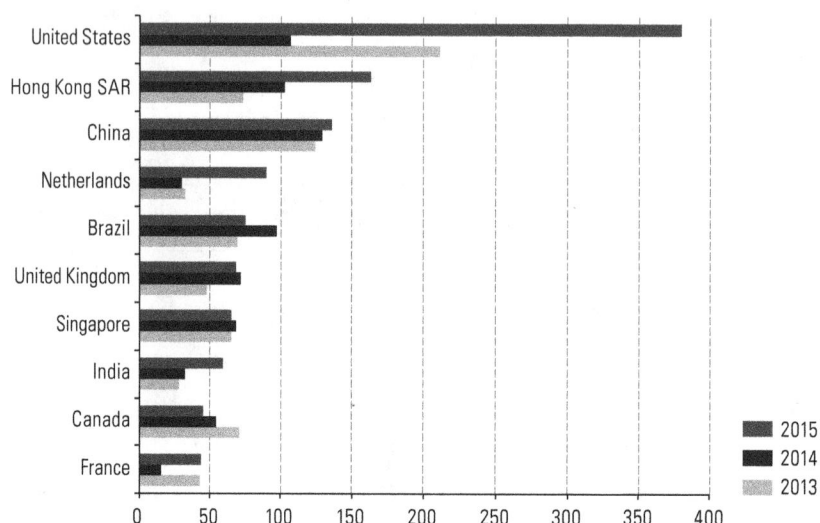

Source: Economic Commission for Latin America and the Caribbean (ECLAC), on the basis of United Nations Conference on Trade and Development (UNCTAD), *Global Investment Trends Monitor*, No. 22, Geneva, 2015; *World Investment Report, 2015* (UNCTAD/WIR/2015), Geneva, 2015; and official figures and estimates as of 27 May 2016.

A good proxy for analysing the dynamics of production investment is found in the announcements of new projects sponsored by foreign investors. In 2015, as noted above, these investments were still showing signs of recovery, led by Asia and the Pacific region, which accounted for 45% of the total amount announced worldwide. Although the United States and the United Kingdom still appear as major recipients of these resources, a number of developing countries are positioning themselves as important destinations for foreign direct investment. In 2015, for the first time, India outpaced China, placing itself as the principal destination for new investment announcements, especially in renewable energy and in coal, oil and natural gas. By contrast, Latin America and the Caribbean, along with Africa, recorded a sharp decline in new investment announcements, reflecting in particular the fall in commodity prices (fDi Intelligence, 2016).

B.   The Latin American and Caribbean region has lost ground

1.   In 2015, foreign direct investment fell by 9.1%

In 2015, most countries in Latin America and the Caribbean switched to the methodology set forth in the sixth edition of the *Balance of Payments and International Investment Position Manual* of the International Monetary Fund (IMF) for preparing their foreign direct investment statistics. This process has meant some significant changes in the figures for previous years, especially in Brazil (see annex I.A1).

Inflows of FDI into Latin America and the Caribbean declined by 9.1% between 2014 and 2015, dropping to around US$ 179.1 billion, the lowest level since 2010.

This performance reflected the drop in investment in natural resource sectors and a slowing of economic growth, particularly in Brazil. Between 2014 and 2015, Brazil, Latin America's largest economy, accounted for a major portion of that drop —23%, equivalent to US$ 21.820 billion. Excluding Brazil, FDI in the region showed a slight increase of 2.8% in nominal terms (see figure I.4).

Figure I.4
Latin America and the Caribbean: foreign direct investment inflows, 1990-2015
(Billions of dollars and percentages of GDP)

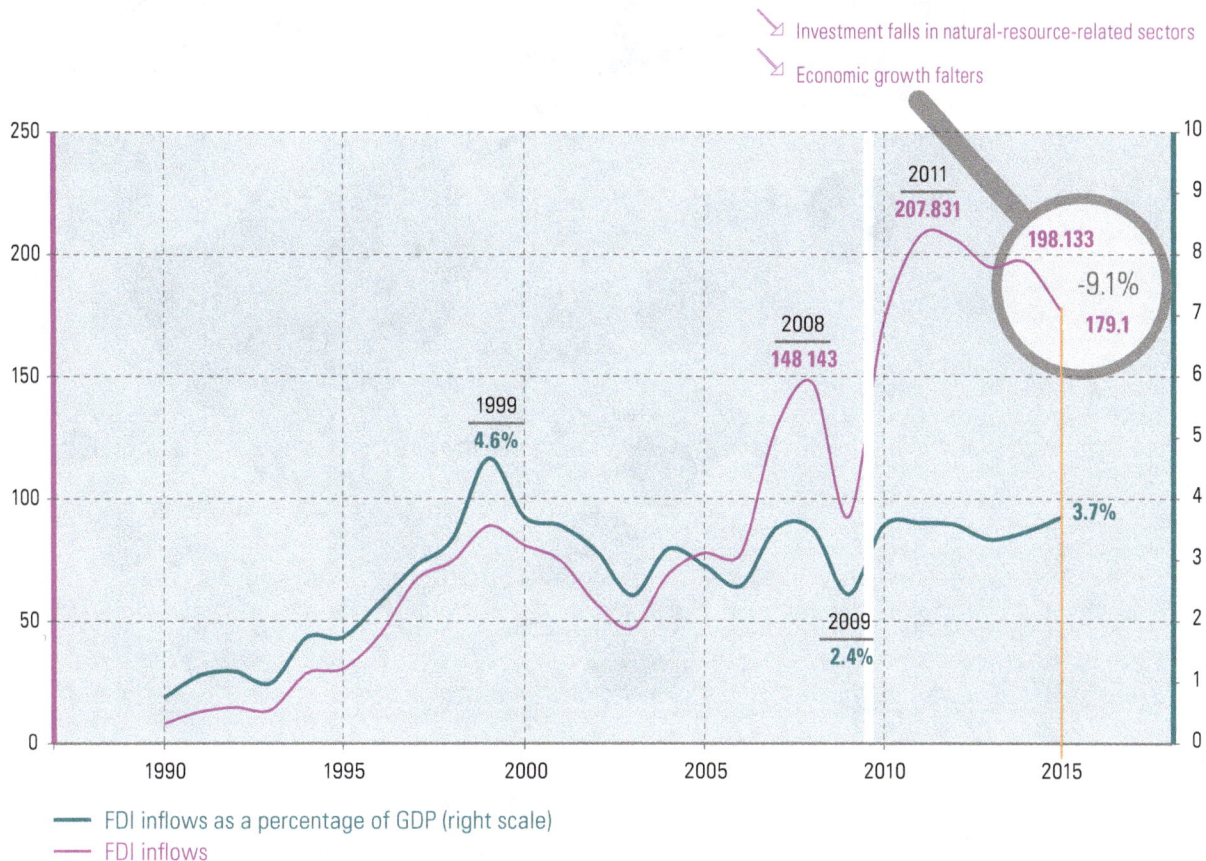

In the last five years, FDI inflows have stabilized at between 3.5% and 3.7% of GDP in the region

Investment falls in natural-resource-related sectors

Economic growth falters

2011
207.831

198.133
-9.1%
179.1

2008
148 143

1999
4.6%

3.7%

2009
2.4%

— FDI inflows as a percentage of GDP (right scale)
— FDI inflows

Source: Economic Commission for Latin America and the Caribbean (ECLAC), on the basis of official figures as of 27 May 2016.
Note: The FDI figures do not include flows into the main financial centres of the Caribbean. FDI figures indicate inflows of foreign direct investment, minus divestment (repatriation of capital) by foreign investors. These figures differ from those set out in the 2015 edition of the *Economic Survey of Latin America and the Caribbean* and the *Preliminary Overview of the Economies of Latin America and the Caribbean,* because they show the net balance of foreign investment, that is, direct investment in the reporting economy (FDI) minus outward FDI. Flows as a percentage of GDP exclude the Bolivarian Republic of Venezuela. From 2010 on, the figures for Brazil include reinvested earnings; as a result, these figures are not directly comparable with those from before 2010. This is represented by a white line on the graph.

In 2015, despite the decline in these inflows, Brazil maintained its lead as the region's main recipient of foreign direct investment. It was followed, some distance behind, by Mexico, Chile, Colombia and Argentina (see map I.1). The greatest increase in FDI inflows in that year was recorded by the Bolivarian Republic of Venezuela, up by 153% in the first three calendar quarters. However, this outcome must be viewed in perspective: first, because it compares with the extremely low level of FDI inflows in 2014, and second because the US$ 1.383 billion in the first three quarters of 2015 amounts to less than half of the average long-term amount. Among the countries receiving the greatest FDI inflows, Argentina recorded the strongest growth, at 130%,[5]

---

[5] This performance is tempered by the fact that the 2012 nationalization of 51% of YPF showed up in Argentina's external accounts only in 2014. Without the impact of that transaction, FDI inflows in 2015 would have been very similar to those for 2014.

followed by Mexico at 18%. On the other hand, Chile, Colombia and Peru saw inflows fall by between 8% and 26%. At the subregional level, Central America increased its inflows by 6%, while the Caribbean showed a decline of 17% (see map I.1).

Map I.1
Latin America and the Caribbean (selected subregions and countries): FDI inflows, 2014-2015
(Billions of dollars)

Brazil alone accounts for more than 40% of FDI inflows to the region

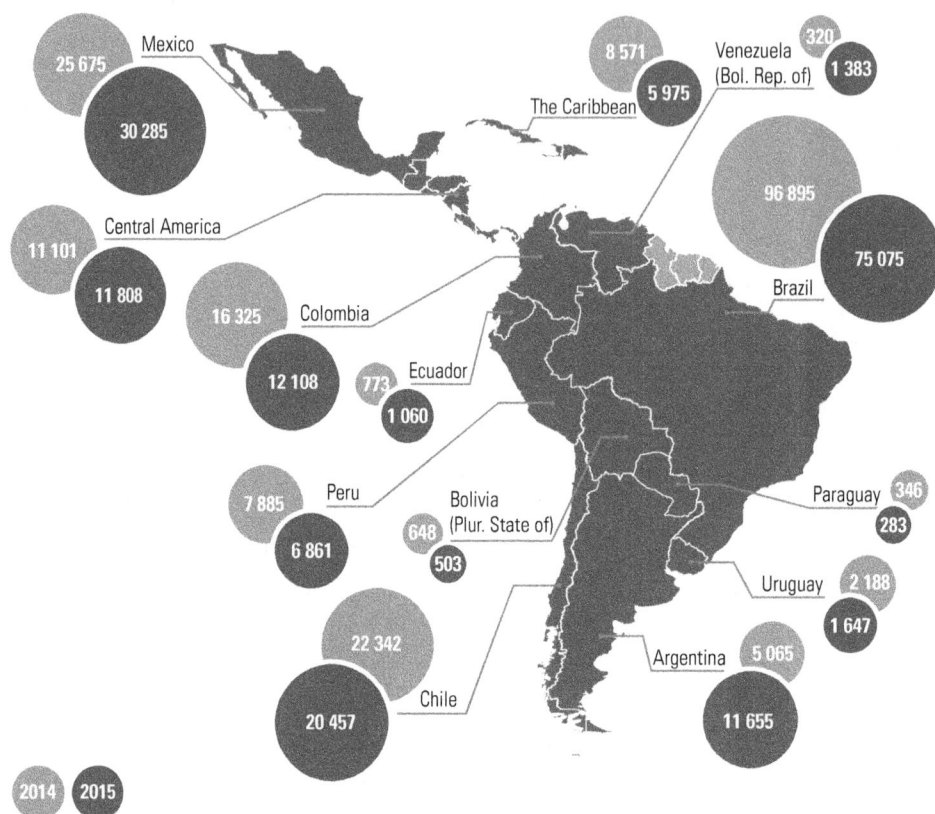

Source: Economic Commission for Latin America and the Caribbean (ECLAC), on the basis of official figures and estimated as of 27 May 2016.
Note: The figures for the Bolivarian Republic of Venezuela and Trinidad and Tobago (included in the Caribbean) correspond to the first three quarters of 2015.

A more detailed look at the fall in FDI inflows to Latin America and the Caribbean reveals a number of interesting findings. In 2015, as discussed in section A, the amount associated with cross-border mergers and acquisitions was especially low in the region. This fact may offer a partial explanation for the decline in FDI inflows, but it could also indicate that that the creation of productive capital was relatively high during 2015. Chapter III discusses more fully the characteristics of FDI and its contribution to productive capital creation. The second explanatory factor is the collapse of international commodity prices. Chapter II offers a detailed analysis of FDI in the mining sector.

Secondly, the decline in reinvested earnings may help to explain the shrinking of FDI inflows (see figure I.5). In fact, the slowing of economic growth in various countries of the region has had a direct impact on business profits. Moreover, many firms have not cut back on the repatriation of profits, and this has had a negative impact on the reinvestment rate in the recent past. In Brazil, this trend has been especially intense.

Between 2010 and 2012, profit reinvestment averaged around US$ 25 billion a year, but then fell to US$ 2.3 billion between 2013 and 2015.

The decline in reinvested earnings reflects the region's deteriorating economic conditions

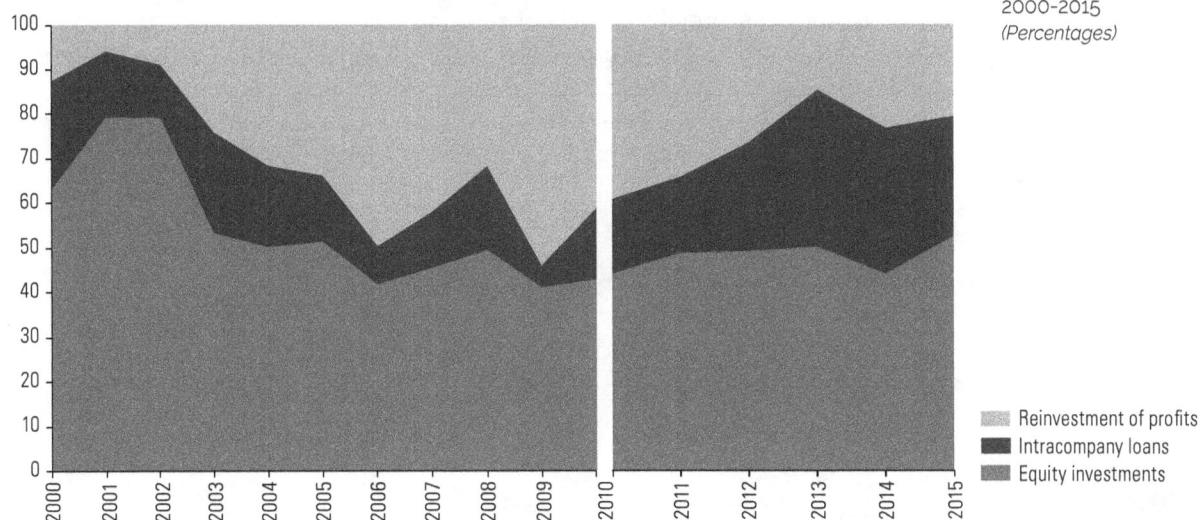

Figure I.5
Latin America and the Caribbean: foreign direct investment by component, 2000-2015
(Percentages)

Reinvestment of profits
Intracompany loans
Equity investments

Source: Economic Commission for Latin America and the Caribbean (ECLAC), on the basis of official figures and estimates as of 27 May 2016.

Note: Data before and after 2010 are not directly comparable, because they refer to a different selection of countries. In both cases, the data exclude Argentina, Belize, the Dominican Republic, Suriname and Trinidad and Tobago; before 2010, they also exclude Brazil.

Intracompany loans also declined substantially in 2015, as a result of which the relative share of capital contributions, or equity investment, rose. Although the statistics before and after 2010 are not strictly comparable, the share of capital contributions had been dropping systematically for several years, and consequently the results for 2015 could point to a shift in this trend.

2.   Less investment in natural resources

Not all countries publish statistics on FDI inflows disaggregated by sector of destination: such statistics are available only for some of the bigger economies and for most Central American countries. For this group of countries, the importance of the extractive sectors has been sinking steadily. Among the countries for which this information is available, in Colombia the share of primary sectors in FDI declined from 51% in 2010-2014 to 31% in 2015 (see figure I.6). In that latter year, the share of natural resources in FDI inflows was 13% in Brazil and only 3% in Mexico. In Central America, the natural resource share of FDI dropped from 13% to 8%.[6] The shrinkage of FDI in natural resources is linked to the collapse of commodity prices, with the end of the commodities super cycle and the slowdown in the world economy.[7]

---

[6]   It is important to note that the generation of energy from renewable sources is not included in the natural resources sector, but as a category under services.

[7]   Chapter II of this publication focuses on metal mining, offering a fuller explanation for the sharp drop in investment in this sector.

On the other hand, the importance of the services sectors would seem to be rising. In Brazil, Colombia and Mexico, FDI in services accounts for 49% of total FDI, and in Central America this figure reaches 65%. Among the services of greatest interest to foreign investors in the most recent period were telecommunications and renewable energy.

Business services also carry considerable weight in the FDI totals in many economies, while the role of financial services varies greatly from one country to the next. There are three specific aspects of services that merit particular attention. First, the renewable energy sector is growing strongly and gaining importance in the region. Second, the telecommunications sector is one in which foreign firms are dominant and investment needs are great. Finally, the retail trade subsector is interesting for its high growth rate and the significant participation of trans-Latin firms.

Figure I.6
Latin America (selected subregions and countries):[a] distribution of FDI by sector, 2010-2015
(Percentages)

As FDI in natural resources declines, the share of services is rising

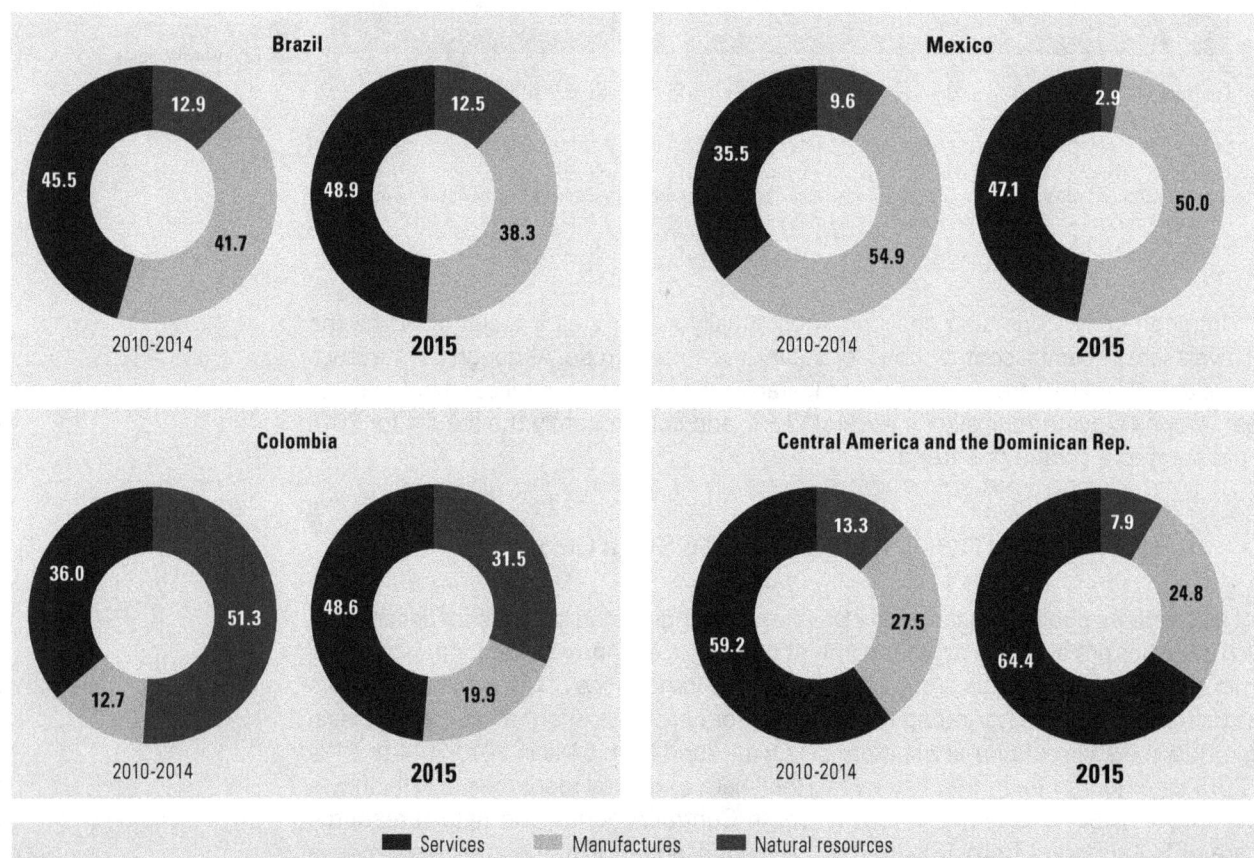

Brazil

2010-2014: 12.9, 45.5, 41.7

2015: 12.5, 48.9, 38.3

Mexico

2010-2014: 9.6, 35.5, 54.9

2015: 2.9, 47.1, 50.0

Colombia

2010-2014: 36.0, 51.3, 12.7

2015: 31.5, 48.6, 19.9

Central America and the Dominican Rep.

2010-2014: 13.3, 59.2, 27.5

2015: 7.9, 24.8, 64.4

■ Services   ■ Manufactures   ■ Natural resources

Source: Economic Commission for Latin America and the Caribbean (ECLAC), on the basis of official figures and estimates as of 27 May 2016.
[a] The data for Central America do not include Panama.

Given the limitations in coverage and detail of national FDI statistics disaggregated by economic activity, the present analysis is supplemented with information from announcements of new FDI projects compiled by the Financial Times publication, *fDi Markets*. As noted earlier, this information is not strictly comparable with the FDI inflows reported in the balance of payments. Nevertheless, it reveals in greater detail the tendency of the medium- and long-term strategies pursued by transnational firms or their announcements of coming investments.

Between 2005 and 2015, there were some major changes in the sectorial distribution of FDI projects announced in Latin America and the Caribbean (see figure I.7).

- New investments announced in the natural resource extraction and processing sectors —essentially mining and hydrocarbons— fell from 74% to 13% of the total between 2005 and 2015.

- In the manufacturing industry, the automotive sector was particularly dynamic. Over the entire period, announced investments for vehicle assembly and parts production rose from 4% to 15% of the total.

- In services, two sectors stand out for their especially strong performance: telecommunications and renewable energy. Between 2005 and 2015, announced investments in the telecommunications sector increased from 4% to 11% of the total, reflecting the rapid deployment of new infrastructure that has enhanced the coverage and quality of modern services in the region. At the same time, announcements of renewable energy projects jumped from 1% to 20% of the total between 2005 and 2015. In fact, renewable energies have been the most important target of new investment announcements in 2015.

Announced new investments in the natural resources sector fell from 74% to 13% of the total over the last 10 years

Figure I.7
Latin America and the Caribbean: distribution of announced FDI projects by sector, 2005-2015
(Percentages)

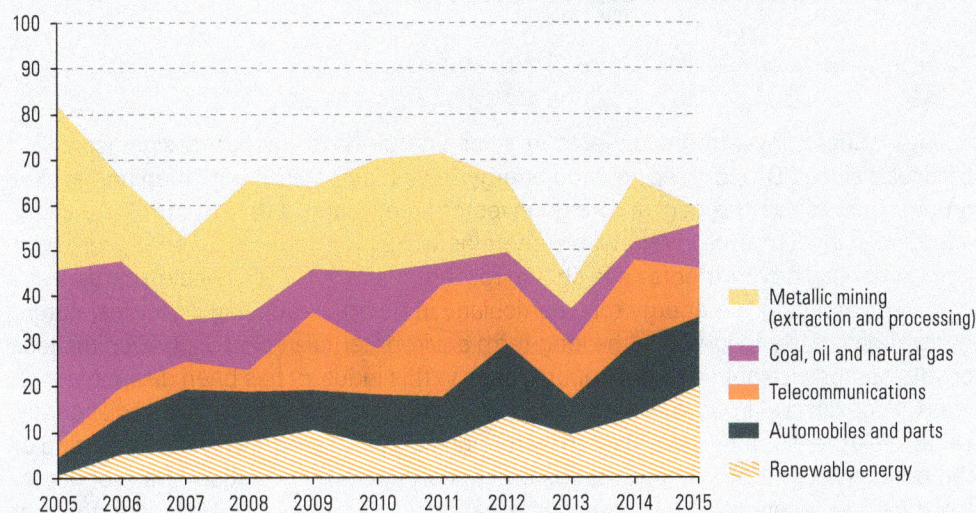

Legend:
- Metallic mining (extraction and processing)
- Coal, oil and natural gas
- Telecommunications
- Automobiles and parts
- Renewable energy

Source: Economic Commission for Latin America and the Caribbean (ECLAC), on the basis of Financial Times, *fDi Markets*.
Note: This analysis excludes the 2013 announcement of the Nicaragua Canal, for a value of US$ 40 billion.

In 2015 more than 50% of the investment announced in renewable energy projects was earmarked for Chile (see figure I.8). During that year, in fact, Chile boosted its installed capacity by 580 MW. Honduras too recorded a strong performance, adding some 500 MW to its generating capacity (Shumkov, 2015). That country's success has been the result of a generous policy of subsidies for capacity installed prior to July 2015, and this has meant a substantial boost in the share of solar energy in the Honduran energy matrix. Other countries of interest here include Brazil, Mexico and Panama. The first two countries are, of course, much bigger markets than Chile, and renewable energy commands a significant share of their energy mix. However, because of the regulatory framework and the presence of large domestic players, there is less international involvement through FDI in those countries than in Chile or Panama. Lastly, investment announcements in the renewable energy sector have increased in most countries, with the exception of Peru, where few projects have been announced in that sector over the last three years.

Figure I.8
Latin America and the Caribbean: FDI projects announced in renewable energies, by country, 2005-2015
(Millions of dollars and percentages of the total)

In 2015 over 50% of the investment announced in renewable energy projects went to Chile

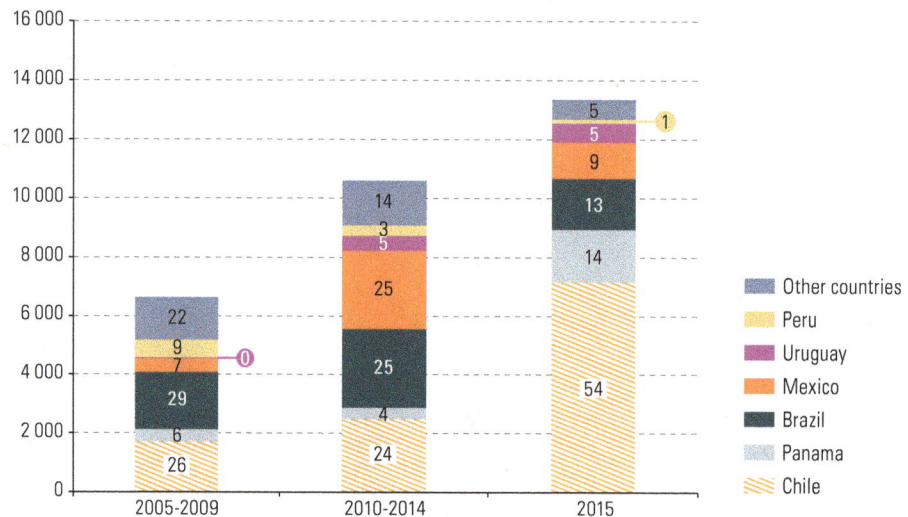

Source: Economic Commission for Latin America and the Caribbean (ECLAC), on the basis of Financial Times, *fDi Markets*.

Announced investment projects in solar energy have increased significantly, in particular since 2010.

Announced investment projects in solar energy have increased significantly, in particular since 2010, displacing wind energy technology, which until then had evoked greater interest on the part of foreign investors (see figure I.9). In 2015, 70% of the announced investments in renewable energies were targeted at solar energy projects. Latin American governments have shown real enthusiasm for renewable energies as a way of diversifying the energy mix, particularly in non oil-producing countries, cutting generating costs and lowering the long-term environmental impact. However, the local private sector's response to the opportunities in this industry has been disappointingly weak. For example, in Chile —one of the world leaders in terms of installed solar energy capacity— the industry is dominated by foreign companies. As a way of capitalizing on the country's competitive advantages and encouraging the creation of a production, logistics and technology platform of international reputation, the Chilean authorities have attempted to coordinate and strengthen local players involved in the solar energy sector, through a "smart specialization" programme.

Between 2013 and 2015, solar energy represented on average more than 50% of total announced investment in renewable energy projects

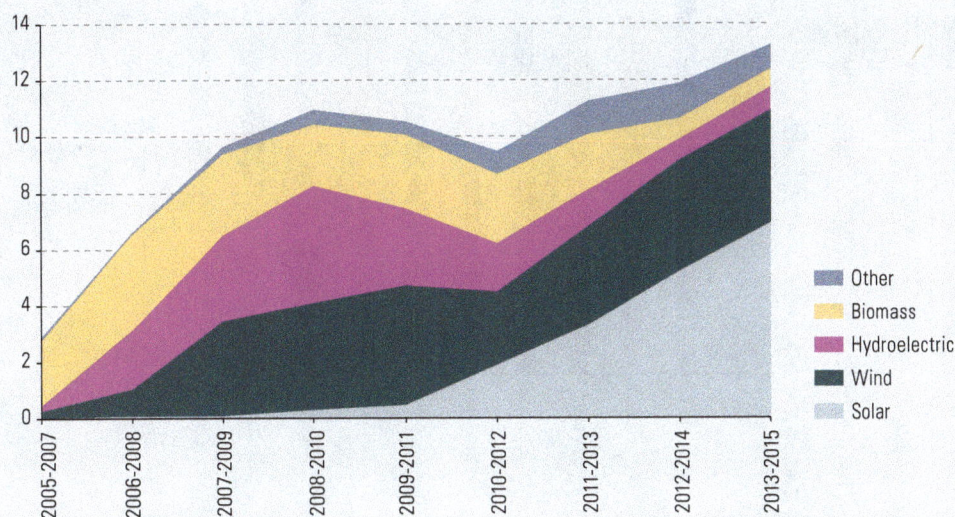

Source: Economic Commission for Latin America and the Caribbean (ECLAC), on the basis of Financial Times, *fDi Markets*.
Note: data represent three-year moving averages.

In Latin America and the Caribbean, telecommunications has been one of the most important services sectors for channelling FDI. Between 2011 and 2015, telecommunications accounted for 17% of all announced foreign investments. There are at least three reasons for this phenomenon:

(i)   The telecommunications sector is very intensive in high-tech infrastructure and hardware, which entails investment on a very large scale. The speed of technological change is obliging companies to invest continuously in order to keep abreast, as in the case of the recent transition from 3G to 4G in mobile telephony.

(ii) It is a sector where competition is fierce and customer loyalty is fickle. Under these conditions, firms must invest to the same degree as their competitors.

(iii) Lastly, it is a sector with a large presence of transnational firms. Within the region, only in Costa Rica, Mexico, Uruguay and the Bolivarian Republic of Venezuela is the local market dominated by a domestic firm. In most Latin American countries, the market is dominated by two foreign companies: América Móvil (Mexico) and Telefónica (Spain) (see figure I.10). In the Caribbean the pattern is very similar. In most of the English-speaking Caribbean there are two major operators: the Jamaican-Irish firm Digicel and Cable & Wireless Communications (CWC) of the United Kingdom. In November 2015, CWC was acquired by the United States-British firm Liberty Global.

Figure I.10
Latin America (selected
countries): distribution
of mobile telephony
customers by company,
2015 or latest available year
(Percentages)

In mobile telephony, two international firms enjoy dominant positions in the majority of regional markets

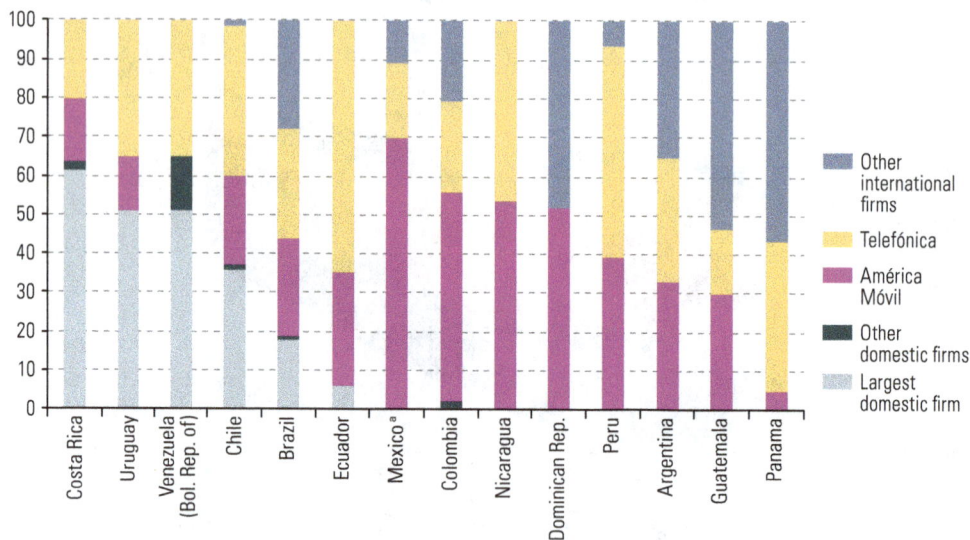

Source: Economic Commission for Latin America and the Caribbean (ECLAC), on the basis of official figures.
[a] In Mexico, América Móvil is the main national player in this market.

> One of the preferred strategies for large retail chains in pursuing their international growth has been to acquire local operators.

In Latin America, a small group of firms is responsible for the bulk of investment. According to data provided by the company, América Móvil has been investing around US$ 10 billion every year, including its home market, Mexico. Between 2012 and 2015, the Spanish firm Telefónica, with its Movistar brand, has invested some US$ 22 billion in the region, while Telecom Italia has disbursed close to US$ 8 billion in Brazil, its main market.

Another service sector that has shown impressive growth is retail trade. In 2015, the amount of announced investments rose by 25% to US$ 3.649 billion. This performance has been driven by capital originating essentially in three countries: the United States (41%), France (17%) and Chile (15%) (see figure I.11). In the most recent period, however, the two leading source countries, and France in particular, have been losing ground. In fact, the bulk of French FDI in Latin America's retail trade sector has been accounted for by operations of the Carrefour supermarket chain (80% of the total announced), a company that has in recent years reversed its strategy of regional expansion. In 2012, Carrefour sold its operations in Colombia for US$ 2.5 billion to the Chilean firm Cencosud, re-focusing its activities on Brazil and Argentina, where it has 876 stores. Similarly, FDI from the United States in retail trade is concentrated essentially in one company —Wal-Mart— the largest company in the world according to the Fortune Global 500 ranking (Fortune, 2015). In recent years Wal-Mart has accounted for 25% of all announced investments in the retail trade sector, and 61% of investments in the region announced by United States firms in this industry. In the case of Chile, three firms account for the majority of FDI announced in the regional retail sector: Cencosud, Falabella and Ripley were responsible for 49%, 32% and 10%, respectively, of all announced investment in this sector by Chilean firms.

Figure I.11

Latin America and the Caribbean: distribution of FDI projects announced in the retail trade sector,
by country of origin and destination, 2003-2015
(Percentages)

In retail trade, Chilean firms have consolidated their position as key players,
while Colombia is becoming an attractive destination for investment

A. By country of origin

B. By receiving country

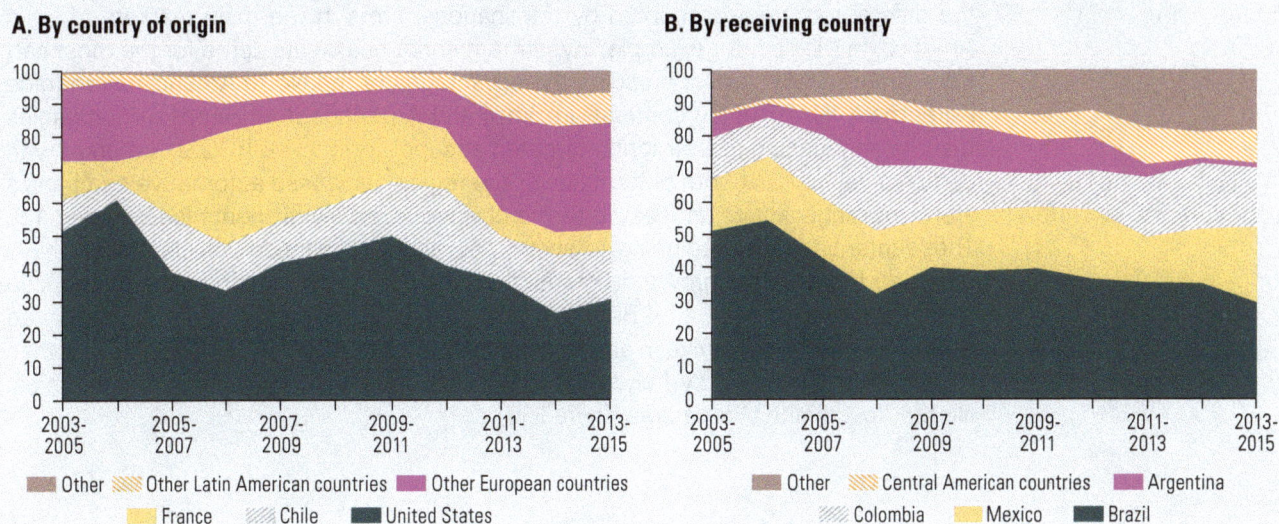

Source: Economic Commission for Latin America and the Caribbean (ECLAC), on the basis of Financial Times, *fDi Markets*.
Note: Data are three-year moving averages.

In terms of the geographical distribution of investments announced in the retail trade sector, the leading destinations are Brazil (38%), Mexico (20%) and Colombia (15%). Market-seeking is the main motivation for FDI by the big retail chains. Thus, when domestic conditions start to deteriorate, business interest also tends to fall off, as demonstrated by the decline in FDI in Argentina since 2010 and the recent drop in Brazil (see figure I.11).

One of the preferred strategies for large retail chains in pursuing their international growth has been to acquire local operators, thereby giving them swift access to new markets and familiarity with local customers and habits. As to the origen of acquiring companies, the pattern is very similar to that of new investment announcements. Between 2003 and 2015, United States firms accounted for 34%, by value, of mergers and acquisitions in this industry, followed by Chilean (28%) and Mexican (9%) companies. The two biggest players are Wal-Mart and Cencosud, which together are responsible for 50% of the mergers and acquisitions completed in Latin America. However, there are some differences between announced investments and M&As when it comes to the geographic destination of these operations. The main destination was Chile, which accounted for 30% of the funds flowing into M&A operations. In this particular case, the lead player is Wal-Mart: through various transactions it has gained control of one of the largest local supermarket chains, D&S, which operates under the trade name Líder. As for Cencosud, it has launched an ambitious strategy for international growth, taking over a number of local chains in Argentina, Brazil, Colombia and Peru.

In the manufacturing sector, the automotive and parts industry remains one of the main focal points of interest for transnational companies, in terms of the volume of investment, although it is highly targeted in geographic terms. Between 2011 and 2015, investments amounting to some US$ 60.279 billion were announced in the Latin American automotive and parts sector, concentrated essentially in three countries: Mexico (61%), Brazil (30%) and Argentina (5%).

Yet, the origin of investments reveals some important distinctions that reflect the different strategies adopted by transnational firms in the main markets of Latin America. In Mexico, for example, investment announcements come for the most part from United States firms, pursuing the advantages of the North American Free Trade Agreement (NAFTA). By contrast, in Brazil and Argentina it is European companies that are announcing investments, targeted at supplying the MERCOSUR market with compact vehicles. At both extremities of the region, Japanese automotive companies are increasingly active, at least in terms of announced investments (see figure I.12). These intentions are beginning to show real results: Japanese vehicle makers have recorded the greatest growth in production, thanks to completion of the announced new factories (see table I.2). Between 2011 and 2015, General Motors of the United States was the most active in announcing new investments, amounting to more than US$ 8 billion, followed by Italy's Fiat (US$ 5 billion) and three Japanese companies: Nissan, Toyota and Honda (see figure I.13).

Figure I.12
Mexico and Brazil: distribution of the total value of announced FDI projects in the automotive sector (including autoparts), by country of origin, 2011-2015
(Percentages)

United States firms dominate the automotive industry in Mexico, while firms from the European Union are key players in Brazil

A. Mexico

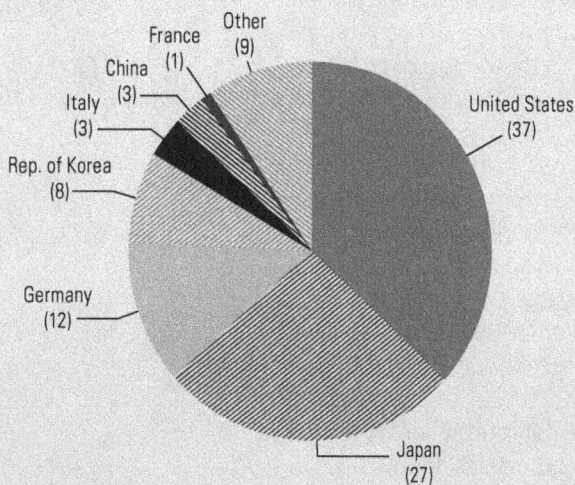

B. Brazil

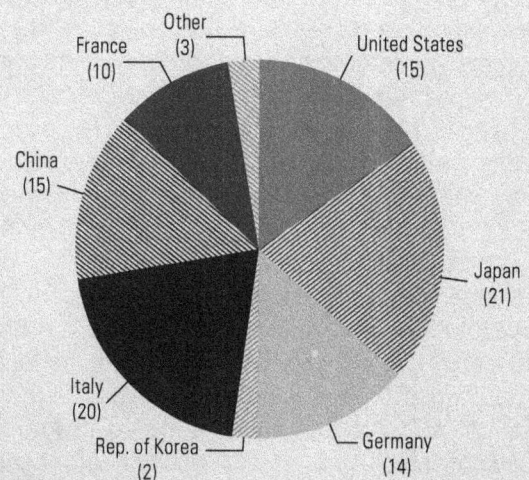

Source: Economic Commission for Latin America and the Caribbean (ECLAC), on the basis of Financial Times, *fDi Markets*.

Table I.2
Latin America and the Caribbean (selected countries): production by the main automotive firms, 2006 and 2014
(Units and percentages)

The region's automobile production is concentrated in Brazil and Mexico

Firm	Brazil		Argentina		Mexico		Share of Latin America in firm's total production (percentages)	
	2006	2014	2006	2014	2006	2014	2006	2014
From the European Union								
- Volkswagen	630 982	500 104	46 815	20 425	348 391	475 121	18.1	10.1
- Fiat	565 988	686 468	3 414	95 538	...	500 247	24.6	26.4
- PSA Peugeot-Citroën	92 515	94 825	96 787	57 609	...	...	5.6	5.2
- Renault	68 423	229 806	52 446	80 854	9 859	...	7.1	13.8
- Daimler	50 194	...	19 839	...	28 722	...	4.8	
Share in production *(percentages)*	**53.9**	**48.0**	**50.8**	**41.2**	**18.9**	**29.0**		
From the United States								
- General Motors	550 183	580 794	70 862	86 931	504 746	678 388	12.6	14.1
- Ford	320 124	304 403	78 785	103 107	330 228	431 613	16.9	14.1
Share in production *(percentages)*	**33.3**	**28.1**	**34.6**	**30.8**	**40.8**	**33.0**		
From Japan								
- Toyota	61 650	161 907	65 280	96 350	33 920	71 398	2.2	3.2
- Nissan	...	34 088	...	...	407 222	805 967	12.6	16.5
- Honda	78 360	127 508	...	6 756	24 300	145 213	2.8	6.2
Share in production *(percentages)*	**5.4**	**10.3**	**15.1**	**16.7**	**22.8**	**30.4**		

Source: Economic Commission for Latin America and the Caribbean (ECLAC), on the basis of information provided by the International Organization of Motor Vehicle Manufacturers (OICA).

Figure I.13
Latin America and the Caribbean: announced value of FDI projects in the automotive sector, by firm, 2011-2015
(Millions of dollars)

A handful of firms account for the majority of announced projects in the automotive industry

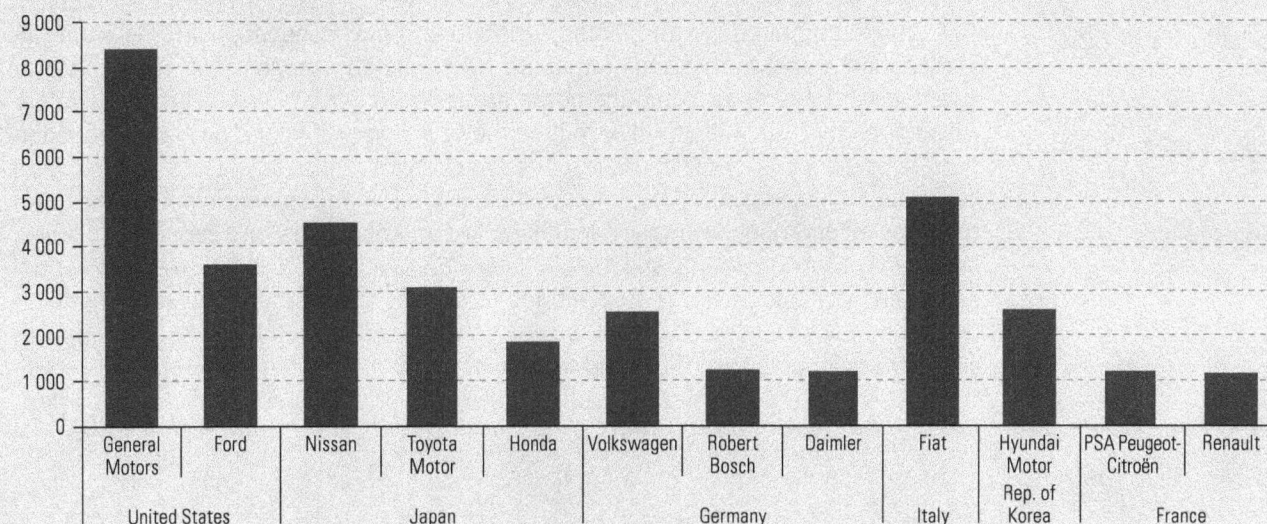

Source: Economic Commission for Latin America and the Caribbean (ECLAC), on the basis of Financial Times, *fDi Markets*.

3.   The United States is once again the principal source

In 2015, the United States became the main source of FDI flows to Latin America and the Caribbean. For those flows that have a clearly identified origin,[8] the United States accounts for 25.7%. The Netherlands is the second most important source, at 15.9%, followed by Spain, at 11.5% (see figure I.14).

Figure I.14
Latin America (selected subregions and countries): origin of FDI, 2015
(Percentages)

From Panama northward, United States firms are responsible for the bulk of FDI

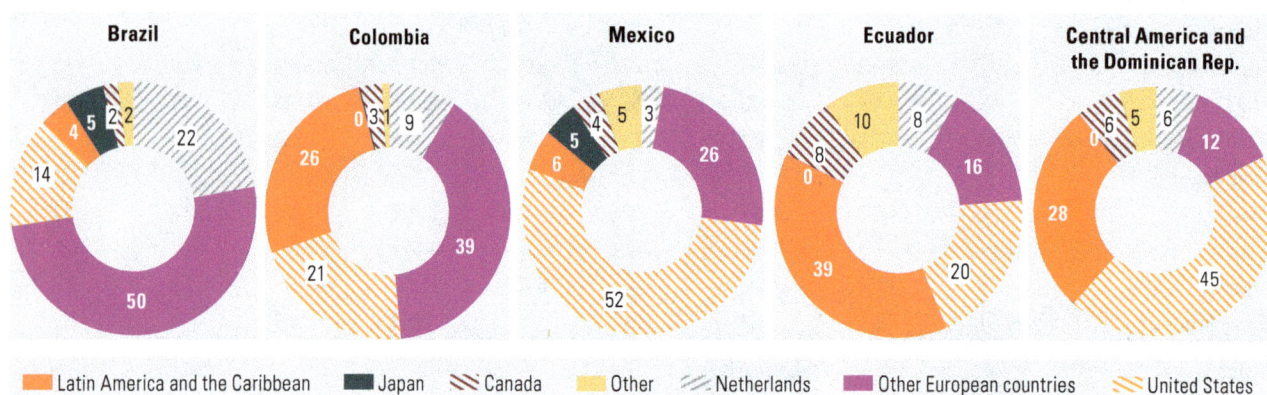

| Brazil | Colombia | Mexico | Ecuador | Central America and the Dominican Rep. |

Legend: Latin America and the Caribbean · Japan · Canada · Other · Netherlands · Other European countries · United States

Source: Economic Commission for Latin America and the Caribbean (ECLAC), on the basis of official figures and estimates as of 27 May 2016.
Note: Central America here includes Costa Rica, El Salvador, Guatemala and Honduras. The figures exclude FDI for which the origin cannot be determined, ie, FDI of unknown origin or originating in tax havens. In countries for which data are available, FDI of undetermined origin accounts for 5.9% of inflows.

The case of the Netherlands is particularly interesting, as its weight in the statistics bears little relationship to the presence of Dutch firms in Latin American economies. This apparent contradiction reflects the fact that many transnational firms establish subsidiaries in the Netherlands, attracted by its tax advantages, and then go on to invest in third countries. Although corporate taxation is high, the Netherlands offers advantages that can substantially reduce the taxes on profits and dividends obtained from subsidiaries in other countries. The Dutch system also has a highly developed network of double-taxation, information sharing and investment agreements with other countries, offering significant tax benefits for financial expenses, and especially for loans between parent companies and their subsidiaries. Lastly, there is the so-called "Dutch sandwich" that allows transnational firms to benefit from preferential agreements in place with tax havens such as the former Netherlands Antilles (*El País*, 2016). Similar situations exist in Luxembourg and Ireland.

---

8   The designation "identifiable investment" includes only figures from countries that disaggregate their statistics by country of origin, and it excludes investments from unidentified countries as well as from so-called tax havens.

There are some major differences between the countries of the region in 2015. In Brazil, 22% of identified flows comes from the Netherlands (although the ultimate origin of many of the investments is unknown), followed by the United States (14%) and Spain (13%). In Mexico, as in many countries of Central America and the Caribbean, the United States is by far the main source of FDI inflows: the United States accounts for 52% of inflows to Mexico, followed by Spain (9%) and Japan (5%). In Central America (excluding Panama and Nicaragua) and the Dominican Republic, 45% of FDI inflows come from the United States, followed by Colombia (8%) and Panama (8%). In Colombia, three countries are the source of slightly over half of FDI inflows whose origin can be identified: the United States (21%), Panama (16%) and Spain (14%).

An alternative and complementary way of analysing the origin of FDI flows is to consider large cross-border mergers and acquisitions (see table I.3). Among the 20 largest transactions concluded in 2015, United States firms were the dominant buyers, and they were particularly important in the telecommunications sector in Mexico. The largest transaction of the year was conducted by Telefónica of Spain, which took over the Brazilian firm Global Village Telecom, owned by the French company Vivendi, for a price tag of US$ 10.285 billion. Next in rank was the purchase, through tender, of the concession to operate the Jupiá and Ilha Solteira hydroelectric plants in São Paulo by China Three Gorges Corporation (CTG), which is the operator of the world's biggest hydroelectric project. In Brazil, CTG is partnered with Energias de Portugal (EDP) in three hydropower stations and 11 wind farms. Also noteworthy was the purchase of Columbus International, a Barbadian telecommunications firm, by Britain's Cable & Wireless (C&W) in what was the biggest acquisition to date in the Caribbean. Subsequently, in November 2015, Liberty Global announced its takeover of the assets of C&W in the Caribbean, for US$ 5.3 billion, but the transaction was not finalized during that year.

On the other hand, Latin America and the Caribbean saw little in the way of sizable divestments in 2015. In fact, there were only three such operations for more than US$ 100 million, and the 10 largest totalled US$ 1.834 billion. This stands in contrast to the US$ 15.242 billion of divestment in 2014, suggesting that there may be fewer incentives for investors to withdraw from the region. The largest transaction was the sale by the Canadian firm Barrick Gold of a 50% interest in a copper mine in Chile, for US$ 1.005 billion: that move was made to improve the firm's overall balance sheet, which had been affected by falling commodity prices and higher operating costs (see table I.4).

Many transnational firms establish subsidiaries in the Netherlands, attracted by its tax advantages, and then go on to invest in third countries.

Table I.3
Latin America and the Caribbean: 20 largest cross-border mergers and acquisitions, 2015

Four of the seven biggest mergers and acquisitions of 2015 took place in the telecommunications sector

Firm/ country of origin	Assets acquired/location of assets (country or subregion)	Sector	Amount (millions of dollars)	Country of seller
Telefónica Spain	Global Village Telecom Brazil	Telecommunications	10 285	France
China Three Gorges Corp. (CTG) China	Central hidroeléctrica Jupiá e Ilha Solteira Brazil	Energy	3 680	Brazil
Cable & Wireless United Kingdom	Columbus International The Caribbean and Central America	Telecommunications	3 025	Barbados
AT&T United States	Grupo Iusacell Mexico	Telecommunications	2 500	Mexico
British American Tobacco (BAT) United Kingdom	Souza Cruz (22%) Brazil	Manufactures	2 422	United Kingdom
Owens-Illinois United States	Vitro Mexico	Manufactures	2 150	Mexico
AT&T United States	Comunicaciones Nextel Mexico	Telecommunications	1 875	United States
Crown Holdings United States	Empaques Ponderosa Mexico	Logistics	1 225	Netherlands
Empresas Públicas de Medellín Colombia	Aguas de Antofagasta Chile	Infrastructure	967	Chile
Colbún Chile	Fenix Power Perú Peru	Energy	786	United States
Heineken Netherlands	Desnoes & Geddes (57%) y otros Jamaica and elsewhere	Manufactures	781	United Kingdom
Grupo Éxito France and Colombia	GPA (19%) and Libertad (100%) Brazil and Argentina	Commerce	758	France
IFM Investors Australia	Organización de Proyectos de Infraestructura (25%) Mexico	Infrastructure	628	Mexico
Brookfield Asset Management Canada	Activos inmobiliarios Brazil	Real estate	593	Brazil
JBS SA Brazil	Tyson de México, Tyson del Brasil Mexico and Brazil	Foods	575	United States
GIC Pte. Ltd. Singapore	Rede d'Or São Luiz (15%) Brazil	Health	523	Brazil
Mitsui & Co. Japan	Petrobras Gas (49%) Brazil	Gas and oil	486	Brazil
Ball Corp. United States	Latapack-Ball Embalagens (40%) Brazil	Manufactures	415	Brazil
Statkraft Norway	Empresa Eléctrica Pilmaiquén (98%) Chile	Energy	404	Chile
Advent International Corp. United States	Lifemiles (30%) Panama	Services	344	Colombia

Source: Economic Commission for Latin America and the Caribbean (ECLAC), on the basis of figures provided by Bloomberg.

Table I.4
Latin America and the Caribbean: 10 largest divestments, 2015

There were no major divestments in 2015

Selling firm/ country of seller	Assets sold/buyer	Sector	Amount (millions of dollars)	Country of buyer
Barrick Gold Canada	Zaldívar, copper mine (50%) Antofagasta PLC	Mining	1 005	Chile
Lafarge France	Cementos Fortaleza (47%) Elementia SAB	Cement	225	Mexico
Iberdrola Spain	Companhia de Eletricidade do Estado da Bahia (9%) Neoenergia	Energy	188	Brazil
QBE Insurance Group Australia	QBE Workers Compensation Werthein Investment Management	Finance	88	Argentina
Affinia Group Holdings United States	Pellegrino, distributor of automobile parts Distribuidora Automotriz	Automobile sector	76	Brazil
Nestlé Switzerland	Mexican ice-cream segment Grupo Herdez	Food	68	Mexico
Ridge Property United States	Two buildings in Monterrey (Mexico) México Real Estate Management	Real estate	58	Mexico
Affinia Group Holdings United States	Affinia Automotiva Private investor	Automobile sector	48	Brazil
Usina Internet Group United States	Sieve Group Brasil (75%) B2W Cia Digital	Technology	42	Brazil
Iberdrola Spain	Companhia Energética do Rio Grande do Norte (7%) Neoenergia	Energy	36	Brazil

Source: Economic Commission for Latin America and the Caribbean (ECLAC), on the basis of figures provided by Bloomberg.

4. Although it is falling, income from FDI is still important

In 2015 the stock of FDI shrank,[9] and earnings fell even further (see figure I.15). As a percentage of the stock of FDI, profits reached their most recent peak in 2011, and then began to drop. In 2015, they stood at 5.0%, the lowest level in 13 years. The collapse of profitability affects not only transnational companies, but firms in the Latin American economies in general. In fact, the profitability of the 500 largest firms in the region has been declining for a decade now (see figure I.16). During that time, the region's best earnings came in 2006, when profitability stood at around 7.2%, or 5.3% excluding natural resources.[10] Subsequently, in 2014, income fell to 2% (or 2.7% excluding natural resources). In that year, profits were down in all sectors, compared to the 2010-2013 average, and the drop was particularly severe in the mining sector (see figure I.16). This trend is beginning to be reflected in a loss of interest in certain resource-intensive activities, primarily mining, as a destination for FDI flows.

Figure I.15
Latin America and the Caribbean:[a] stock and average profitability of FDI, 2000-2015
(Billions of dollars and percentages)

The profitability of FDI in the region has fallen in recent years

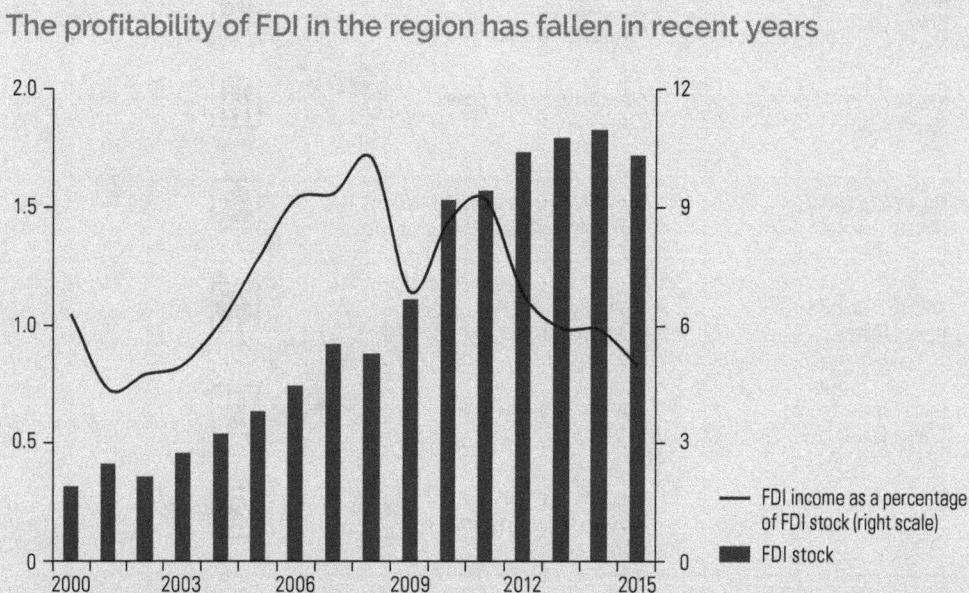

— FDI income as a percentage of FDI stock (right scale)
▪ FDI stock

Source: Economic Commission for Latin America and the Caribbean (ECLAC), on the basis of official figures and estimates as of 27 May 2016.
a Does not include data for Cuba, Jamaica, Trinidad and Tobago, the Bolivarian Republic of Venezuela or the member countries of the Organisation of Eastern Caribbean States (OECS).

---

[9]   Between 2014 and 2015, the stock of FDI fell from US$ 1.91 billion to US$ 1.8 billion. Among other factors, this outcome reflects the devaluation of many Latin American currencies. The shrinkage of the FDI stock was especially significant in Brazil. Between the beginning of January and the end of December 2015, the exchange rate rose from 2.7 reais to 3.9 reais to the dollar, and this had a significant impact on the value of assets denominated in dollars.

[10]   As discussed in chapter II, the mining industry yields high profits: 24.9% in 2006. The hydrocarbons sector, which also falls well outside the average excluding natural resources, recorded profits of 7.2% in 2006.

Figure I.16
Latin America and the Caribbean: company earnings, median and by sector
(Percentages)

Profits have declined across all sectors in real terms

A. Average returns, 2005-2014

B. Returns by sector, 2010-2014

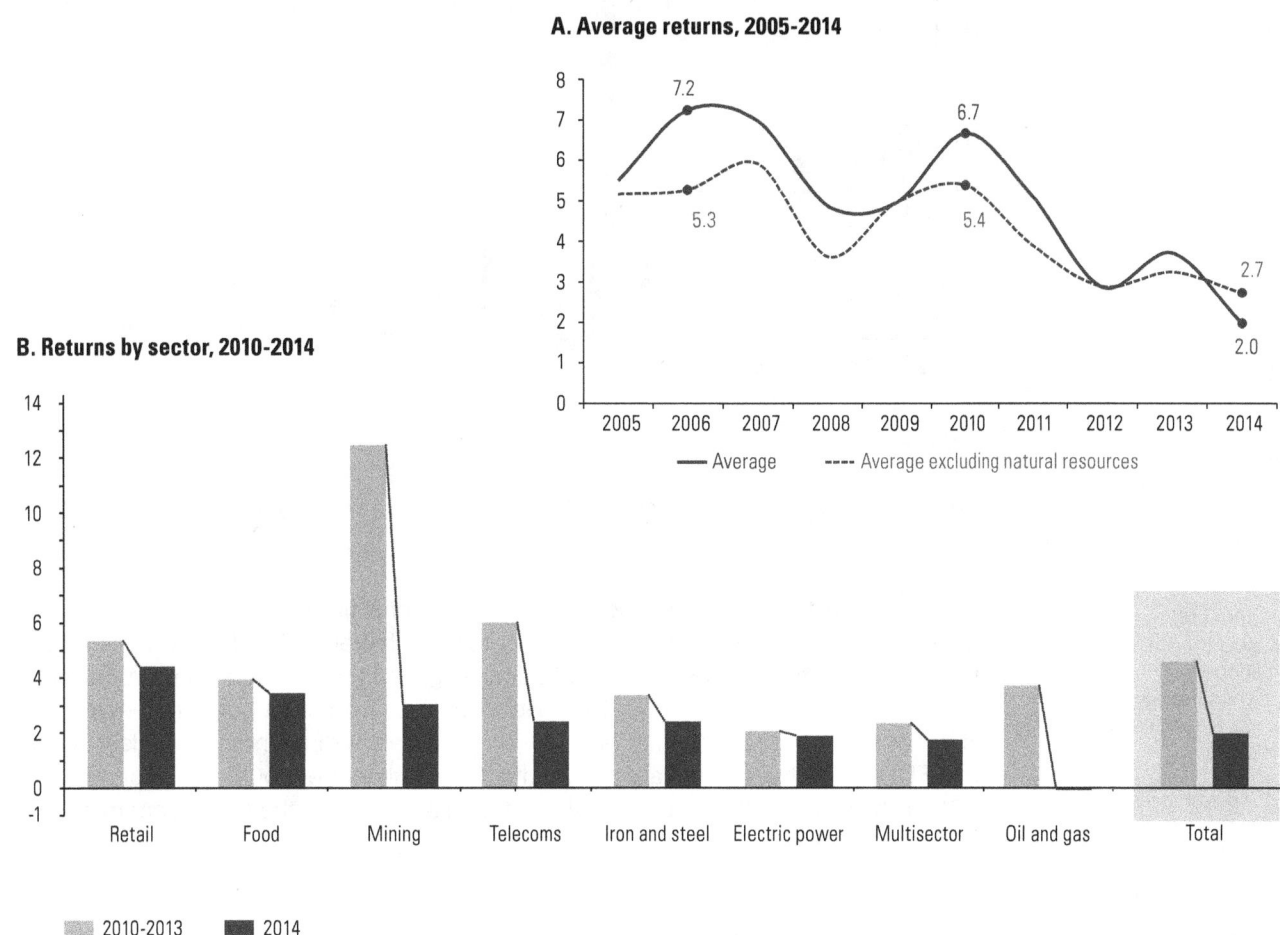

2010-2013   2014

Source: Economic Commission for Latin America and the Caribbean (ECLAC), on the basis of *América Economía* magazine.
Note: The data show results for the 500 biggest firms in Latin America and the Caribbean, excluding those firms that do not publish specific data on their subsidiaries abroad. The data cover cross-border, national and state-owned firms. The sectors included in figure B are the eight sectors with the largest sales volumes, according to *América Economía*.

An analysis of the situation by country shows that the greatest declines in profitability occurred in countries with substantial mining activity (Chile, Colombia, Peru and the Plurinational State of Bolivia). However this trend is not confined to mining economies. In fact, for the great majority of countries, FDI profits in 2015 were lower than the average for the period 2010-2014 (see figure I.17). Only in Panama was income slightly higher in the last year. Finally, profitability levels also reflect the characteristics of countries' production and business structure. Generally speaking, the larger economies, with more diversified productive structures and more competitive local firms, show lower levels of FDI profitability.

Figure I.17
Latin America and the
Caribbean (selected
countries): FDI income as
a proportion of FDI stock,
2010-2015
(Percentages)

Countries with substantial mining activity recorded the greatest fall in FDI income

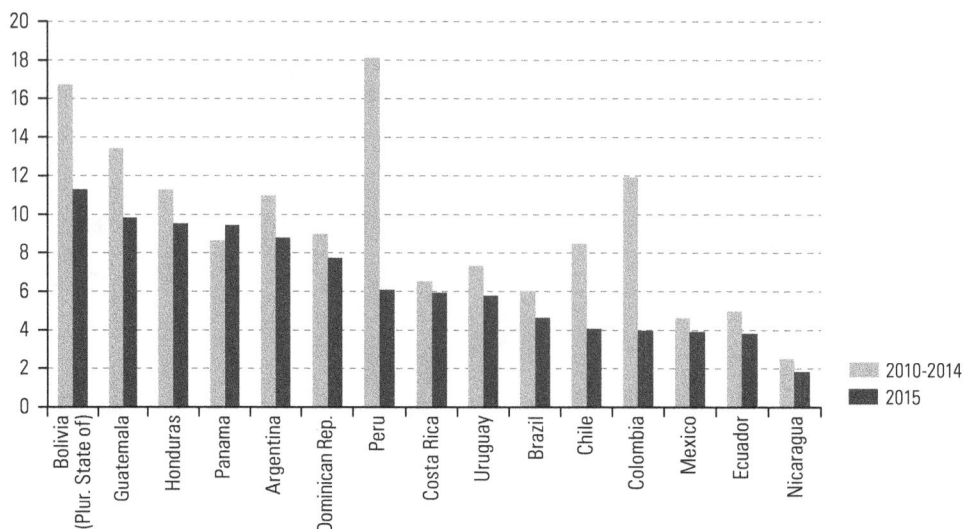

Legend: 2010-2014, 2015

Source: Economic Commission for Latin America and the Caribbean (ECLAC), on the basis of official figures and estimates as of 27 May 2016.

Figure I.18
Latin America and the
Caribbean: [a] FDI income
and distribution between
income reinvested and
repatriated
*(Billions of dollars
and percentages)*

In a context of shrinking FDI earnings, transnational firms have at least two options: to reinvest a smaller proportion of profits or to remit fewer profits. In Latin America and the Caribbean, the reinvestment rate is declining, and this can be a negative factor for the host economies (see figure I.18). Nevertheless, from a longer-term viewpoint, it is important to assess the effects of FDI on the balance of payments. While it is clear that FDI inflows have an initial positive effect, the subsequent outflows of profits from FDI will have a negative impact on the external accounts of the host economies.

The bulk of income is repatriated

A. FDI income, 2000-2015
(billions of dollars)

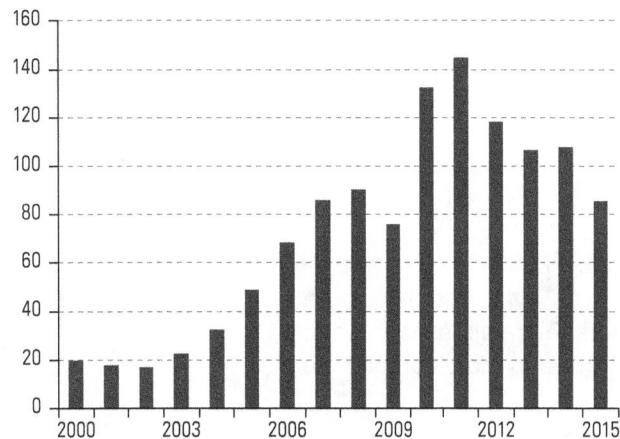

B. Distribution of FDI income between reinvestment and repatriation, 2010-2015
(percentages)

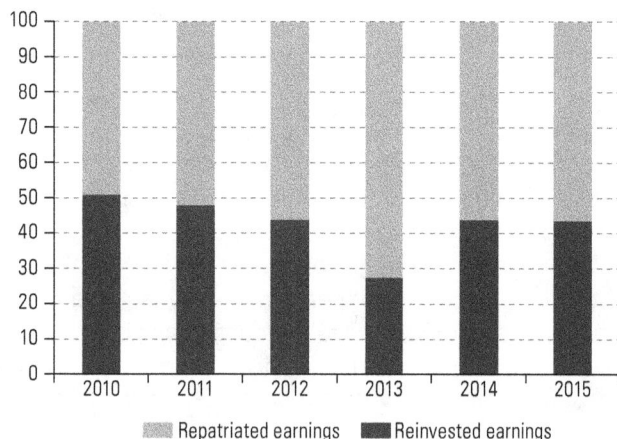

Legend: Repatriated earnings, Reinvested earnings

Source: Economic Commission for Latin America and the Caribbean (ECLAC), on the basis of official figures and estimates as of 27 May 2016.
[a] The graph in panel A includes data from Argentina, Brazil, Chile, Colombia, Costa Rica, Dominican Republic, Ecuador, Guatemala, Honduras, Mexico, Nicaragua, Panama, Plurinational State of Bolivia and Uruguay. The graph in panel B includes data from Brazil, Chile, Colombia, Costa Rica, Ecuador, Guatemala, Honduras, Mexico, Panama, Plurinational State of Bolivia and Uruguay.

On the financial account, FDI has been a very important and stable component of capital inflows. At US$ 179.10 billion, FDI represented 70% of foreign capital inflows in 2015. Yet in that same year, while FDI declined by 9.1%, inflows of portfolio and other investments dropped by 59% and 51% respectively. These last two components are more sensitive to the economic cycle and to short-term expectations (see figure I.19)

Figure I.19
Latin America and the Caribbean: cross-border capital inflows, 2005-2015
(Billions of dollars)

FDI is the principal and most stable component of capital inflows

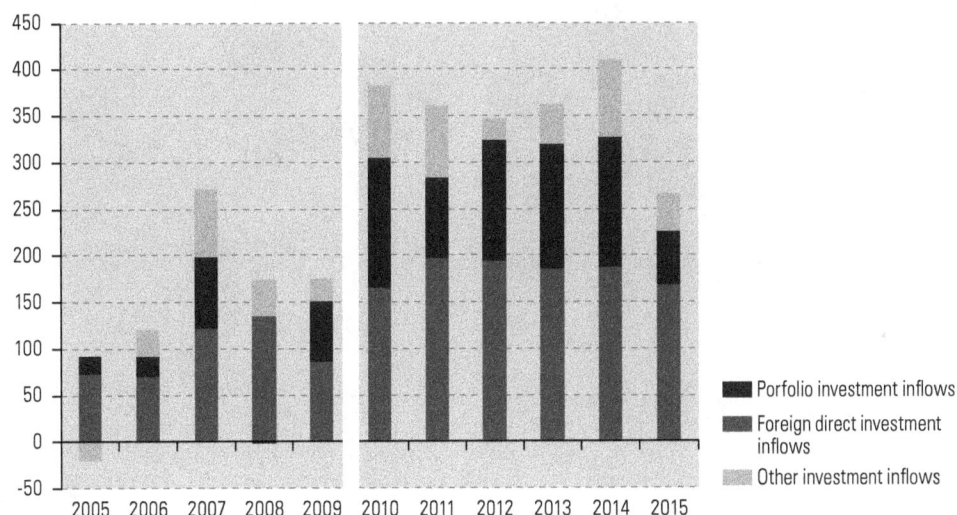

- Porfolio investment inflows
- Foreign direct investment inflows
- Other investment inflows

Source: Economic Commission for Latin America and the Caribbean (ECLAC), on the basis of official figures and estimates as of 27 May 2016 and *Preliminary Overview of the Economies of Latin America and the Caribbean, 2015* (LC/G.2665-P), Santiago, December 2015.

Note: Data prior to 2010 are not directly comparable with those for 2010 and later. Includes data from Argentina, Bahamas, Brazil, Chile, Colombia, Costa Rica, Dominica, Ecuador, El Salvador, Grenada, Guatemala, Honduras, Jamaica, Mexico, Nicaragua, Panama, Paraguay, Peru, Saint Kitts and Nevis, Saint Lucia, Saint Vincent and Uruguay.

The current account of the balance of payments has been deteriorating gradually in recent years, and in 2015 it showed a deficit of 3.3% of GDP (see figure I.20). Under this scenario, the income balance is the component with the largest deficit, and the one that produces the greatest net outflows of funds abroad. Within this item, the biggest component is the repatriation of FDI income by firms to their parent companies abroad. The situation is complicated by the steady deterioration in the goods balance, which historically has helped to finance the income balance deficit. In absolute terms, the surplus on the goods balance was greater than the deficit on the income balance until 2006. Since then, the goods balance has deteriorated swiftly, and the surplus disappeared in 2013 (see figure I.21). In 2015, the goods balance recorded its worst performance since 2001 (ECLAC, 2015b).[11] In fact, the negative trend in the region's export prices —in line with the collapse of commodity prices— cut into the earnings of transnational companies operating in the region, and as a result it also reduced the share that they remit to their parent companies.

---

[11]   In 2015, the deterioration in the goods balance resulted from a sharp drop in the value of exports together with a decline in the value of imports, the absolute magnitude of which was not sufficient to offset the drop in exports (ECLAC, 2015b).

Figure I.20
Latin America and the Caribbean: balance-of-payments current account
by component, 2010-2015
(Percentages of GDP)

The balance-of-payments current account remains in deficit and the goods balance is deteriorating

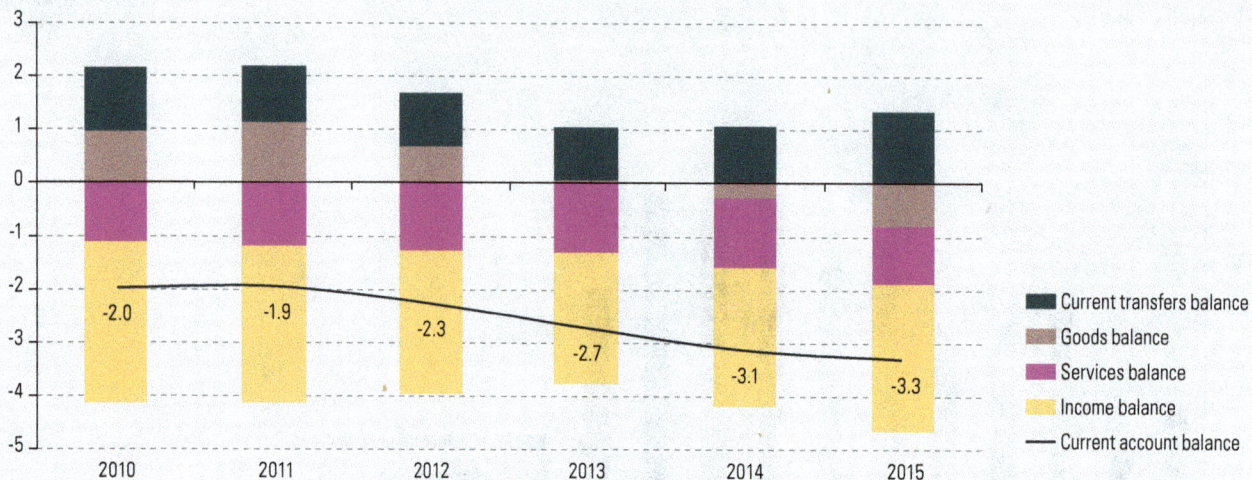

Legend:
- Current transfers balance
- Goods balance
- Services balance
- Income balance
- Current account balance

Values on chart: -2.0 (2010), -1.9 (2011), -2.3 (2012), -2.7 (2013), -3.1 (2014), -3.3 (2015)

Source: Economic Commission for Latin America and the Caribbean (ECLAC), on the basis of *Preliminary Overview of the Economies of Latin America and the Caribbean, 2015* (LC/G.2665-P), Santiago, December 2015.

Figure I.21
Latin America and the Caribbean: selected items of balance-of-payments current account, 2006-2015
(Billions of dollars)

The income balance is improving, but the decline in the goods balance is accelerating

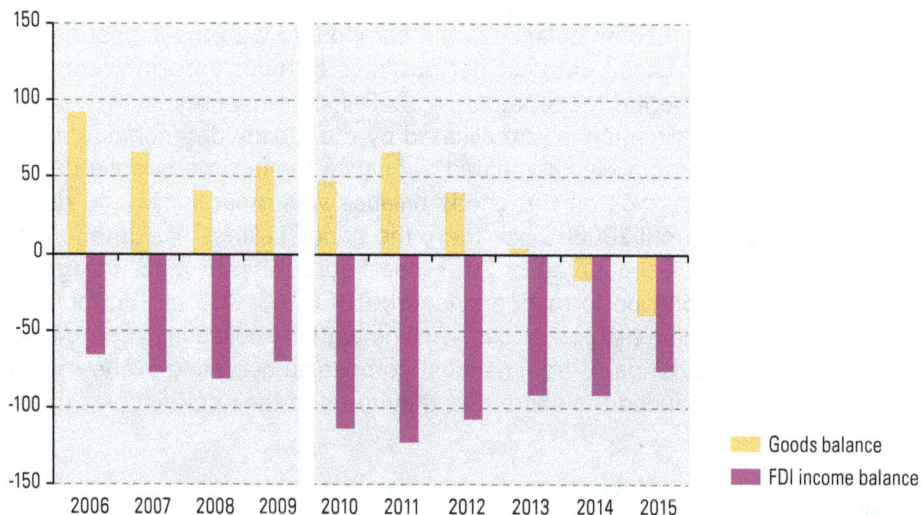

Legend:
- Goods balance
- FDI income balance

Source: Economic Commission for Latin America and the Caribbean (ECLAC), on the basis of *Preliminary Overview of the Economies of Latin America and the Caribbean, 2015* (LC/G.2665-P), Santiago, December 2015.
Note: Data prior to 2010 are not directly comparable with those for 2010 and later. This is represented by a white line on the graph.

Lastly, when FDI inflows are combined with outflows of FDI income, their impact on the balance of payments becomes clear. In most countries, the impact is positive. However, even if FDI inflows were to contract sharply, the existing FDI stock is of such a size as to produce income outflows that could be very significant. At the present time, the Bolivarian Republic of Venezuela, Guatemala, Peru and the Plurinational State of Bolivia are already experiencing a negative impact from FDI on their balance of payments (see figure I.22).

For many countries the FDI balance is virtually nil

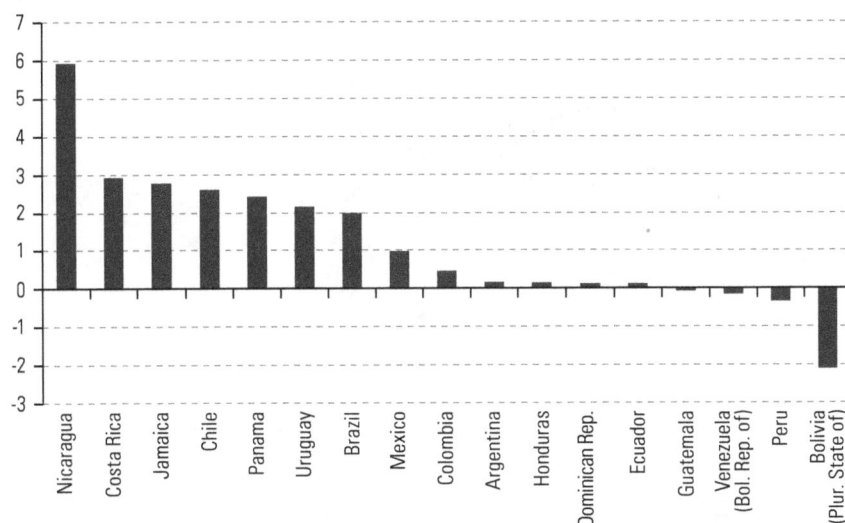

Figure I.22
Latin America and the Caribbean (selected countries): balance between FDI inflows and FDI income outflows, average for the period 2010-2015
(Percentages of GDP)

Source: Economic Commission for Latin America and the Caribbean (ECLAC), on the basis of official figures and estimates as of 27 May 2016.

C. Outward investment by trans-Latin firms is slowing

In 2015, outward FDI flows from Latin American and Caribbean countries declined substantially to US$ 47.362 billion, down by 15% from the previous year. Although the decline is real, it was accentuated by corrections and methodological changes introduced in the statistics, especially with the use of the sixth edition of the *Balance of Payments and International Investment Position Manual* of IMF (2009). Adoption of the sixth edition sparked major changes in the statistics of Brazil, especially those concerning Brazilian investments abroad (see section D of this chapter for further details). The impact of these changes can be appreciated from a comparison of regional figures with and without Brazil (see figure I.23).

Prior to adoption of the sixth edition of the IMF *Balance of Payments Manual*, Brazilian statistics showed great volatility, and this had repercussions on the regional aggregates. By excluding Brazil from the Latin American and Caribbean total, trends can be identified more clearly. First, outward direct investment shows a steady increase between 2007 and 2012. Trans-Latin firms took advantage of the sound conditions in their domestic economies and the opportunities that began to appear in some of the main regional markets, for example, with the resurgence of a number of transnational firms from beyond the region that had been affected by the international financial crisis. Outward direct investment flows began to shrink in 2012, with the cooling of regional growth and changes in the international commodity markets where some of the biggest trans-Latin firms were active. In 2015, the collapse of commodity prices accelerated and countries' economic conditions worsened. Outward direct investment by Brazilian firms declined more sharply than that of their peers in other countries of the region (see table I.5).

Figure I.23
Latin America and the Caribbean: outward FDI flows, 2005-2015
(Billions of dollars)

Outward direct investment from Latin American countries is slowing

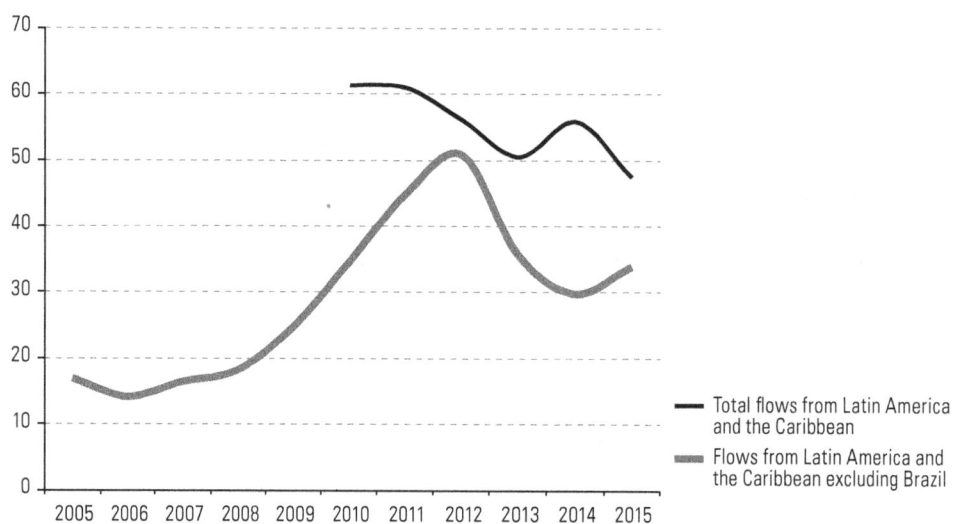

Source: Economic Commission for Latin America and the Caribbean (ECLAC), on the basis of official figures and estimates as of 27 May 2016.

Note: Because the data prior to 2010 do not include the reinvestment of profits by Brazilian firms, the data before and after 2010 are not directly comparable.

Three countries account for over 85% of outward direct investment from the region. In 2015, Chile was the source of the greatest outflows of direct investment, illustrating the vigour of Chilean trans-Latin firms. Chile was followed by Brazil and Mexico, which were responsible for 28% and 26% of the total, respectively (see table I.5).

Figures for the stock of outward direct investment help to place the annual flow statistics in perspective (see figure I.24). In fact, the stock of such investment reveals the rapid growth of the two countries that are home to the largest firms with international operations: Brazil and Mexico. As well, those figures reveal the weakening role of the Bolivarian Republic of Venezuela as a source of direct investment.

Table I.5
Latin America and the Caribbean (selected countries): outward FDI flows, 2005-2015
(Millions of dollars and percentage variation)

In 2015, Chile was the region's most active outward direct investor

	2005-2009[a]	2010	2011	2012	2013	2014	2015	Absolute variation 2015-2014 (millions of dollars)	Relative variation 2015-2014 (percentages)
Argentina	1 471	965	1 488	1 055	890	1 921	1 139	-782	-41
Brazil[b]	14 067	26 763	16 067	5 208	14 942	26 040	13 498	-12 541	-48
Chile	5 117	9 461	20 252	20 555	9 872	12 915	15 794	2 879	22
Colombia	2 786	5 483	8 420	-606	7 652	3 899	4 218	319	8
Mexico	6 250	15 050	12 636	22 470	13 138	7 463	12 126	4 663	62
Trinidad and Tobago	282	0	1 060	1 681	2 061	1 275	717[c]	145[c]	25[c]
Venezuela (Bolivarian Republic of)	1 438	2 492	-370	4 294	752	1 024	-1 112[c]	-2 142[c]	...
Latin America and the Caribbean[d]	32 091	61 302	60 919	55 993	50 465	55 803	47 362	-8 441	-15

Source: Economic Commission for Latin America and the Caribbean (ECLAC), on the basis of official figures and estimates as of 27 May 2016.
[a] Simple averages.
[b] The 2005-2009 figure for Brazil does not include reinvestment of profits, and is therefore not directly comparable to the figures from 2010 onward.
[c] Trinidad and Tobago and the Bolivarian Republic of Venezuela have published data only for the first three quarters of 2015. The change from 2014 to 2015 is calculated for the first three quarters of both years.
[d] For the region overall, the variation between 2014 and 2015 for the cases of Trinidad and Tobago and the Bolivarian Republic of Venezuela was calculated taking only the first three quarters of those years.

Brazil and Mexico are the countries that invest the most beyond their borders

Figure I.24
Latin America (selected countries): stock of FDI abroad, 2005-2015
(Billions of dollars)

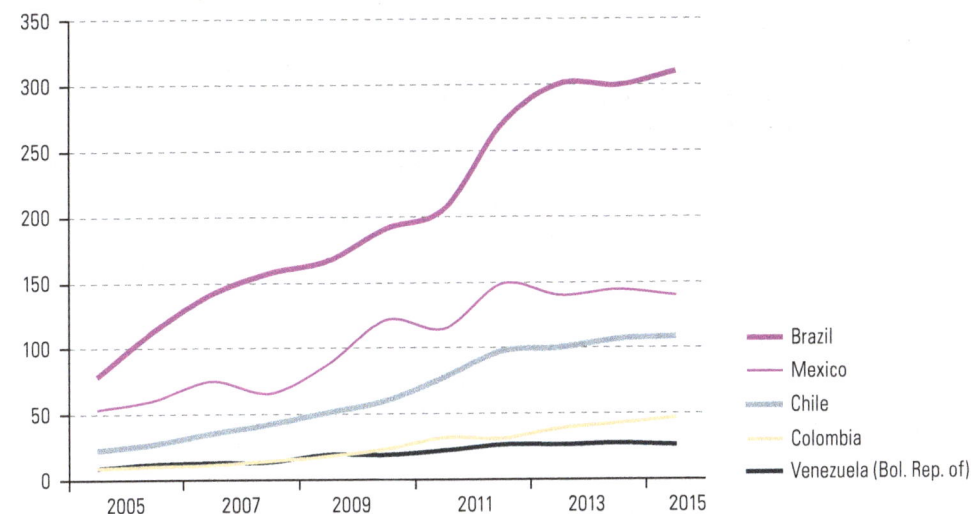

Source: Economic Commission for Latin America and the Caribbean (ECLAC), on the basis of official figures and estimates as of 27 May 2016.

In 2015, outward direct investment by Chilean companies rose 22%, to US$ 15.794 billion. Chile thus became the largest source of direct investment in the region. Capital outflows occasioned by investments abroad took the form primarily of deposits and loans extended by firms resident in Chile to their foreign subsidiaries: these amounted to US$ 10.621 billion (Central Bank of Chile, 2016). Among the most significant acquisitions by Chilean firms abroad were the purchase of City National Bank of Florida by the Banco de Crédito e Inversiones (BCI), for US$ 947 million, and the takeover of 100% control of the Peruvian thermoelectric generating company Fenix Power by a consortium headed by the electrical company Colbún (of the Grupo Matte) for US$ 786 million (see table I.6). The principal firms in the retail trade sector, which in the past have adopted ambitious globalization strategies, remained very active during 2015. Cencosud, Parque Arauco, Falabella and Ripley continued to expand their presence in countries where they already had operations: Argentina, Brazil, Colombia and Peru. This process persisted in the early months of 2016. Falabella announced an agreement with Soriana, operator of the second-largest supermarket chain in Mexico, which will give it entry to the Mexican market through the chain of home improvement stores with the Sodimac trademark, and a financial services business. However, there have also been some retreats: Ripley, for example, announced that it was abandoning the Colombian market because performance was falling short of expectations.

In second place was Brazil, which mobilized US$ 13.498 billion in outward direct investment. In 2015, Brazilian firms were involved in six of the 15 largest M&A transactions by trans-Latin firms (see table I.6). It should be noted, however, that four of the six operations featured the same firm, JBS SA, the world's leading meat processing company, which made acquisitions in the United States, New Zealand, Mexico and the United Kingdom. Moreover, JBS SA announced additional investments in the amount of US$ 150 million to boost its operations in Mexico. Another particularly dynamic sector has been the cement industry. In 2015, Camargo Corrêa announced investments of US$ 250 million in a new cement plant in Mozambique, and Votorantim Cimentos revealed its intention to invest some US$ 153 million in Turkey. Moreover, some of Brazil's biggest firms, such as Vale, have continued to pursue ambitious strategies for international expansion.

In 2015, outward direct investment by Mexican firms climbed sharply to US$ 12.126 billion, representing a jump of 62% from the previous year. As noted above, the telecommunications firm América Móvil was particularly active, given the competitive and technological demands of the sector. In fact, of the investments announced over the two years 2014-2015, América Móvil was responsible for US$ 6.166 billion, or 45% of the total. The cement firm CEMEX, for its part, announced an investment of US$ 300 million in the Philippines, while at the same time announcing divestments of US$ 1 billion in Europe. In general, Mexican firms have given priority to the United States market, and this trend continued in 2015. Among the principal firms, the announcements of the Grupo Posada attracted particular attention.

Lastly, Colombian firms have shown a noteworthy capacity to exploit external markets in recent years. They have a growing presence in the Central American market, which was the main destination for Colombian investment between 2000 and 2014 (accounting for 22.5% of all Colombian outward FDI), during which time Colombian firms built up US$ 9.231 billion in investment stock in the subregion (Cordero, 2015). In 2015, outward investment from Colombia reached US$ 4.218 billion, up by 8% from the previous year. Among the most important transactions were the purchase of the Chilean water company Aguas de Antofagasta by Empresas Públicas de Medellín, for US$ 967 million.

Lastly, there has been a notable process of integration among the smaller countries in the region. In this regard, most of outward FDI from the Central American and Caribbean countries remains within the respective subregion. These transactions, generally not very large, are mainly market-seeking investments in the most dynamic sectors.

Table I.6
Latin America and the Caribbean: the 15 largest cross-border acquisitions by trans-Latin firms, 2015

The Brazilian food processing firm JBS SA was responsible for four of the 10 largest acquisitions by trans-Latin firms in 2015

Firm/ country of origin	Assets acquired/ country of assets	Sector	Amount (millions of dollars)	Country of seller
BTG Pactual Brazil	BSI Switzerland	Finance	1 680	Italy
JBS S.A. Brazil	Moy Park Holdings (Europe) United Kingdom	Food	1 507	Brazil
JBS S.A. Brazil	Cargill pork business United States	Food	1 450	United States
JBS S.A. Brazil	Primo Group Holding New Zealand	Food	1 258	Hong Kong (Special Administrative Region of China)
Empresas Públicas de Medellín Colombia	Aguas de Antofagasta Chile	Infrastructure	967	Chile
Banco de Crédito e Inversiones Chile	City National Bank of Florida United States	Finance	947	Spain
Colbún Chile	Fenix Power Perú Peru	Energy	786	United States
Grupo Éxito Colombia/France	GPA (19%) and Libertad (100%) Brazil and Argentina	Retail	758	France
Private investor Mexico	Over 4,600 apartments in the United States United States	Real estate	650	United States
JBS S.A. Brazil	Tyson de México, Tyson do Brasil Mexico and Brazil	Food	575	United States
Inmobiliaria Carso Mexico	Realia Business (25%) Spain	Real estate	457	Spain
Casa Cuervo Mexico	Bushmills United Kingdom	Food	408	United Kingdom
Pluspetrol S.A. Argentina	Apco Oil and Gas International Inc. United States	Natural gas and oil	399	United States
Camargo Corrêa Brazil	Grupo Tavex S.A. (50%) Spain	Manufactures	389	Spain
Alfa S.A.B. de C.V. Mexico	Campofrío Food Group (37%) Spain	Food	354	China

Source: Economic Commission for Latin America and the Caribbean (ECLAC) on basis of Bloomberg.

Box I.1
Trans-Latin firms shopping in Europe: a complex adventure

In general, trans-Latin firms initially focused their globalization strategies on neighbouring country markets. As they have grown and become more competitive, they are now beginning to explore more distant markets. Several recent transactions by Latin American firms in Europe illustrate this trend. Between 2010 and 2015, according to figures from Bloomberg, trans-Latin firms have made acquisitions in the old continent amounting to US$ 49.310 billion.

Brazilian and Mexican trans-Latins have been the most active in this process, followed at a certain distance by Chilean and Colombian companies. The favourite European host country for Latin American acquisitions has been Portugal, essentially thanks to its strong economic and cultural ties with Brazil. In second place is Spain, where Mexican firms are most active.

European Union: value of mergers and acquisitions by trans-Latin firms, 2010-2015
(Billions of dollars)

Acquisitions by Brazilian firms in Portugal represent the majority of such transactions in the European Union

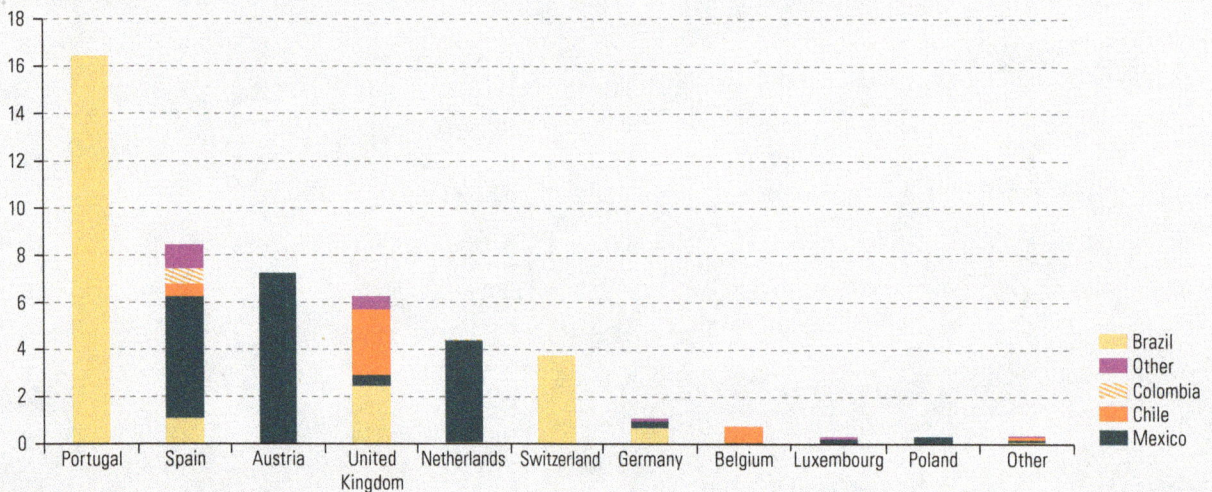

Source: Economic Commission for Latin America and the Caribbean (ECLAC), on the basis of information from Bloomberg.

Among the Brazilian companies that have been most active in the European Union are the telecommunications operator Oi, the Camargo Corrêa group and the Safra banking entity. In 2014, Oi acquired PT Portugal for US$ 8.056 billion. That venture, however, turned out to be more difficult than expected and in June 2015 Oi sold its share in PT Portugal to the French operator Altice, for 4.9 billion euros (€). Between 2010 and 2012, Camargo Corrêa acquired more than 90% ownership of the Portuguese cement company CIMPOR, in a series of transactions for which it paid out more than US$ 7 billion. In another series of transactions, Camargo Corrêa acquired all the shares of Grupo Tavex, the world's leading denim manufacturer. Some time later, however, the Brazilian group divested itself of Tavex operations in the United States, Mexico, Europe and North Africa, retaining only those in South America, which were generating around 75% of total sales. In a number of operations conducted between 2012 and 2013, the Safra banking entity acquired the Swiss concern Bank Sarasin. Subsequently, Safra purchased the operations of Morgan Stanley in Switzerland.

The most active Mexican firm in the European Union has been América Móvil which, after consolidating its position in the principal Latin American markets, has sought to position itself as a world leader through strategic acquisitions of European operators. In 2012, it acquired an important share in the Dutch operator KPN, for US$ 3.301 billion, and between 2012 and 2014 if purchased around a third of the shares of Telekom Austria, for US$ 7.253 billion.

Source: Economic Commission for Latin America and the Caribbean (ECLAC).

D. The fall in FDI was heaviest in South America

In 2015, Latin America and the Caribbean experienced a decline of 10.0% in FDI inflows, and this had a particular impact in some countries of South America. The regional figures were affected by the contraction of inward FDI in Brazil, Colombia and Uruguay, where it fell by 23%, 26% and 25% respectively. The most notable increases occurred in the Bolivarian Republic of Venezuela (up by 153% between the first three quarters of the two years 2014 and 2015) and in Argentina (130%), followed by Suriname (69%) and Grenada (59%) (see table I.7). These outcomes confirmed the cyclical nature of FDI: the two economies that showed the greatest increases in 2015 had recorded some of the sharpest drops in the previous year.

Table I.7
Latin America and the Caribbean: FDI inflows by receiving country and subregion, 2005-2015
(Millions of dollars and percentage variation)

The decline in FDI in 2015 was concentrated in South America

	2005-2009[a]	2010	2011	2012	2013	2014	2015	Absolute difference 2015-2014 (millions of dollars)	Relative difference 2015-2014 (percentages)
South America[b]	**68 016**	**135 066**	**167 923**	**168 253**	**132 133**	**152 786**	**131 032**	**-21 208**	**-14**
Argentina	6 204	11 333	10 840	15 324	9 822	5 065	11 655	6 590	130
Bolivia (Plurinational State of)	259	643	859	1 060	1 750	648	503	-144	-22
Brazil	32 331	88 452	101 158	86 607	69 181	96 895	75 075	-21 820	-23
Chile	11 891	15 510	23 309	28 493	19 362	22 342	20 457	-1 885	-8
Colombia	8 894	6 430	14 648	15 039	16 209	16 325	12 108	-4 217	-26
Ecuador	465	165	644	567	727	773	1 060	287	37
Paraguay	131	216	557	738	72	346	283	-63	-18
Peru	4 978	8 455	7 665	11 918	9 298	7 885	6 861	-1 023	-13
Uruguay	1 461	2 289	2 504	2 536	3 032	2 188	1 647	-540	-25
Venezuela (Bolivarian Republic of)[c]	1 403	1 574	5 740	5 973	2 680	320	1 383	837	153
Mexico	**25 293**	**26 431**	**23 649**	**20 437**	**45 855**	**25 675**	**30 285**	**4 609**	**18**
Central America	**5 867**	**6 304**	**9 061**	**9 229**	**10 848**	**11 101**	**11 808**	**708**	**6**
Costa Rica	1 584	1 907	2 733	2 696	3 555	3 064	3 094	30	1
El Salvador	714	-230	218	482	179	311	429	118	38
Guatemala	640	806	1 026	1 244	1 295	1 389	1 209	-180	-13
Honduras	742	969	1 014	1 059	1 060	1 144	1 204	59	5
Nicaragua	394	490	936	768	816	884	835	-49	-5
Panama	1 792	2 363	3 132	2 980	3 943	4 309	5 039	729	17
The Caribbean[b]	**6 643**	**5 171**	**7 198**	**8 741**	**6 946**	**8 571**	**5 975**	**-1 255**	**-17**
Antigua and Barbuda	237	101	68	138	101	155	154	-1	0
Bahamas	1 311	1 148	1 533	1 073	1 111	1 596	385	-1 211	-76
Barbados	416	446	362	313	-35	486	254	-231	-48
Belize	131	97	95	189	95	133	59	-73	-55
Dominica	45	43	35	59	25	35	36	1	2
Dominican Republic	1 782	2 024	2 277	3 142	1 991	2 209	2 222	13	1
Grenada	117	64	45	34	114	38	61	22	59
Guyana	135	198	247	294	214	255	122	-134	-52
Haiti	69	178	119	156	160	99	104	5	5
Jamaica	882	228	218	413	595	591	794	203	34
Saint Kitts and Nevis	136	119	112	110	139	120	78	-42	-35
Saint Lucia	108	97	86	115	160	110	121	11	10
Saint Vincent and the Grenadines	183	127	100	78	95	93	95	2	2
Suriname	-141	-248	70	174	188	163	276	113	69
Trinidad and Tobago[c]	1 232	549	1 831	2 453	1 995	2 488	1 214	67	6
Total[b]	**105 819**	**172 973**	**207 831**	**206 660**	**195 782**	**198 133**	**179 100**	**-17 918**	**-9.09**

Source: Economic Commission for Latin America and the Caribbean, on the basis of official figures and estimates as of 27 May 2016.
[a] Simple averages. Due to methodological changes, data prior to 2010 are not directly comparable with data for 2010 and after.
[b] The totals and subtotals include only the first three quarters of 2015 in the cases of the Bolivarian Republic of Venezuela and Trinidad and Tobago. The variation between 2014 and 2015 for the region was calculated using 2014 data for the first three quarters for these two countries.
[c] The 2015 data for Trinidad and Tobago and the Bolivarian Republic of Venezuela relate only to the first three quarters. The differences between 2014 and 2015 are calculated on the basis of the first three quarters of each year.

Despite a decline of 23%, Brazil remains the leading recipient of FDI in the region, accounting for 42% of the total. At a considerable distance behind come Mexico (17%) and Chile (11%). These figures confirm the persistent pattern of concentration within the region: five countries account for 84% of total FDI inflows.

In general, the smaller economies receive amounts of FDI that are larger in relation to their GDP, thus giving transnational firms a particularly important role. In Saint Vincent and the Grenadines, for example, while inward FDI is modest in amount, it has a great impact given the size of the economy. FDI inflows represent up to 10% of GDP in Chile, Nicaragua and Panama (see figure I.25). Some exceptional operations can have a great repercussion on inward FDI in certain economies, especially the smaller ones. Mergers and acquisitions tend to have a greater impact on the annual FDI figures than new investments, because the first usually take place in a relatively short period of time, while large investments in new plant take several years.

Figure I.25
Latin America and
the Caribbean: FDI as
a proportion of GDP, 2015
(Percentages)

Foreign direct investment tends to have a greater impact in smaller countries

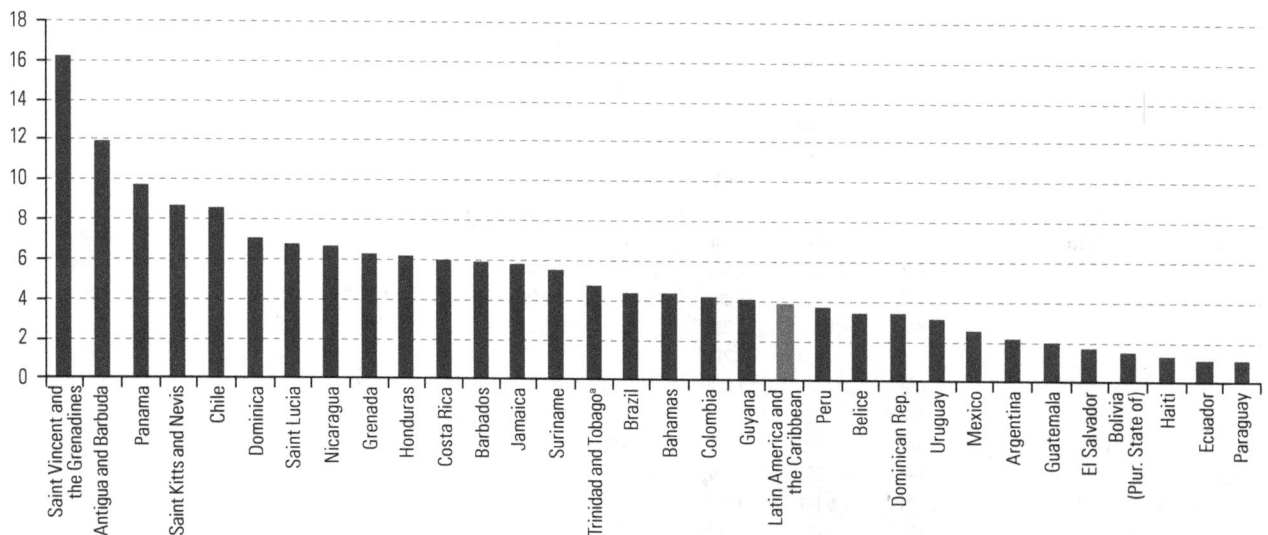

Source: Economic Commission for Latin America and the Caribbean, on the basis of official figures and estimates as of 27 May 2016.
ª The figure for Trinidad and Tobago refers to the first three quarters of 2015 only.

1.   Brazil: uncertainty hits domestic market investment in 2015

As noted above, the methodological changes introduced in Brazil have had an impact on the statistics. In 2015, as measured according to the sixth edition of the IMF *Balance of Payments Manual*, FDI inflows declined by 22.5%, to US$ 75.075 billion. This drop was especially pronounced in intracompany lending, which fell by 52% (mainly because of a significant increase in amortization payments) in the face of a 33% reduction in reinvested earnings and a 4% increase in capital contributions.

The analysis of intracompany lending reveals some interesting developments. In recent years, the cost of capital in Brazil has been fairly high, and as a result many investments were financed through transfers from the parent company. In fact, it is less costly to finance a business through the parent company than via the local market. However, this trend seems to have shifted in 2015, when intracompany loans declined as a result of a sharp increase in amortization of those loans. In other words, Brazilian subsidiaries of transnational corporations were prepaying loans provided by their parent company. There are at least three explanations for these findings in 2015: a reduction in the relative cost of capital in Brazil, a dearth of investment opportunities in the country and falling investor confidence owing to political instability. Between 2010 and 2015, reinvested earnings fell from US$ 34.865 billion to US$ 7.145 billion, lending support to the notion of a possible decline in investment opportunities in Brazil. It is plausible to assume that transnational firms have been saving a portion of their profits for some time now, and that deteriorating economic conditions have convinced them of the need to reduce the weight of their loans in the country.

The sheer size of Brazil's domestic market remains a key factor in the investment decisions of international firms. Brazil has not been immune to the effects of collapsing commodity prices, which have affected sectors such as mining, that in recent years were a major attraction for FDI. These opposing effects had varying results for different economic activities. In 2015, mining experienced significant divestment, while the automotive, food and energy sectors saw a sharp increase in investment. The last two years were marked by the acquisition of 22% of Souza Cruz SA by the United Kingdom-based British American Tobacco, for US$ 2.422 billion, and the takeover of the Jupiá and Ilha Solteira power-generating concession by China Three Gorges Corporation (CTG), for US$ 3.680 billion.

Of the 20 mergers and acquisitions completed during 2015, nine occurred in Brazil, including the two largest ones. In addition to the CTG takeover of the Jupiá and Ilha Solteira power-generating concession, there was the acquisition from the French company Vivendi of Global Village Telecom by Telefónica of Spain, for US$ 10.285 billion. As this last transaction took place between two foreign companies, it did not involve any inflow of investment to Brazil, but merely a change of ownership.

As with the balance of payments statistics, the figures for announced investments have also declined. Between 2014 and 2015, the number of announced projects valued at more than US$ 100 million fell from 43 to 34 (see figure I.26). In 2015, the majority of announcements were concentrated in financial services, while there was a sharp contraction in some sectors that were traditionally of great interest for FDI, such as telecommunications and the automotive industry, reflecting perhaps the deteriorating expectations for the performance of the Brazilian economy in the near future.

An analysis of the origin of FDI places the Netherlands and Luxembourg among the three main sources of investment, ranking first and third respectively. As suggested earlier, transnational companies are using these countries to "triangulate" their investments, and to reap tax benefits in the process. Consequently, it is difficult to identify the source for a very significant portion of the capital flowing into Brazil in the form of FDI. In any case, some traditional investing countries such as Germany, Spain and the United States remain in the top rank.

Figure I.26
Brazil: projects announced valued at over US$ 100 million, by sector, 2012-2015
(Number of announcements)

The number of projects announced is declining in some of the largest sectors
of the Brazilian economy

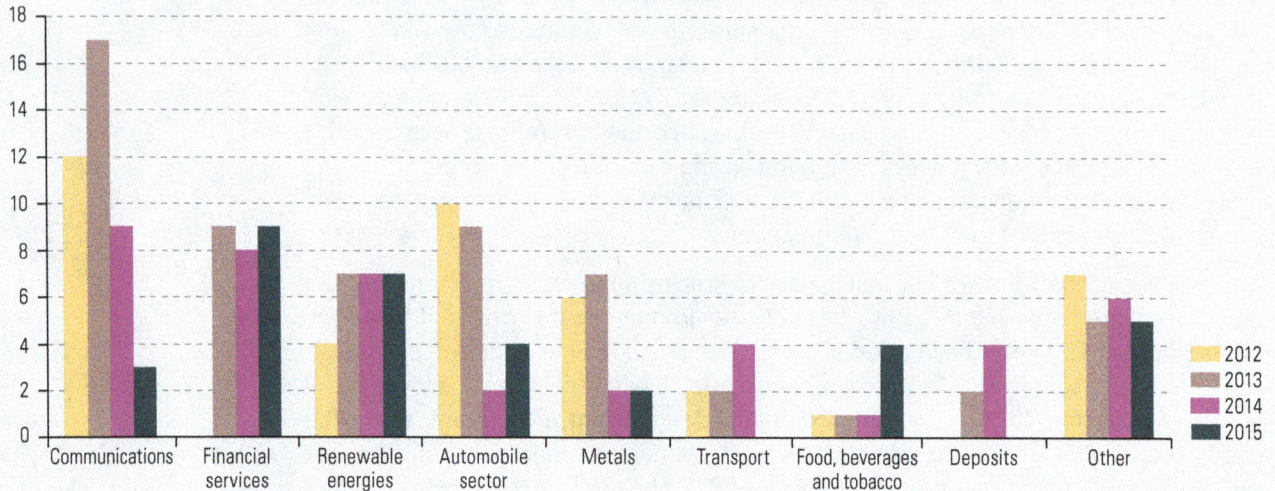

Source: Economic Commission for Latin America and the Caribbean (ECLAC), on the basis of Financial Times, *fDi Markets*.

2. The Andean and Southern Cone countries: the bottom of the commodity cycle

Despite a slight decrease in inflows, **Chile** still recorded the third-highest amount of inward FDI among Latin American economies in 2015. These capital flows declined by 8% to US$ 20.457 billion, a level similar to that for previous years. Although information disaggregated by economic sector was not available at the time of publication of this document, other sources point to a continued contraction of investment in mining, which had been the most important sector for foreign investment in recent years. Between 2009 and 2011, the mining sector accounted for 58% of inward FDI, a share that fell to 36% between 2012 and 2014. This proportion is likely to have shrunk further in 2015.

There have been no major announcements of new investments in Chilean mining, and the sector is declining in importance as an FDI destination. As of December 2015, there were eight projects under way for a total estimated investment of some US$ 15.122 billion, 27% of which came from foreign companies (Mining Council, 2015). Foreign companies account for 74% of the estimated US$ 35.879 billion in investments now under consideration for projects down the road.

There has also been a notable decrease in cross-border mergers and acquisitions, the value of which dropped from US$ 6.748 billion to US$ 1.979 billion between 2014 and 2015. Highlights of that latter year included the purchase of Aguas de Antofagasta by the Colombian concern Empresas Públicas de Medellín, for US$ 967 million, and the acquisition of 98% of Empresa Eléctrica Pilmaiquén S.A. by the Norwegian company Statkraft, for US$ 404 million (see table I.3).

Announced investments were up by 36% in 2015, according to data from fDi Markets, with renewable energies standing out as the largest recipient sector: 95% of the total amount announced was for the energy sector, and of this 80% was for renewable energies. In 2014, the respective shares of the energy sector, and of renewable energies, in announced investments were 45% and 37%.

A major project in this area is the construction of a power transmission line for the Interconnected System of the North (SING) and the Central Interconnected System (SIC). The Spanish firm Red Eléctrica de España and the French ENGIE (previously known as GDF Suez) are in charge of these works, with an estimated investment of US$ 780 million. The initiative, which is now in execution, involves a 500 kV power line, 600 km in length, that will come on stream in the second half of 2017 (pv Magazine, 2015).

According to the Ministry of Energy of Chile (2016), 2015 saw the completion of renewable energy projects that will introduce some 580 MW of generating capacity, to which will be added around 2,500 MW in 2016. In January 2016, Chile had a total generating capacity of 19,971 MW, and the new renewable energy projects will thus have a great impact on the future energy mix and on price trends. At the end of 2015, the United States-based First Solar completed construction of Luz del Norte, the biggest solar power park in Chile and, indeed, in Latin America. The project has a generating capacity of 141 MW, enough to supply 174,000 households, and it involved an investment of approximately US$ 370 million. The Spanish firm Acciona has begun construction of an even bigger solar farm —El Romero— with a capacity of 247 MW and an investment of US$ 343 million, which is to begin operation in the second half of 2017.

There was a great deal of activity in the insurance market in 2015. Talanx, Germany's third largest insurance firm, has been seeking out strategic markets as a way of countering the economic stagnation in Europe, and it acquired Aseguradora Magallanes for US$ 204 million. Colombia's Grupo Sura, through its insurance affiliate Suramericana, purchased all the Latin American assets of the British insurer RSA for some US$ 620 million, thereby positioning itself as one of the leading insurance firms in the region and making itself a strong force in the markets of Argentina, Brazil, Chile, Mexico and Uruguay. Lastly, in 2015 the British United Provident Association Ltd. (Bupa) took control of Bupa Chile, through the purchase of 17% of locally held shares and a subsequent tender offer, involving an investment of US$ 590 million.

FDI in **Colombia** fell by 26% in 2015 to US$ 12.108 billion, the lowest level in five years. As in other countries of the region that were hit by the collapse of commodity prices, the decline in FDI in Colombia was especially pronounced in the natural resources sector (see chapter II).

Nonetheless, Colombia saw much movement in other economic areas. Several Chilean groups have become actively involved in Colombia's retail trade: Cencosud, Falabella and Parque Arauco are investing to expand and upgrade their facilities in the country. In the hotel sector, the Spanish group NH acquired 87% of Hoteles Royal for around US$ 96 million. Confident of a recovery in international trade, the Danish firm APM Terminals, the port operator of the Maersk Group, is planning to invest some US$ 200 million in the port of Cartagena, after signing an agreement with the Compañía de Puertos Asociados, Compas S.A. In the manufacturing sector, General Motors of the United States has announced its intention to invest some US$ 100 million in its Colombian plant in the next few years, while the Spanish firm Cementos Molins and the Colombian group Corona have agreed to the joint production of cement in Colombia, for which they have announced investments of US$ 370 million.

In recent years, Colombian firms have shown a real determination to expand their operations beyond their country's borders. Colombian investment abroad rose by 8%

in 2015, to US\$ 4.218 billion. Important outward investments include the purchase of the Chilean sanitation company Aguas de Antofagasta by Empresas Públicas de Medellín for US\$ 967 million, and the acquisition by the Grupo Éxito (in which France-based Casino holds 54%) of 55% of GPA (Grupo Pão de Açúcar) in Brazil, and 100% of Libertad in Argentina (owned by Casino) for US\$ 1.826 billion. Yet another important investment was the purchase of the Latin American assets of the British firm RSA by Grupo Sura, for US\$ 617 million, a transaction that, because it was only completed in 2016, is not included in the figures for 2015.

In 2015, FDI in **Argentina** was up by 130%, at US\$ 11.655 billion. While this growth is impressive, it is tempered by the fact that the 2012 nationalization of 51% of YPF showed up in Argentina's external accounts only in 2014, in which year it represented a divestment of around US\$ 6 billion.[12] Without the impact of that transaction, FDI inflows in 2015 would have been very similar to those for 2014.

There has recently been a rapid increase in the interest shown by some international companies in the exploration and exploitation of hydrocarbons in Argentina. In fact, vast shale deposits of oil and natural gas have been discovered. In December 2015, Exxon Mobil announced investments of US\$ 229 million to develop the Vaca Muerta field. If the initial tests prove positive, the company could invest up to US\$ 13.8 billion. Other companies, including China's SINOPEC and Gazprom of the Russian Federation, are pursuing new exploration initiatives. Trafigura Beheer, the Dutch trading company for metals and hydrocarbons, has announced an investment of US\$ 350 million to build a port and a metals warehouse.

When it comes to sectors not related to natural resources, Spain's Telefónica invested US\$ 941 million in 2015 to upgrade its 3G and 4G services in the country. The Spanish telecommunications company has announced its intention to invest an additional US\$ 3.7 billion between 2016 and 2018. The French automaker Renault, for its part, will invest around US\$ 100 million in its plant in the city of Córdoba.

FDI in **Peru** declined for the third consecutive year. In 2015, FDI inflows dropped by 13%, to US\$ 6.861 billion. The component that saw the greatest retreat was intracompany loans, primarily because of the increase in amortization payments. In Peru, as in other countries with significant extractive industries, the relative importance of the mining sector in inward FDI has shrunk. Nevertheless, there was important movement in other sectors, and significant M&A activity.

The most important transaction was the purchase of the power generator Fénix Power by a consortium headed by the Chilean company Colbún, for US\$ 786 million. This was in fact one of the biggest cross-border M&A transactions recorded in Latin America and the Caribbean in 2015 (see table I.3). At the beginning of 2016, the Mexican firm Arca Continental, Coca Cola's second-largest bottling company in Latin America, completed its purchase of 48% of Corporación Lindley, with a transaction of US\$ 760 million. In pursuit of its regional expansion policy —focused especially on Chile, Colombia, Mexico and Peru— Canada's Scotiabank acquired the Peruvian assets of United States-based Citibank for US\$ 295 million. As well, the Chinese firm Tangshan Jidong Cement Co., the world's sixth-largest cement maker, announced its intention to buy Cementos Interoceánicos. Finally, there was great activity involving changes of ownership among foreign firms engaged in smaller-scale mining operations.

In telecommunications, following the acquisition of Nextel in 2013, the Chilean firm Entel has invested around US\$ 500 million to upgrade its network. Spain's Telefónica has invested some US\$ 8.5 billion in recent years and has announced new investments

---

[12] The figure of US\$ 6 billion represents two transactions: the first for US\$ 5 billion in payment for 51% of YPF, made on 26 February 2015, and the second for US\$ 1.311 billion in payment for 12.34% of YPF, made on 7 May 2015.

amounting to US$ 2 billion for the period 2015-2017. According to the Sociedad Hoteles del Perú (SHP), hotel investment in that country should amount to US$ 1.211 billion between 2015 and 2018 (involving 102 projects that would add some 7,676 rooms in 3-, 4- and 5-star hotels). This performance stands in contrast to the investments made in the period 2010-2014, which amounted to US$ 550 million.[13] Lastly, the Spanish oil company Repsol invested US$ 215 million in modernizing the La Pampilla refinery, and Norway's Statkraft inaugurated the new Cheves hydroelectric plant, following an investment of US$ 636 million.[14]

FDI in **Uruguay** dropped by 25% in 2015, to US$ 1.647 billion, the lowest level since 2009. In recent years, the country has received heavy investments in the energy sector, and this has modified its energy mix considerably. At the present time, 95% of power generating capacity comes from renewable sources, and there are several solar and wind power projects in the development stage. In 2015 the 65 MW Artilleros wind farm was inaugurated, representing an investment of US$ 107 million by a joint venture between the Uruguayan state-owned electric utility Administración Nacional de Usinas y Trasmisiones Eléctricas (UTE) and Brazil's Petrobras. In parallel with the progress in renewable energy, the search for hydrocarbons is also underway in Uruguay. Exxon Mobil acquired a 35% share of the offshore "concession 14" which was awarded to the French company Total. In 2016, work started on the drilling of a well at the Uruguayan marine platform. This well, which is expected to require an investment of some US$ 200 million, will be the deepest in the world.

After three years of exploration activity, the British oil company BP decided to abandon Uruguay in light of the collapse in world oil prices and the high risks involved in exploration.

A highlight for the manufacturing sector was the decision by United States-based Velcro Companies, the world's largest fastener systems producer, to build a new plant in Uruguay. This was Velcro's biggest investment in recent years, and one of the largest private investments in Uruguay in 2015. Another important development was the return of the Italian firm Parmalat, after its controlling company, France's Lactalis, acquired the Mexican company Esmeralda, which has a plant in Mexico, another in Argentina, and two in Uruguay. This transaction amounts to around US$ 105 million. The Uruguayan plants operate under the same Indulacsa.

The complicated political and economic situation in the **Bolivarian Republic of Venezuela** has had an adverse impact on inward FDI. Figures for the fourth quarter are not yet available, but official data show that during the first three quarters of 2015 the country received US$ 1.383 billion, 153% more than in the first three quarters of 2014. In July 2014, during the official visit of the President of China, Xi Jinping, it was announced that China would invest US$ 20 billion in the country, with the support of the Export Import Bank of China and the China Development Bank. Within this framework, the Chinese firm Zhengzhou Yutong Bus Co. will invest US$ 417 million to build a bus assembly plant in Yaracuy, with the capacity to produce some 3,600 buses a year. Other Chinese firms have shown interest in investing in the Bolivarian Republic of Venezuela, including Sinotruck (in a plant that will produce heavy trucks) and Sany Group (with a construction machinery factory). On the other hand, some foreign firms operating in the manufacturing sector are beginning to abandon the country. Companies from other countries are still active in the petroleum sector, but international firms have written off the bulk of their manufacturing investments. Due to the lack of raw materials for vehicle assembly, Ford Motor Co. and General Motors were forced to halt production at

---

13   See "Hotel investment to reach US$ 1.211 billion from 2015-2018", 2015 [online] http://www.peruthisweek.com/news-hotel-investments-to-reach-us-1211-billion-from-2015-2018-108377.

14   Repsol has invested some US$ 350 million since 2012 in modernizing the La Pampilla refinery, and has announced that, between 2016 and 2018, it will invest a further US$ 333 million in this operation (*El Comercio*, 2015).

the end of 2015. In fact, Ford Motor has segreagated its operations from its Venezuelan subsidiary. With this move, it was seeking to prevent its accumulated debt (some US$ 800 million) from affecting the company's financial balance, and this could well mean the definitive closure of operations in the country (*Automotive News*, 2015).

Ecuador recorded a historic high in inward FDI in 2015, with inflows rising by 37% to US$ 1.06 billion. The oil sector remains the main destination for FDI, although its share of the total dropped to 32% in 2015, ahead of the manufacturing industry at 24%. The Government of Ecuador expects to obtain around US$ 500 million in mining investment in 2016, and up to US$ 1.5 billion in 2017.[15] In December 2015, the French oil company Schlumberger announced investments of some US$ 4.9 billion.[16] Schlumberger will invest US$ 3.1 billion in the initial years to optimize and boost production from block 61, operated jointly with the state-owned Petroamazonas EP, and it will assume US$ 1.8 billion in operating costs over a period of 20 years. For its part, the World Bank's arbitration tribunal, the International Center for Settlement of Investment Disputes (ICSID), ordered Ecuador to pay slightly more than US$ 1 billion to Occidental Petroleum of the United States in compensation for the cancellation in 2006 of a contract to produce oil in the Amazon zone. If this payment is made, it will mean a divestment in that amount. The United States remained the leading source of FDI inflows to Ecuador in 2015, accounting for 18% of the total, followed closely by Peru and China with 16% and 9%, respectively.

Among the most important cross-border M&A transactions concluded in 2015 was the purchase of 64% of Unión Cementera Nacional (UCEM) by the Peruvian company Cementos Yura, part of the Grupo Gloria, for US$ 230 million. The Colombian infrastructure management and development company Grupo Odinsa took control of the concessionaire for the Mariscal Sucre Airport in Quito (Corporación Quiport), through the purchase of the 46% holding of the Canadian concern Aecon Group, for US$ 232 million. Lastly, Mexico's Sigma Alimentos, belonging to the Grupo Alfa, acquired the Ecuadorian company Elaborados Cárnicos (ECARNI), engaged in the production and marketing of frozen meats. This purchase follows upon the acquisition of the sausage maker Juris by Sigma Alimentos in November 2014.

In 2015, inward FDI in the **Plurinational State of Bolivia** declined by 22%, to US$ 503 million. The hydrocarbons sector is still the most important for foreign capital, with intensive activity in natural gas exploration and exploitation. Of note here are the announcement by the French oil company Total that it will invest some US$ 800 million between 2016 and 2018, and the coming start-up of joint production by Gazprom of the Russian Federation and Tecpetrol of Argentina at the Incahuesi field in July 2016. In the first stage, the extraction of gas from the Incahuesi deposit is expected to reach 6.7 million m³ a day. As well, the Spanish firm Repsol has announced that it will invest US$ 1.5 billion following the increase in production at the Margarita field. British Gas Group (BG Group) has announced the investment of US$ 300 million by 2019 for geological exploration in various zones of the country, while Gazprom and Petrobras have also announced huge investments of more than US$ 2 billion for exploration in the coming years.

In the telecommunications sector, the Swedish company Millicom announced investments of US$ 130 million in its local operator, Tigo, primarily to expand the fibre-optic network and to service 100,000 new households. Spain remains the leading source of FDI inflows to the Plurinational State of Bolivia, but data for 2015 have not

---

[15] See "Ecuador Hoping To Attract US$ 1.5 Billion Investment In Mining Sector", 28 October 2015 [online] http://oilprice.com/
      Finance/investing-and-trading-reports/Ecuador-Hoping-To-Attract-15-Billion-Investment-In-Mining-Sector.html.

[16] See "Schlumberger to invest US$ 4.9 bn in Ecuador", December 2015 [online] http://latino.foxnews.com/latino/politics/2015/12/16/
      schlumberger-to-invest-4-bn-in-ecuador/.

yet been published. Chinese companies have also shown interest in the country, and are estimated to have invested around US$ 3 billion[17] in recent years.

Inward FDI to **Paraguay** declined by 18%, to US$ 283 million. A number of companies have undertaken exploration work in the country's hydrocarbons sector. They include the Franco-Russian Riviera SA, which announced its intention to invest an initial US$ 25 million to get two wells operating, and a further US$ 100 million in the near future. In the telecommunications sector, the Swedish firm Millicom, through its trademark Tigo, has purchased several pay-TV operators. These transactions have allowed it to expand its presence and the services it offers in the country.

Brazilian firms are still the main investors in Paraguay. In 2015 Intercement, and the Brazilian owner of Cimentos de Portugal (CIMPOR) sold 16% of Yguazú Cementos SA to the local concern Concret-mix, for US$ 35 million, as part of a corporate reorganization and sale of nonstrategic assets. Even so, the firm retains a majority shareholding interest (51%) in Yguazú. In the hotel sector, the United States chain Hilton has announced the construction of two new hotels in Paraguay, one in Asunción (US$ 30 million) and the other in Ciudad del Este (US$ 50 million). Finally, Germany's Grob Aerospace intends to establish a small aircraft assembly plant in Paraguay.

3. Mexico: the region's strongest investment growth

FDI inflows to Mexico rose 18% in 2015, to US$ 30.285 billion, the second highest level for the last seven years after the US$ 45.855 in 2013.[18] For the second year running, profit reinvestment declined, dropping to 30% of total FDI. On the other hand, capital contributions and intracompany loans were up substantially. Mexico accounted for a large portion of the cross-border mergers and acquisitions recorded in Latin America and the Caribbean (see table I.3). In 2015, the United States again became the principal investor country, and was responsible for 52% of the total, up from 30% in 2014. Next in the ranking, but well behind, came Spain (9%) and Japan (5%). Canada retreated as a source of FDI, dropping from 12% of the total in 2014 to 4% in 2015, as a result of the stagnation in mining investment. Brazil was the largest investor in Mexico from the Latin American and Caribbean region in 2015, with US$ 993 million.

The manufacturing sector was the leading destination of FDI inflows to Mexico, accounting for 50% of the total. The largest segment within this is the automotive industry, responsible for 43% of manufacturing FDI. In recent years, the world's leading vehicle brands, especially those from the United States, Japan and the European Union, have announced many new investments. These announcements have been materializing gradually over the years, and have sparked heavy inflows of FDI. In 2015 this trend persisted, and the coming years will likely witness significant new FDI inflows in the automotive industry. In 2015, the Korean automaker Hyundai announced US$ 800 million in investments to install two new plants. Similarly, Japan's Toyota announced an investment of US$ 1 billion to build a new plant in Guanajuato, where it will undertake assembly of the Toyota Corolla model. Ford Motor of the United States announced investments of US$ 2.5 billion to build two new plants, one of which will also be in Guanajuato.

---

[17] See *"La inversión china en Bolivia supera los US$ 3.000 millones"* ["Chinese investment in Bolivia exceeds US$ 3 billion"], 1 October 2015 [online] http://www.paginasiete.bo/economia/2015/10/1/inversion-china-bolivia-supera-3000-millones-71917.html.

[18] The growth rate of 18% is obtained by comparing the definitive figures for 2014 with the preliminary figures for 2015. The definitive figures are generally higher than the preliminary figures. Alternatively, comparing the preliminary figures for both 2014 and 2015 yields a jump of 26% in FDI inflows in 2105.

Other manufacturing industries showing notable activity have included the food and glass businesses. The United States company Owens-Illinois purchased the Vitro glassmaking firm for US$ 2.150 billion. The Danish company Lego announced its intention to expand production capacity in Mexico, for which it will invest some US$ 800 million.

In services, the telecommunications sector was a leader during 2015, thanks in particular to the ambitious acquisitions strategy of United States-based AT&T. Until the recent reforms in the sector, the Mexican telecommunications market had maintained heavy restrictions on the entry of new international players, and on the convergence between different technological platforms (fixed telephony, mobile telephony, broadband and pay television). This context has given rise to one of the leading players in the region's telecommunications market: Telemex/América Móvil. Recent regulatory changes have helped to overcome domestic market rigidities by encouraging competition and the offer of better and more modern services to users. In 2014, AT&T sold its interest (around 8%) in América Móvil for US$ 5.566 billion, allowing it to finalize the purchase of the satellite TV provider DirecTV, a move that entailed a divestment of US$ 4.03 billion in Mexico. These transactions reflect an expansion strategy on the part of AT&T, designed to meet heavy competition in the United States market. This approach has not been restricted to the United States market, however, and the company has also sought opportunities abroad. Thus, AT&T began to implement an ambitious strategy of acquisitions to reinforce its position in the Mexican market, not as a minority shareholder of the dominant provider but rather as the entity controlling fiercely independent operators. In 2015, according to data from Bloomberg, AT&T consummated the purchase of Iusacell and Nextel for US$ 2.5 billion and US$ 1.875 billion respectively, and it also announced investments totalling US$ 3 billion to upgrade the services of both companies.

Finally, as with telecommunications, the energy reform launched by the Government of Mexico is opening new opportunities for private sector participation. While this is not yet apparent in the official FDI figures, there have been many announcements recently in which international firms have declared their intention to invest in Mexico. This is the case with the Spanish company Abengoa which, before its financial problems surfaced, had announced a number of projects, both traditional and in nonconventional renewable energies, totalling several billion dollars. The Italian firm ENEL has also shown interest in investing in Mexico's flourishing energy industry, and it announced construction of two wind farms of 100 MW and 129 MW, with investments of US$ 220 million and US$ 250 million, respectively. Finally, the Spanish company Iberdrola announced construction of a 53 MW power plant, for which it will invest some US$ 84 million jointly with the chemicals firm Dynasol.

Outward direct investment by Mexican firms rose by 62%, to US$ 12.126 billion. Mexico remains one of the principal investor countries of Latin America, and some of its firms are indeed world leaders in their industries. According to data from Bloomberg, one of the largest transactions of 2015 was the acquisition of properties in the United States by a group of private Mexican investors, in the amount of US$ 650 million. Thanks to its wide presence in Latin America and, more recently, in Europe, in a sector that is highly competitive and demands constant technological upgrading, América Móvil is perhaps the biggest direct investor outside Mexico. In the food sector, a number of Mexican firms with an international presence continued to expand their operations. The Grupo Bimbo, for example, acquired Canada's Saputo Bakery for US$ 103 million, and Sigma, owned by the Alfa SAB group, bought 37% of the Spanish firm Campofrío Food Group for US$ 354 million.

4. Central America: a shift in the energy mix

FDI flows in Central America were up by 6% in 2015, at US$ 11.808 billion. With 43% of the total, Panama is still the most important destination of FDI in the subregion, followed by Costa Rica (26%), Honduras (10%) and Guatemala (10%) (see map I.2). In the last year, renewable energies and the financial sector have stood out as the principal targets of inward FDI in the subregion. In October 2014, Citibank announced its intention to sell its assets in five Central American countries (Costa Rica, El Salvador, Guatemala, Nicaragua and Panama) and in Peru. Among those interested in acquiring the Central American assets, valued at some US$ 1.5 billion, were Spain's Banco Popolar and the Colombian institutions Aval and Banco Promérica. Negotiations collapsed, however. In the end, the Citibank assets were sold in separate batches: Canada's Scotiabank purchased the operations in Costa Rica and Panama, the Honduran group Ficohsa bought the assets in Honduras and Nicaragua, the Nicaraguan group América took over the operations in Guatemala, and the Honduran group Atlántida acquired the assets in El Salvador. For its part, the United States-based insurance company American International Group Inc. (AIG) sold its operations in the subregion (El Salvador, Guatemala, Honduras and Panama) to the Panamanian firm ASSA, which already had activities in Costa Rica, El Salvador, Nicaragua and Panama. The fact that the assets of Citibank and AIG were sold primarily to Central American entities will help to further business integration in the subregion.

Map I.2
Central America: FDI received, 2014-2015
(Millions of dollars)

Panama is the main recipient of FDI in Central America

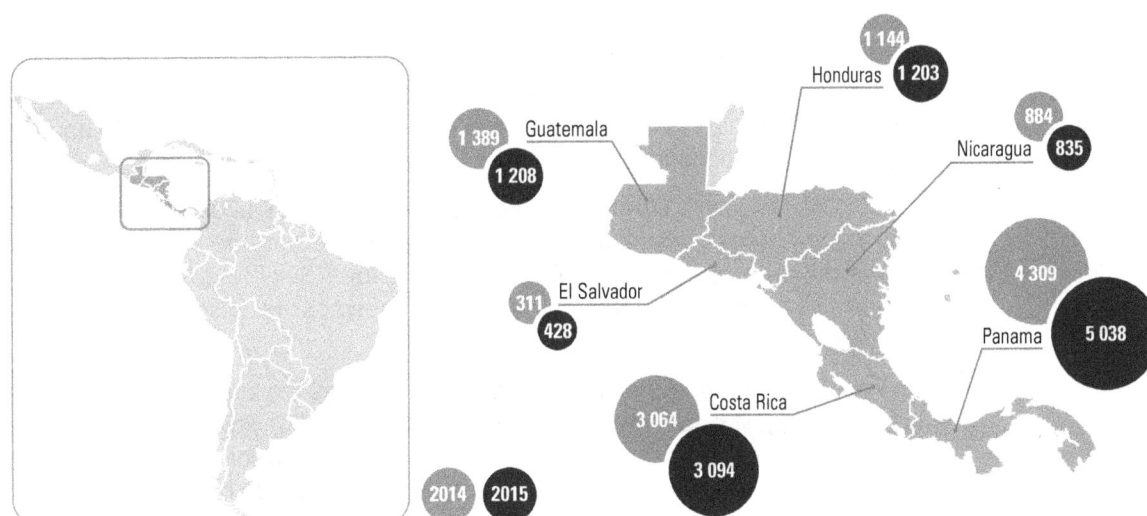

Source: Economic Commission for Latin America and the Caribbean (ECLAC), on the basis of official figures and estimates as of 27 May 2016.

In 2015, FDI flows to **Panama** rose by 17%, and stood at US$ 5.039 billion. This figure constitutes a record high, positioning the country as the leading recipient in Central America, and the seventh in Latin America and the Caribbean. During 2016, the work of widening of the Panama Canal will be completed and a number of firms involved in Canal-related activities have made major investments to expand their capacities. For its part, Avianca of Colombia has sold 30% of the LifeMiles customer loyalty business, headquartered in Panama, to the United States-based Advent International for US$ 344 million.

Energy projects have been one of the most dynamic areas for foreign investment in Panama, as in other Central American countries. InterEnergy of the United States purchased 55% of the 55 MW Latin Power III generating plant in Pedregal from Conduit Capital Partners, also of the United States. During 2015, the same company pursued construction of a wind farm that will generate 215 MW, with an estimated investment of US$ 430 million. The Canadian company SkyPower announced construction of a 500 MW solar energy generating plant, at a cost of US$ 1 billion, to which maybe added another US$ 50 million for installation of a research centre on solar energy and other environmental issues. Lastly, the Chinese firm Solar Power Inc. (SPI) announced construction of a 100 MW solar plant.

In 2015, FDI inflows to **Costa Rica** rose by 1% to US$ 3.094 billion. The country has benefited from a real estate development boom, focused essentially on the tourism industry and retirement communities, in which a few foreign investors have been key players. In early 2015, the United States chain AMResorts, a subsidiary of Apple Leisure Group, inaugurated the Las Mareas resort, in which it invested US$ 130 million, and it also took over management of the Papagayo Resort & Spa (previously known as the Hilton Papagayo Costa Rica Resort & Spa).

In recent years, thanks to an aggressive strategy for attracting investments, Costa Rica has been able to influence the decisions of firms seeking locations. In 2015, Germany's Bosch announced an investment of US$ 30 million to establish a business services centre. Like other countries of the subregion, Costa Rica has also received investment in renewable energies. SunEdison of the United States invested US$ 350 million to acquire 100% of Globeleq Mesoamerica Energy (GME) from a consortium led by the British firm Actis, with renewable energy assets throughout the subregion.[19] Lastly, the United States chain Wal-Mart announced a US$ 100 million investment to upgrade and expand its operations in the country.

In 2015, FDI inflows to **Guatemala** dropped by 13% to US$ 1.209 billion. The fall-off in intracompany lending was particularly steep. Over the last two years, the energy sector was the main destination for FDI, accounting for 31% of total inflows, followed by manufacturing, with 16%. The main source of these capital flows was the United States (29%), followed by Colombia.

An important development in the electricity sector was the purchase of Energuate, the country's biggest power distributor, by the Israeli firm I.C. Power Ltd., part of the Kenon Holdings Group, from the British investment fund Actis, for some US$ 554 million.[20] This purchase added to the assets that the Israeli group already held in the country's

---

[19] In 2010, Actis acquired 70% of Globeleq Mesoamerica Energy (GME) and thereby took control of the first wind farm in Latin America, Planta Eólica Tilarán (PESA) in Costa Rica. The Costa Rican firm Mesoamérica Energía acquired the remaining 30%. Since this acquisition, Actis and Mesoamérica have expanded capacity from 24 MW in operation to 314 MW in operation and under construction.

[20] Energuate embraces two power distribution companies that together supply 1.6 million customers, or around 60% of connected users in Guatemala. Distribuidora de Electricidad de Oriente, S.A. (DEORSA) and Distribuidora de Electricidad de Occidente, S.A. (DEOCSA) cover 19 of the country's 22 departments. This acquisition marks the third change in ownership of the power distributors, after the partial privatization of the Instituto Nacional de Electrificación (INDE) in 1999. The first owner was Spain's Unión Fenosa, followed by the British investment fund Actis and finally I.C. Power of Israel.

power generating segment (CMI, 2016). In the banking sector, in addition to the sale of Citibank's assets in the subregion, the year was marked by the acquisition of an additional 20% in Banco Agromercantil by Bancolombia for US$ 180 million, bringing the latter's participation to 60%.[21] While this transaction does not represent a new investment, but merely a change of ownership, it represents a vote of confidence in the Guatemalan market. Lastly, two firms announced new investments: Germany's Bayer, to improve and expand its local operations in the area of over-the-counter medicines and agricultural inputs (US$ 28 million), and Peru's Ransa, for construction of a specialized logistics centre for receiving and fitting out imported passenger and commercial vehicles (US$ 60 million).

In **Honduras**, FDI rose by 5% in 2015, to US$ 1.204 billion. The biggest increases were in the financial sector, real estate and business services. The sector of greatest interest, however, was renewable energy. An expansion plan has been drawn up for renewable energy generation and distribution, aimed at increasing these energies' share of the country's power generation matrix to 80%. In the framework of this plan, the Government of Honduras announced a special rate for the first 300 MW of solar energy generated before 31 July 2015. This programme proved very successful during 2015: 500 MW in new capacity was created (GTM, 2015), while it is expected that about 700 MW on new capacity will come on stream by 2017. Among the many new projects is one headed by SunEdison of the United States, which had already acquired the Central American assets of Globeleq Mesoamerica Energy (GME) and had built an 82 MW generating plant for which it invested US$ 145 million. In 2015, Honduras became the second most important market for solar energy in Latin America, behind Chile but ahead of Mexico. In this way, and with the new investments in wind energy, the energy mix in Honduras has undergone some significant changes. Between 2007 and 2015, renewable energy increased its share from 6% to 47% of the total (Mercados y Tendencias, 2015).

In infrastructure, the Colombian-Honduran company Autopistas del Atlántico SA (ADASA) announced investments amounting to US$ 260 million for maintenance and improvement of a highway in the north of the country, which has been targeted by the government for development of the tourism sector.[22] The Goldlake Group of Italy announced an investment of US$ 230 million to reactivate an iron ore deposit (US$ 30 million) and build a ferro-cement plant for export (US$ 200 million).

In 2015, FDI flows to **Nicaragua** declined by 5%, to US$ 835 million. Since 2014, Nicaragua's *maquiladora* (assembly plant) industry has felt the effects of the change in United States policy, which entailed removal of the tariff preference level (TPL) provisions. It is estimated that some 3,000 jobs have been lost and textile exports have fallen by 5% as a result of this change. To counter the effects of that measure, the Government of Nicaragua is in discussions with Canada and the Republic of Korea to move forward with trade negotiations. If those efforts are successful, the Nicaraguan authorities estimate that the next few years could bring some US$ 160 million in new investment.[23] Moreover, in March 2015 Japan's Yazaki Group, a manufacturer of wire harnesses and auto parts, announced a substantial investment in expanding its operations, with the creation of 3,300 jobs.

The telecommunications sector saw the greatest activity in 2015, thanks in particular to the investments made by Movistar and América Móvil. In the financial sector, Grupo Financiero Ficohsa of Honduras purchased the assets of Citibank, thus adding Nicaragua to its existing operations in Guatemala, Honduras and Panama and

[21]   With this operation, Bancolombia is pressing ahead with its strategy for expansion in Central America: El Salvador, Guatemala and Panama.

[22]   ADASA is a company formed by Grupo Empresarial Grodco of Colombia and the Honduran firm Profesionales de la Construcción (PRODECON).

[23]   See "Nicaragua seeks textile investments to grow exports", 7 September 2015 [online] http://www.just-style.com/analysis/nicaragua-seeks-textile-investments-to-grow-exports_id126100.aspx.

continuing its expansion in Central America. And in manufacturing, Mexico's Sukarne inaugurated a new meat processing plant in which it invested US$ 115 million.

In 2014, work began on the biggest project in the country's history, the Nicaragua Canal. As of the date of publication of this paper, however, there were still many unknowns as to its continued viability (International Business Times, 2015).

In 2015, FDI inflows to **El Salvador** rose by 38%, to US$ 429 million, or more than twice the inflows recorded in 2013. Most of the new investments received by El Salvador are the result of small-scale projects. The biggest acquisition was the US$ 100 million purchase of Grupo CYBSA, a packaging manufacturer, by the Irish company Smurfit Kappa, in order to expand its presence in Central America. In recent years, the country's mineral resources have attracted interest from international investors in metal mining; however, strong opposition was mounted amid environmental concerns, chiefly in relation to water resources, which led the government to halt mining operations in the country. Some of the firms involved, such as Canada's Pacific Rim Corporation, a subsidiary of OceanaGold, brought legal actions against El Salvador, whose outcomes were still unknown at the time of publication.

5.   The Caribbean: tourism maintains its share in FDI

FDI in the Caribbean was down by 17%, to US$ 5.975 billion (see table I.7).[24] In 2015, the subregion's main recipient of FDI was the Dominican Republic, with 39% of the total. Somewhat behind came Trinidad and Tobago (20%, but counting only the first three quarters) and Jamaica (13%). The countries of the Organization of Eastern Caribbean States (OECS) received together 9% of FDI inflows to the subregion (see map I.3).

When it comes to FDI, the Caribbean economies can generally be divided into two groups: those dependent on tourism and those specialized in the exploitation of natural resources. Experience suggests that very few countries are able to attract FDI simultaneously into tourism and natural resources, and sector diversification is rare. However, strong activity in the telecommunications sector has modified this pattern in the recent past. In 2014, with a view to strengthening its growth strategy, the British firm Cable & Wireless Communications (CWC) announced its intention to acquire Columbus international Inc., a Barbadian firm with operations in various countries of the Caribbean (Antigua and Barbuda, Barbados, Curaçao, Grenada, Jamaica, Saint Vincent and the Grenadines, St. Lucia, and Trinidad and Tobago).[25] In March of 2015, this acquisition was completed, after payment of some US$ 3.025 billion. To fulfil the conditions imposed by the regulatory authorities, CWC undertook to sell 49% of Telecommunications Services of Trinidad and Tobago, a move that had not yet been finalized as of the date of publication of this paper. A few months later, Liberty Global of the United States and the United Kingdom announced its intention to acquire CWC for some US$ 5.3 billion.[26] These transactions are sure to have an impact on FDI statistics for the subregion, but it will probably be minor, as the operations involve changes of ownership among foreign companies. However that may be, as a result of these operations the Caribbean will be left with only two significant telecommunications operators, Liberty Global and Digicel, a situation that could affect the level of competition in some markets of the subregion.

---

[24]   In the case of Trinidad and Tobago, fourth-quarter data are lacking for 2015. The comparison presented here covers the first three quarters of 2014 and 2015.

[25]   See "CWC agrees to acquire Columbus International Inc. to accelerate growth strategy and deliver superior customer service" [online] http://www.columbusbusiness.co/en/el-salvador/news/cwc-acuerda-adquirir-columbus-international-inc-para-acelerar-la-estrategia-de-crecimiento-y-entregar-un-servicio-de-atencion-al-cliente-superior/53.

[26]   Liberty Global and CWC have one very important factor in common: one of the pioneers of the cable television industry in the United States, John Malone. He is president and majority shareholder of Liberty Global, and has acquired a share of approximately 13% of CWC, after that company took over Columbus International.

Map I.3
The Caribbean: FDI received, 2014-2015
(Millions of dollars)

The Dominican Republic is the principal recipient of FDI in the Caribbean

OECS countries, 11%

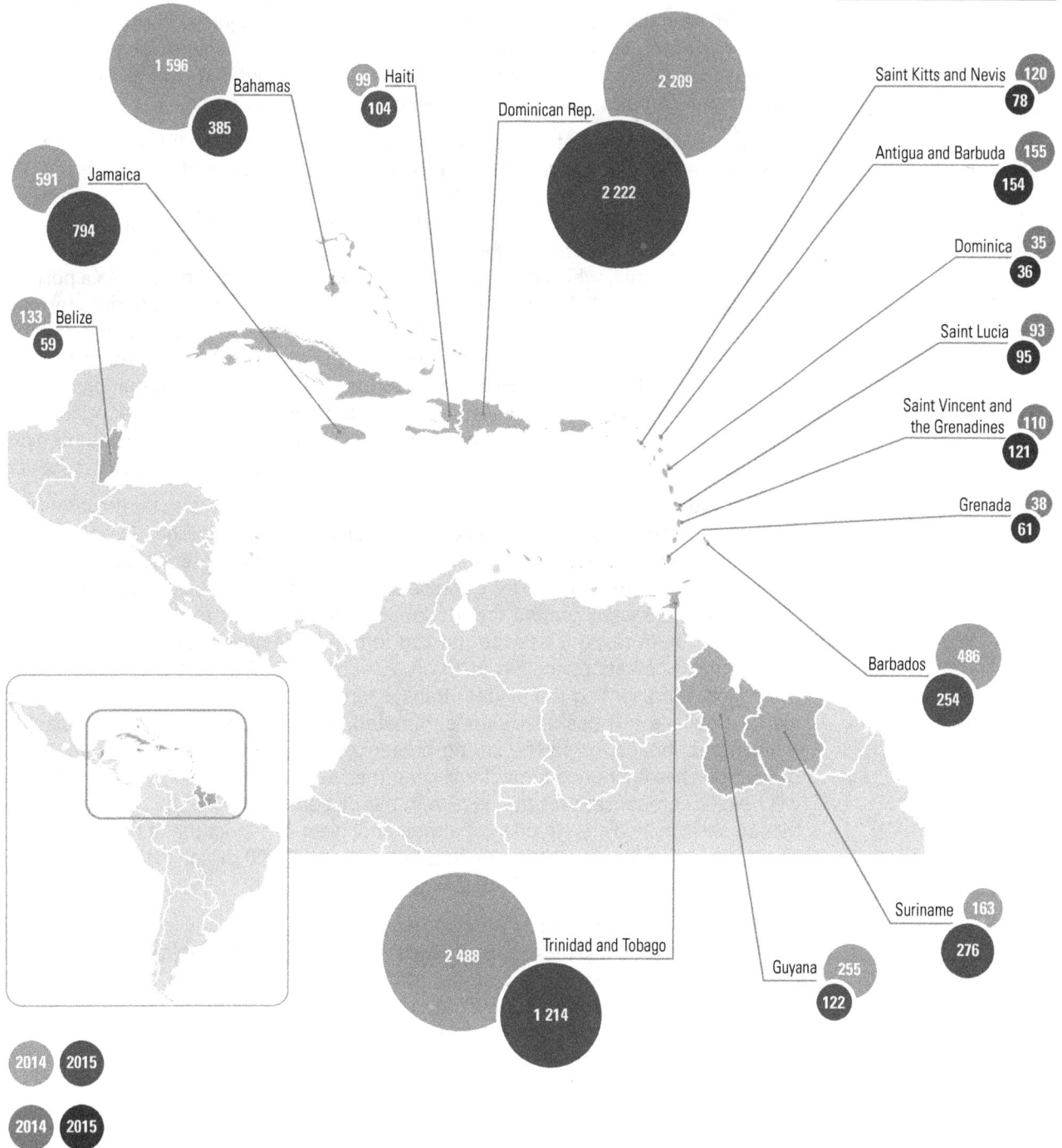

- 1 596
- Bahamas
- 385
- 99 Haiti
- 104
- 2 209
- Dominican Rep.
- 2 222
- 591 Jamaica
- 794
- 133 Belize
- 59
- Saint Kitts and Nevis 120
- 78
- Antigua and Barbuda 155
- 154
- Dominica 35
- 36
- Saint Lucia 93
- 95
- Saint Vincent and the Grenadines 110
- 121
- Grenada 38
- 61
- Barbados 486
- 254
- Suriname 163
- 276
- 2 488
- Trinidad and Tobago
- 1 214
- Guyana 255
- 122

2014 2015

2014 2015

Source: Economic Commission for Latin America and the Caribbean (ECLAC), on the basis of official figures and estimated as of 27 May 2016.
Note: The 2015 figure for Trinidad and Tobago refers only to the first three quarters of the year.

The **Dominican Republic** recorded a slight increase (1%) in FDI inflows, which amounted to US$ 2.222 billion. Investment in 2015 was centred in tourism-related activities and in real estate development, which together accounted for 49% of the total. For example, the United States-based cruise operator Carnival Corporation inaugurated a new terminal at Puerto Plata, for which it invested US$ 85 million. The Amber Cove terminal will be the port of departure for the first vessel of the Fathom brand, which Carnival Corporation will launch in 2015. The shipping company is planning to have 23 vessels of its different brands arrive at the new cruise terminal during the first year, carrying some 350,000 tourists. The German group Lopesan has acquired around 20 ha in the tourism centre of Bávaro-Higüey (La Altagracia), for US$ 30 million, where it will build a hotel with more than 1,000 rooms. The acquired site is located in the most desirable zone of Playa Bávaro, on the beachfront and next to the IFA Villas Bávaro hotel complex, which the German company already owns.

Other major sectors of activity including telecommunications (15%) and free zones (11%), while the importance of mining has evaporated: it dropped from 47% to 0.3% of FDI inflows between 2011 and 2015. In telecommunications, the Mexican operator América Móvil announced its intention to invest around US$ 245 million in 2015, and a total of US$ 800 million over the next three years. In the power sector, AES Corp. of the United States, which generates 40% of the country's electricity, has a portfolio of projects for some US$ 125 million. These include expansion of the Andrés terminal for the export of liquefied natural gas, and the construction of a gas pipeline that will allow the generation of 1,000 MW of energy: both projects are supposed to be ready in the second half of 2016. Lastly, as proof of the problems facing international mining companies, the Swiss concern Glencore sold its participation in a nickel mine in the Dominican Republic to Americano Nickel Ltd. (ANL). In fact, due to the low price of nickel and the high cost of energy, Glencore has cut back and at times suspended production.

In **Trinidad and Tobago**, information for the fourth quarter is not yet available. In the first three quarters of 2015, the country received US$ 1.214 billion, up by 55% over the same period of the previous year. Even so, inflows may not record any significant increase for the full year, given the collapse of oil prices: the hydrocarbons sector, which has contracted sharply around the world, accounts for close to 90% of FDI inflows (89% in 2015). In response to the marked retreat in oil prices, the Anglo-Dutch firm Royal Dutch Shell announced in 2015 an agreement to acquire British Gas (PG) for €64 billion, representing the biggest transaction in the oil and gas sector for at least the past decade.[27] If this deal is consummated, it could have a significant impact on Trinidad and Tobago, given the strong presence of BG in the country. In fact, Royal Dutch Shell has announced that it will keep the BG operation running. In a move that will help to compensate for the decline in the oil sector, in 2015 the Japanese group Mitsubishi launched construction of a methanol plant, a project that it had announced two years earlier. The company has invested some US$ 990 million in that plant, which is to come on stream in early 2019 (Mitsubishi Corp., 2015).

Some of the services sectors were also recipients of FDI inflows. In telecommunications, Jamaica-based Digicel is making major investments in its network infrastructure in order to upgrade its services in the country. At the beginning of 2016, Digicel announced that it would invest some US$ 300 million in deploying "fiber to the home" (FTTH) infrastructure, in preparation for the launch of new pay TV and fixed broadband services. Lastly, the Salvadoran retail group Unicorner has begun construction of a distribution centre that will involve an investment of around US$ 60 million.

In the first three quarters of 2015, the United States was the source of 60% of FDI inflows to Trinidad and Tobago. Next, but well behind, came Canada, with 8% of the total.

---

[27]   This huge operation has coincided with the collapse of oil prices, sparked by the nonconventional oil boom in the United States and the decision of Saudi Arabia not to cut back production. The situation is similar to the one that prevailed at the beginning of the millennium, which witnessed a number of major mergers: British Petroleum bought Amoco and Arco, Exxon acquired Mobil, and Chevron merged with Texaco.

Inward FDI in **Jamaica** rose 34% in 2015, reaching US$ 794 million. In that year, the tourism sector proved particularly attractive, accounting for the bulk of investment projects announced by foreign firms. Among the most important developments was the announcement by the Mexican chain Karisma Hotels & Resorts that it would invest US$ 900 million to build nine hotels with a total of 4,000 rooms over the next 10 years. The first hotel is to open its doors in 2018. The Spanish-Canadian chain Ocean by H10 Hotels announced the construction of two luxury hotels, for which it will invest some US$ 200 million.[28] The Jamaican government agreed to hand over a 486 ha property to the China Harbour Engineering Company (CHEC) to build three luxury hotels with 2,500 rooms, in exchange for constructing a 67 km highway to the north coast of the island. The four-lane road, popularly known as the "Beijing Highway", will cost US$ 600 million (Financial Juneteenth, 2016). The same Chinese company has participated in another major project on the Caribbean island, the development of a transshipment port in Portland Bight, on Goats Island, where it will invest some US$ 1.5 billion. This initiative, however, has aroused great resistance in the community, given the status of Goats Island as a protected zone, and this poses much uncertainty as to its future. On another front, the French company CMA CGM, one of the world's leading container carriers, signed a 30-year agreement with the Government of Jamaica to manage the container terminal at the Port of Kingston, for which it is committed to investing around US$ 600 million (Jamaica Observer, 2015a). Lastly, a new free zone is to be constructed in Spanish Town, under the aegis of the Jamaican Logistics Hub Initiative, which seeks to create a logistics centre in Jamaica and take advantage of the island's communications links by manufacturing products destined for regional markets. This project will involve US$ 350 million in investments covering productive activities related to oil derivatives, vehicle assembly, food and tobacco, and pharmaceuticals (IIS, 2015).

The 2015 edition of this document examined the process of concentration in the beer market in Latin America and around the world (ECLAC, 2015a). Until 2015, Jamaica seemed an exception to this global trend. However, during the past year the Dutch firm Heineken, the world's second-biggest brewer, completed acquisition of two companies that it held jointly with the British firm Diageo PLC, for US$ 781 million. Thus, Heineken acquired 57.9% of the local firm Desnoes & Geddes (D&G), thereby achieving 73.3% ownership. This transaction is part of the Dutch bottling company's strategy for coping with a global market dominated by the major brands, and with declining consumption in some key markets including the United States. This in fact turned into one of the largest cross-border M&A operations in Latin America and the Caribbean in 2015 (see table I.3). Lastly, there have been some significant investments in fairly unconventional activities. First, with the partial decriminalization of marijuana, the Jamaican authorities are implementing a series of rules and regulations intended to regulate a flourishing pharmaceuticals industry based on cannabis. In this context, the Canadian firm Timeless Herbal Care (THC) announced an investment of US$ 100 million to produce marijuana for medical purposes (Jamaica Observer, 2015b). In line with other regional initiatives, WRB Enterprises of the United States announced an investment of US$ 60 million in a 20 MW photovoltaic plant with 98,000 panels that will be the biggest solar generator in the English-speaking Caribbean.

In 2015. FDI inflows to the **Bahamas** declined by 76%, to US$ 385 million.[29] As in other Caribbean countries, tourism is the most important industry for FDI entering the Bahamas. Of particular interest here is the Baha Mar project, which was to involve investments of US$ 3.5 billion. This initiative fell into bankruptcy in 2015 (see box I.2). In addition to this megaproject, there are a number of initiatives in the tourism sector that entail significant investments. These include: expansion of the Deep Water Cay Fishing Resort, operated by the Dutch firm Six Senses, which calls for an investment of US$ 160 million; the Malai

---

[28] Established in 2007, Ocean by H10 Hotels is a joint venture between the Spanish hotel chain H10 and Vacances Air Transat, a Canadian tour operator.

[29] The statistics from the Central Bank of the Bahamas are not fully comparable with those of other countries. In this document, FDI data represent the sum of two items on the financial account: direct investment and other private flows.

Resorts World, with US$ 600 million in the Bimini Resort (Caribbean Journal, 2015); Aman Resorts of the United Kingdom is investing some US$ 350 million to construct a luxury hotel complex, Mat Lowe's Cay, and China Construction America (CCA) has announced construction of a 200 room hotel in Nassau, The Pointe, with an investment of around US$ 250 million. At the end of 2015, the Italian firm Mediterranean Shipping Company (MCS), the second largest cruise operator in the world, undertook to build a cruise ship port, with an investment of US$ 100 million, at Sandy Cay (Tribune 242, 2015). Some weeks later, the Government of the Bahamas awarded MCS a 100-year concession to transform a desert island into a high-end beach destination, for which it will invest around US$ 200 million (Daily Mail, 2015). Finally, MCS and Hutchison of the Hong Kong Special Administrative Region of China have undertaken to expand facilities of the Freeport Container Port (FCP), for which they will invest some US$ 280 million (The Nassau Guardian, 2015). Despite all this activity, it must be noted that the soaring crime rate in the country could pose a potential risk when it comes to attracting new investments (Tribune 242, 2016).

Box I.2
Foreign direct investment: yes or no? The case of Baha Mar

The Bahamas receives around 5 million visitors every year, including cruise ship passengers, making the island one of the prime tourism destinations of the Caribbean. This has imprinted a marked pattern of specialization on the economy, in which the bulk of jobs depends directly or indirectly on the tourism industry. At the same time, new tourism undertakings generate huge inflows of FDI.

At the present time, the biggest project in the Caribbean area is unfolding in the Bahamas: the Baha Mar resort, near Nassau, with 3,000 rooms and an estimated investment of US$ 3.5 billion. The project was launched in 2010, and a year later the cornerstone was laid. This undertaking would become the second mega-resort in the Bahamas, after Atlantis Resort, located a few kilometres away. The Baha Mar is intended to breathe new life into tourism in the Bahamas and to broaden the country's tourism options. The Atlantis is geared to family tourism, while Baha Mar targets an adult clientele, with a large casino as its prime attraction. In contrast to other projects, moreover, this undertaking is intended to draw visitors from Asia.

The project was conceived by local entrepreneurs, although it had the backing of the Government of China. The company responsible for construction is China Construction of America (CCA), which used thousands of Chinese workers. Most of the financing for the project was provided by the Export Import Bank of China, through a loan of US$ 2.45 billion.

From the balance of payments perspective, this project would not represent FDI since, although it has external financing and was built by a foreign company, the owner is a local firm. This shows that some international financial flows do not represent FDI, a topic that is discussed in further detail in Chapter III. Similarly, a foreign investor can finance itself locally and "create" FDI without any cross-border movement of funds.

During 2015, when the Baha Mar complex was practically completed, the project began to encounter severe problems. In June, the firm responsible for the undertaking filed for protection under the Chapter 11 of the United States bankruptcy law in the District of Delaware. The judge hearing the case dismissed the filing and the project was placed in the hands of a liquidator in Nassau. The suspension of activities had an immediate impact on the country's economy, with a significant jump in unemployment and a decline in economic growth. The estimated value of the project was in fact equivalent to 40% of GDP. Apparently, the project's failure was sparked by disputes between CCA, the Export Import Bank of China, the local investors and the government. However, it must be noted that the economic feasibility of the project was questionable, to say the least. A few years previously, the Atlantis resort had been so burdened with debt that it was declared bankrupt, and this obliged the South African company Kerzner International Holdings to transfer ownership to the Canadian investment administrator Brookfield Asset Management. It would seem, then, that there is not enough room in the Bahamas for two initiatives of the scale.

Box I.2 (concluded)

Given the damage that the project has suffered after work was suspended, it is now expected to require perhaps US$ 1 billion in additional spending to complete it and make it operational. Yet there are no potential investors on the horizon capable of assuming the challenges posed by the project. In recent months, different options have appeared, prime among which are Kerzner International Holdings, referred to above, and China's Fosun Group, which has operations in the Bahamas.

This is a very interesting project from the viewpoint of FDI statistics. As noted at the outset, the project does not currently represent an inflow of FDI to the Bahamas. However, if it were taken over by a foreign firm, it would become an FDI project. If this alternative should come to pass, it could result in an extremely large inflow, even if the money were used to pay off the loans from the Export Import Bank of China. In the end, the situation shows once again that large, short-term movements of FDI do not necessarily translate into new investments in productive capital.

Source: Economic Commission for Latin America and the Caribbean (ECLAC), on the basis of Tribune 242, "Idb: Baha Mar To Up Jobless Rate 2%", 16 December 2015 [online] http://www.tribune242.com/news/2015/dec/16/idb-baha-mar-jobless-rate-2/ and "China Provides 'No Baha Mar Comfort'", 21 December 2015 [online] http://www.tribune242.com/news/2015/dec/21/china-provides-no-baha-mar-comfort/; *The Economist,* "The bankruptcy of a big resort buffets the Bahamas", 23 January 2016 [online] http://www.economist.com/news/americas/21688935-bankruptcy-big-resort-buffets-bahamas-no-dice.

In 2015, FDI flows into **Suriname** rose by 69%, to US$ 276 million.[30] This outcome reflected the fact that the United States company Alcoa Inc. had disinvested heavily in 2014, under the impact of shrinking bauxite reserves and rising energy costs. The process continued in 2015, when Alcoa sought to transfer its bauxite refining operations to a state-owned enterprise. Negotiations collapsed, however, and Alcoa closed its plant in November. At the present time, the country's main economic source of attraction is shifting to gold mining. The United States mining concern Newmont is committed to investing US$ 1 billion to develop the Merian gold deposit, which is to come on stream at the end of 2016. In the same vein, Australia's Mariana Resources was promoting the Nassau Gold Project, located some 20 km from Merian, but it abandoned the undertaking at the beginning of 2016.

Among developments in other sectors of the Suriname economy, the Royal Bank of Canada sold RBC Royal Bank to Republic Bank Ltd. (RBL) of Trinidad and Tobago for some US$ 40 million.[31] The Chinese construction company Broad began operations on the outskirts of Paramaribo, producing inputs for the construction industry (The Guardian, 2015).

Barbados recorded a decline of 48% in FDI, which in 2015 amounted to US$ 254 million. As noted earlier, the largest transactions in the Caribbean subregion took place in Barbados. The first was the purchase of Columbus International by Cable and Wireless (CWC), followed by the acquisition of CWC by Liberty Global. As a result of these transactions, investments of US$ 100 million were announced for improving the network infrastructure in Barbados.[32] The Jamaican telecommunications firm Digicel, as part of its expansion and diversification strategy, acquired a majority shareholding in Prism Holdings, a company that has operations in several countries of the Caribbean and is specialized in payment systems, information management, data centres and

[30] The Central Bank of Suriname has revised FDI figures for recent years. The original estimate for 2012 was US$ 4 million, while the revised figure rose to US$ 163 million.

[31] See "Republic Bank Limited To Acquire RBC Royal Bank (Suriname) N.V", 1 April 2015 [online] https://www.republictt.com/news/republic-bank-limited-acquire-rbc-royal-bank-suriname-nv.

[32] See "Flow begins significant roll out; launches US$ 160 investment in Barbados", 17 June 2015 [online] fhttp://www.stlucianewsonline.com/flow-begins-significant-roll-out-launches-us160-investment-in-barbados/.

other services. In addition, the Canadian electric company Emera Inc. acquired 19.3% of Emera (Caribbean) for around US$ 55 million, giving it 100% ownership.

As is the case in other Caribbean countries, Barbados is experiencing an investment boom in the tourism sector. Investment of close to US$ 1 billion is expected in the next few years, adding some 2,300 rooms to the country's hotel offerings. The Jamaican company Sandals recently opened a new luxury resort, Sandals Barbados, in which it has invested around US$ 300 million. In addition, Wyndham Hotels and Resorts announced construction of a 5-star hotel with 450 rooms, to open in 2018.

In 2015, FDI flows to **Guyana** dropped by 52%, to US$ 122 million. The mining sector remained the most important destination for these capital flows, accounting for around 30% of the total (compared to 28% in 2014). In October 2015, the Government of the Bolivarian Republic of Venezuela notified the Canadian company Guyana Goldfields of possible legal action against its operations, located in a territory that has been the subject of a century-long dispute with neighbouring Guyana. Guyana Goldfields has been working the Aurora mine since 1996 and, after investing US$ 277 million, it finally began to extract gold in 2015. In that year gold production began at the Karouni project headed by Australia's Troy Resources, following an investment of around US$ 100 million. At the present time, Guyana produces no oil, but new discoveries could change this picture. In 2015, an international consortium led by Exxon Mobil discovered an oil deposit of 700 million barrels on the Esequibo coast, valued at some US$ 40 billion. This discovery has exacerbated the dispute with the Bolivarian Republic of Venezuela, and has heightened the uncertainty prevailing in the country (PI you, 2016).

Haiti received US$ 104 million in FDI in 2015, 5% more than in the previous year. FDI is targeted at two priority sectors: the maquiladora industry and tourism. The first is a traditional destination, while the second has become important more recently. In the maquiladora industry, the Korean clothes maker Hansae announced the opening of a new, export-oriented factory in the Sonapi industrial park, where it is eligible for the tariff benefits that Haiti enjoys in the United States. This initiative will create some 5,000 jobs. As one of the world's largest clothing manufacturers, Hansae employs some 60,000 workers in 11 countries, and its customers include Nike, Gap, H&M, Uniqlo, and Abercrombie & Fitch. As well, several Chinese companies have shown interest in transferring a portion of their basic manufacturing activities to Haiti. In the tourism sector, a number of important investments are coming to fruition. In 2015, the first Marriott hotel was opened in Port-au-Prince, with 175 rooms, as the result of a joint initiative with the Clinton Foundation, the Jamaican company Digicel, and the Marriott chain, with an investment of US$ 45 million. The government is actively encouraging investment in the tourism sector, especially in large-scale projects. Prime examples are the undertakings at Ile-à-Vache and Côtes-de-Fer, although both have drawn criticism from neighbouring residents.

In FDI flows to **Belize** declined in 2015 by 55%, to US$ 59 million. The Spanish-Guatemalan group Santander Sugar has been particularly active recently, committing US$ 150 million to produce sugar for export. The new sugar mill will begin operations in 2016 and will produce up to 100,000 tons a year. At the same time it will use molasses to produce up to 16 MW of electricity annually, representing 20% of the country's power generation. The outsourcing of business processes is another activity that has expanded rapidly among domestic firms, although the government is hoping for a major foreign investment in this sector. A number of tourism projects are under development. The United States actor Leonardo DiCaprio is sponsoring the construction of an ecological resort in Blackadore Caye, in which there are plans to invest some US$ 283 million. Also of interest are the projects at Itz'ana (US$ 43 million) and Mahogany Bay (US$ 75 million). Lastly, the Norwegian shipping company Norwegian Cruise Line has purchased 30 hectares of land in the south of the country to develop a US$ 50 million project that will open its doors in late 2016.

As in other countries of Latin America and the Caribbean, the Central Bank of the Eastern Caribbean has begun to prepare FDI statistics using the methodology from the sixth edition of the IMF Balance of Payments Manual. This methodological change has meant some amendments to the overall figures for previous years. In 2015, the member countries of the Organization of Eastern Caribbean States (OECS) received a total of US$ 545 million, representing a slight reduction (of 1%) from the previous year.

In 2015, FDI in **Antigua and Barbuda** declined by 0.5% to US$ 154 million. As with the great majority of Caribbean countries, tourism is the most important activity for foreign investors. Major projects include one headed by the Chinese company Yida Investment Group for construction of an enormous real estate complex with a number of luxury hotels, more than 1,000 residential units, golf courses and other facilities, for which around US$ 2 billion will be invested. However, although it was announced in 2014, construction work had not yet started as of the date of publication of this document. In a similar situation is an undertaking headed by Canadians of the Sunwing Travel Group to build a 500 room hotel in Deep Bay, with an investment of around US$ 400 million. Slightly more advanced is the Pearns Point project, involving an investment of US$ 300 million, which finally saw shovels in the ground in 2015. Lastly, a project with an estimated cost of US$ 200 million, headed by the United States actor Robert DeNiro on the island of Barbuda, is to begin construction in 2016, thanks to legal changes introduced by the government that should forestall a pending legal challenge (The Daily Observer, 2015). Many projects in Antigua and Barbuda are financed under the "citizenship by investment" model that gained prominence some years ago. However, it is also clear that several of these projects are drawing criticism from various segments of society, either because of their environmental impact or because of the costly tax incentives granted them by the government.

In **Saint Vincent and the Grenadines**, FDI inflows rose by 10% to US$ 121 million in 2015. For this Caribbean island, the lack of an international airport that would connect it with the principal markets of North America and Europe still constitutes a great drawback. For that reason, the authorities sponsored an international competition for the construction of a new airport, with a budget of around US$ 300 million. The Argyle International Airport will at last start operating in 2016. It is hoped that this government-sponsored investment will boost tourism arrivals and attract the interest of international investors. Similar thinking underlies the construction of the Pink Sands Club, a luxury resort headed by English investors at an estimated cost of US$ 120 million. Saint Vincent and the Grenadines is the only member state of the OECS that does not have a "citizenship by investment" programme.

Saint Lucia received US$ 95 million in FDI in 2015, representing an increase of 2% over the previous year. Like other Caribbean countries, Saint Lucia depends heavily on the tourism trade. In 2015, the Canadian Sunwing Group announced the renovation of the Smuggler's Cove Hotel to transform it into the Royalton Resort & Spa, with an estimated investment of US$ 120 million. Work has also been progressing without any major setbacks on construction of the Harbour Club Hotel, led by Swiss investors. In 2015, the government issued a surprise announcement offering citizenship by investment, a step that the island's authorities had previously rejected. However, Saint Lucia's policy differs from that of other countries in the subregion, as it requires potential investors to demonstrate a certain degree of wealth before they are granted citizenship.

Although it recorded a drop in FDI in 2015, **Saint Kitts and Nevis** continues to receive a particularly high volume in relation to the size of its economy. FDI inflows last year amounted to US$ 78 million, down by 35% from 2014. This outcome reflects the success of the citizenship by investment programme. Among the projects under development is one headed by the Hilton chain of the United States, which is building an Embassy Suites-brand hotel with 227 rooms at a cost of around US$ 140 million. The Kittitian Hill project, for US$ 400 million, and the Park Hyatt St. Kitts undertaking, with an estimated cost of US$ 150 million, are also moving forward.

In 2015, FDI inflows to **Grenada** rose by 59% to US$ 51 million. In the tourism sector, the Egyptian entrepreneur Naguib Sawaris is building at least two new hotels.[33] In 2015 work started on the renovation of the Silver Sands and the refurbishing of the old Hotel Riviera, for which some US$ 120 million will be invested. At the beginning of 2016 the Jamaican chain Sandals announced a US$ 10 million investment in its LaSource Resort & Spa facilities.

Lastly, FDI in **Dominica** was up by 2% to US$ 36 million in 2015. In August of that year, tropical storm Erika wrecked havoc on the island, causing damage measured at around 90% of GDP (World Bank, 2015). In October 2015 Range Resorts of the United Arab Emirates began construction of the Cabrits Resort Kempinski, slated to open in 2018, and work began on the Tranquility Beach Resort, another undertaking headed by the Hilton chain.

E. The interaction between corporate governance and mergers and acquisitions

In an international context of growing mergers and acquisitions activity, which involves access by agents (companies) to alternative financial sources beyond the traditional ones, there is a need for thorough and efficient corporate governance structures to keep tabs on that activity and thereby to offer greater certainty to investors and their guarantors. There must also be levels of transparency sufficient to reduce the asymmetries of information between investors in the different countries where these transactions take place.[34] Both aspects presuppose the existence of regulatory frameworks that will spell out the responsibilities of the parties involved in M&A transactions.

Transactions associated with foreign direct investment, and cross-border mergers and acquisitions in particular, can influence corporate governance practices in the host countries. Some authors suggest that FDI operations involving cross-border M&A have positive spillover effects for the sector in which the target firm operates, in terms of corporate governance, market valuation and productivity of rival firms (Albuquerque et al., 2013). The evidence shows that these spillover effects are more pronounced when the acquiring firm is from a country with stronger shareholder protection.

At the same time, mergers and acquisitions can benefit from better corporate governance regimes. The volume of M&A activity is relatively greater in those countries where there is stronger shareholder protection and better accounting standards (Rossi and Volpin, 2004). In cross-border operations, on average, firms that have higher levels of shareholder protection come from countries with better corporate governance systems.

---

[33] See "Camerhogne Park to be relocated", 2016 [online] http://nowgrenada.com/2016/01/camerhogne-park-relocated/.
[34] According to Di Giovanni (2004), information costs, which reflect information asymmetries between investors, can obstruct cross-border asset flows, and this becomes a significant investment cost that tends to be greater when the target firm is located in a developing country.

A broad definition of corporate governance includes the operating parameters of the firm's decision-making body and its ownership structure, geared primarily to ensuring the efficient use of capital.[35] In this respect, it is important to take a comprehensive view of the business, one that is concerned not only with internal management but also with fostering transparency, reducing corrupt practices, counteracting the power of company officers (executives and managers) and contributing to the resolution of disputes between shareholders (principals) and executives and managers (agents), and between majority and minority shareholders. This makes it important to ensure greater coordination among the various areas of the business, as well as to take into account the interests of minority investors and related groups, and to protect the interests of investors (internal and external, private and governmental), thereby encouraging the market in general to pay more for shares and securities.[36]

Implementation of a corporate governance model that considers all the elements mentioned above will not always guarantee sound performance by the company's decision-making bodies. In most countries, some standards and rules are mandatory and others are discretionary. This means that firms, rather than account fully for their actions, need only report to the market on their governance practices (the principle of "comply or explain" enshrined in the corporate governance principles of the Organization for Economic Cooperation and Development (OECD) and in most national legislation). Providing incomplete information will often lead to higher operating costs for firms.

At the present time, the normative frameworks for corporate governance are confined to securities market aspects, and this limits their observance to those firms that are publicly traded or listed on stock exchanges. Moreover, every country has its peculiarities, and while most countries make it mandatory to have a board of directors, there are some countries that do not.

The Economic Commission for Latin America and the Caribbean (ECLAC, together with the Latin American Development Bank (CAE) and the Inter-American Development Bank (IDB), has designed a benchmark indicator that measures the level of corporate governance in corporate debt issuance. That benchmark was adapted to analyse the level of a country's regulation over corporate governance in the particular case of mergers and acquisitions.[37]

The benchmark proposed by ECLAC covers four areas of measurement: (i) the role of the board of directors, (ii) the structure of the board of directors, (iii) the role of its chair, and (iv) the corporate committees (including the audit and risk committees). It also includes two crosscutting categories that permeate action at all levels by the Board of Directors: transparency and equitable treatment of shareholders,[38] and it covers as well some other general aspects of business affairs. To obtain the value of corporate governance, each category is assigned a weighted value as a function of its importance.[39] The sum of the values of the different categories is 10, the maximum score that can be earned.

---

[35]   For Salas (2002), efficiency means net wealth creation. The reference covers both static efficiency, which relates to the proper use of existing resources, and dynamic efficiency, which involves the growing accumulation of ever more productive resources.

[36]   La Porta et al. (1997) argue that potential investors are ready to pay a higher price if their rights are more solidly protected, particularly against expropriation.

[37]   For the methodology used to design the benchmark, see Núñez and Oneto (2012).

[38]   The OECD principles of corporate governance used in the benchmark refer to the structure and composition of the board of directors, and to two basic principles, which are the rights and equal treatment of shareholders and third parties, and transparency in the disclosure of information and in the functions of the board. Shortcomings in terms of transparency and disclosure can contribute to unethical behaviour and loss of market integrity, at high cost to the firm and its shareholders, and to the economy as a whole. Disclosure also helps improve public understanding of the structure and activities of companies, their corporate policies, and their environmental performance and ethical standards and their relationship with the communities in which they operate (OECD, 2015).

[39]   The definition of the weightings used in the corporate governance benchmark for firms merged or acquired is that of Núñez and Oneto.

The objective of the benchmark is to standardize corporate governance models, to allow their comparison, and to identify, among other elements, any room for improvement in their performance. The benchmark matrix makes it possible to evaluate the role of corporate governance in the entire ownership structure, the financing strategies and decisions, and risk management of the companies' affairs in the valuation of a merger or acquisition, as well as to study the path of the corporate governance variable over time, both for the acquiring company and for the target firm.

Table I.8 shows the first results of measurement of the general level of corporate governance regulation for mergers and acquisitions in seven countries of Latin America: Argentina, Brazil, Chile, Colombia, Ecuador, Mexico and Peru. As to the role of the institutions responsible for overseeing the performance of corporate governance (superintendencies and stock markets), there is a general effort on the part of regulatory entities in the seven countries to improve their standards of corporate governance.[40] The countries that have the lowest indices are Brazil and Ecuador. In Brazil, risk committees received the lowest evaluation. Furthermore, one third of the board of directors may be executives of the company, which may generate a potential conflict of interests. The corporate governance rules in Ecuador are confined to banks and financial (essentially insurance) institutions. In the absence of a strong code for nonfinancial companies, the regulatory authorities recommend that companies follow the principles of the Andean Code of Corporate Governance, although it is not compulsory, and there is moreover no mechanism for the authorities to monitor compliance. Table I.8 shows that, between 2004 and 2015, Colombia made the greatest number of improvements to its corporate governance regulations. Of all the countries considered, Peru showed the highest level of corporate governance. In general, between 2013 and 2014 there were significant changes in corporate governance regulations in the four member countries of the Integrated Latin American Market (MILA) —Chile, Colombia, Mexico and Peru— probably in the context of harmonizing capital markets legislation between the countries that are part of the securities markets integration initiative.

Table I.8
Latin America (selected countries): indicator of standards on corporate governance, 2004-2015

In Latin America, the rules on corporate governance have improved

	2004	2005	2006	2007	2008	2009	2010	2011	2012	2013	2014	2015
Argentina	4.66	4.66	4.66	4.66	4.92	4.92	4.92	4.92	4.92	7.65	7.65	7.65
Brazil	4.27	4.27	4.27	5.06	5.06	5.06	5.06	5.06	6.14	6.14	6.14	6.14
Chile	2.56	2.56	2.56	2.56	2.56	2.56	3.06	3.06	3.58	6.84	6.84	7.25
Colombia	0.93	0.93	2.99	2.99	5.12	5.12	5.12	5.12	5.12	5.12	5.12	7.66
Ecuador	3.15	4.05	4.05	4.05	4.05	4.05	4.05	4.05	4.87	5.39	6.15	6.15
Mexico	4.48	4.48	6.19	6.19	6.19	6.19	6.19	6.45	6.45	6.45	6.71	7.12
Peru	4.39	4.39	4.39	4.39	4.39	4.39	4.39	4.39	4.39	4.39	7.76	7.76

Source: Economic Commission for Latin America and the Caribbean (ECLAC).
Note: The maximum possible value is 10.

[40]   The information needed to respond to the questions on the basis of which the level of corporate governance is calculated in each country is found in the laws and regulations (regulatory framework) and in the governmental entities responsible for supervising countries' financial systems. In addition, use is made of information from the codes of good corporate governance practices issued by the supervisory entities, the general principle of which is "comply or explain".

Corporate governance regulations that are limited to securities markets are confined in their scope to companies registered or listed on those markets. In recent years there have been some important changes in the legal frameworks: however, these have not been sufficient to broaden the coverage to the entire business spectrum. In the case of mergers and acquisitions where the majority of firms acquired were not originally listed on the exchange, the evaluation of corporate governance regulations prior to the transaction can give an idea of the level of governance prevailing within a group of firms, including those that are State-owned, which in many countries are the yardstick for the remainder of the market and may influence companies' investment decisions.

Lastly, given the limited coverage of corporate governance rules, these should be coordinated with regulations, such as those governing competition, that are broader and where the scope of action goes beyond governance, allowing their application to be extended to a greater number of companies.

F.   The aim: to attack higher investment in a slow-growth context

In nominal terms, foreign direct investment inflows into Latin America and the Caribbean show clear signs of stagnation. In 2015, for the fourth year running, the region recorded no significant increase in FDI inflows.

In the current global conditions, FDI flows into Latin America and the Caribbean will likely shrink again in 2016. The Economic Commission for Latin America and the Caribbean (ECLAC) has estimated a 0.6% contraction in output, which will continue to dampen investment in supplying domestic demand at the regional level. The South American economies will be the hardest hit, owing to their specialization in primary goods, especially oil and minerals, and their strong trade integration with China. In fact, signs of a slowdown in China and low raw material prices have already paralysed investment in areas relating to natural resources exports. Conversely, prospects are brighter for Mexico and Central America, with average GDP growth estimated at 2.6% in 2016, just below the previous year's rate. The upturn in the United States economy has led to new investment announcements, particularly in export manufacturing. Overall, therefore, ECLAC estimates that FDI flows into the region could drop by as much as 8% in 2016.

> ECLAC estimates that FDI flows into the region could drop by as much as 8% in 2016.

The productive specialization of an important segment of Latin American economies, together with the collapse of commodity prices, has had a substantial impact on FDI inflows. Moreover, this complex scenario has been accentuated by the slowdown of economic growth in various countries of the region.

Foreign direct investment can constitute a driving force for development, which will have positive effects on the host economies. Of particular interest is the function of FDI as a complement to domestic savings and a source of new capital contributions and of benefits in terms of transfers of technology and management systems for productive modernization. However, the positive fallout from FDI does not occur automatically and, in some cases, there are some significant gaps between the expectations generated and the outcomes obtained.

In Latin America and the Caribbean, FDI in natural resources, exports and modern services has made a key contribution to underpinning the pattern of international integration of the countries of the region. However, it has had only a moderate and not very extensive impact in terms of technological content, innovation and research and development (R&D). Many of the effects achieved are associated, on one hand, with the productive and technological capacities and human capital of each country and, on the other hand, with the sector regulatory frameworks, particularly in the services area. Overall, these factors make up a system that can enhance or diminish the benefits of foreign investment in the host countries. Consequently, the adoption of strategies that combine FDI attraction with policies that promote economic modernization and productive diversification would not only foster the establishment of transnational firms in sectors with greater possibilities for developing and strengthening capacities, but would also facilitate the integration of those companies into local economies and would promote economic growth with social inclusion and environmental sustainability.

When policies to attract foreign direct investment are coordinated and integrated with development policies, a country can enhance the conditions that make it attractive to foreign investors, on one hand, and it can also take maximum advantage of the potential benefits of FDI. In this case, the country will define strategies and FDI will help to achieve them. In the context of international competition to attract investments, then, a country can modify and adapt its offerings according to its needs. It can also monitor, through a series of indicators, the impact of FDI, the progress of policies and their performance vis-à-vis the principal competitors. Lastly, the policies adopted will be geared not only to attracting FDI but also to generating conditions for absorbing its benefits. To this end, it is essential to boost the competitiveness of local firms, so that they can integrate themselves into the production and marketing networks of foreign companies.

Bibliography

Albuquerque, R. and others (2013), "International Corporate Governance Spillovers: Evidence from Cross-Border Mergers and Acquisitions", *IMF Working Papers*, No. 13/234, International Monetary Fund (IMF).

Automotive News (2015), "GM cuts Venezuela workforce by 13%; Ford halts output", 28 April [online] http://www.autonews.com/article/20150428/GLOBAL/150429791/gm-cuts-venezuela-workforce-by-13-ford-halts-output.

Caribbean Journal (2015), "Resorts World Planning $600 Million in Bimini Investments", 23 November [online] http://caribjournal.com/2015/11/23/resorts-world-planning-600-million-in-bimini-investments/#.

Central Bank of Chile (2016), *Balanza de pagos, posición de inversión internacional y deuda externa de Chile, resultados al cierre del 2015*, Santiago, March [online] http://si3.bcentral.cl/estadisticas/Principal1/Informes/SE/BDP/BalanzaPagos_cuarto_trimestre2015.pdf.

Chackiel, J. E. and J. Sandoval (2013), "Metodología de medición de la inversión extranjera directa en las estadísticas externas de Chile", *Estudios Económicos Estadísticos*, No. 102, Santiago, October [online] http://si3.bcentral.cl/estadisticas/Principal1/Metodologias/SE/BDP/see102.pdf.

CMI (Centro de Medios Independientes) (2016), "¿Quién está detrás de la compra de Energuate?", 26 January [online] https://cmiguate.org/quien-esta-detras-de-compra-de-energuate/.

Cordero, M. (2015), *La inversión colombiana en Centroamérica* (LC/MEX/L.1190), Mexico City, ECLAC subregoinal headquarters in Mexico, September.

Daily Mail (2015), "Cruise ship giant reveals plans for $200m 'island marine reserve' in the Bahamas complete with a 2,000-seat amphitheatre, restaurants, bars, zip wire and spa", 17 December [online] http://www.dailymail.co.uk/travel/travel_news/article-3364007/MSC-Cruises-reveals-plans-new-beach-destination-Bahamas.html#ixzz48wXvLbxM.

Deloitte (2015), *The Deloitte M&A Index 2016: Opportunities amidst divergence*, London, December [online] https://www2.deloitte.com/content/dam/Deloitte/global/Documents/Finance/gx-finance-m-and-a-index-q4-2015.pdf.

Di Giovanni, J. (2004), "What drives capital flows? The case of cross-border M&A activity and financial deepening", *Journal of International Economics*, No. 65.

ECLAC (Economic Commission for Latin America and the Caribbean) (2015a), *Foreign Direct Investment on Latin America and the Caribbean, 2015* (LC/G.2641-P), Santiago [online] http://repositorio.cepal.org/bitstream/handle/11362/38215/S1500534_en.pdf?sequence=4.

___(2015b), *Preliminary Overview of the Economies of Latin America and the Caribbean, 2015* (LC/G.2655-P), Santiago [online] http://repositorio.cepal.org/bitstream/handle/11362/39559/S1501386_en.pdf?sequence=94.

EIU (The Economist Intelligence Unit) (2016), "Country Report Guyana, 1st Quarter 2016", London [online] http://portal.eiu.com/FileHandler.ashx?issue_id=913864675&mode=pdf.

El Comercio (2015), "Así moderniza Repsol la Refinería La Pampilla", Lima, 7 November [online] http://elcomercio.pe/economia/negocios/asi-moderniza-repsol-refineria-pampilla-video-noticia-1854284.

El País (2016), "La inversión extranjera en España usa Holanda para eludir impuestos", Madrid, 25 January [online] http://economia.elpais.com/economia/2016/01/24/actualidad/1453671308_267191.html.

Fama, E. F. and M. Jensen (1983), "Separation of ownership and control", *Journal of Law and Economics*, vol. XXVI, The University of Chicago, June.

fDi Intelligence (2016), *The fDi Report 2016: Global Greenfield Investment Trends*, The Financial Times, London, April [online] file:///C:/respaldo/Desktop/My%20Local%20Documents/DOCUMENT/Informe%202016/CAPITULO%201/Documentos%20de%20apoyo/2016-FDiIntelligence-The_fDi_Report_2016.pdf.

Financial Juneteenth (2016), "Why Is China Doing Business With Jamaica?", 1 January [online] http://financialjuneteenth.com/china-business-jamaica/.

Fortune (2015), *Fortune Global 500* [online] http://fortune.com/global500/.

Galbraith, J. K. (1967), *The New Industrial State*, Princeton University Press.

GTM (Green Tech Media) (2015), "Honduras Emerges as Central America's Solar Success Story", 7 September [online] http://www.greentechmedia.com/articles/read/honduras-emerges-as-central-americas-solar-success-story.

International Business Times (2015), "Nicaragua Canal Project: Construction Put On Hold As Chinese Investor's Fortunes Dwindle", 26 November [online] http://www.ibtimes.com/nicaragua-canal-project-construction-put-hold-chinese-investors-fortunes-dwindle-2201304.

IMF (International Monetary Fund) (2009), *Balance of Payments and International Investment Position Manual (BPM6)*, Washington, D.C. [online] https://www.imf.org/external/pubs/ft/bop/2007/pdf/bpm6.pdf.

Jamaica Observer (2015a), "New firm investing US$600 m in port upgrade", 8 April [online] http://www.jamaicaobserver.com/news/New-firm-investing-US-600-m-in-port-upgrade_18714798.

___(2015b), "US$100-m ganja deal", 15 September [online] http://www.jamaicaobserver.com/news/US-100-m-ganja-deal.

Jensen, M. and W. Meckling (1976), "The Theory of the Firm: Managerial Behavior, Agency Costs and Ownership Structure", *Journal of Financial Economics*, vol. 3, No. 4, Harvard University Press.

JIS (Jamaica Information Service) (2015), "JAMPRO Facilitates US$350 Million Free Zone Investment", octubre [online] http://jis.gov.jm/jampro-facilitates-us350-million-free-zone-investment/.

JP Morgan (2016), *2016 M&A Global Outlook. Higher deal count drives continued strength*, New York, February [online] https://www.jpmorgan.com/country/US/EN/insights/maglobaloutlook.

___(2015), *Cross-Regional M&A: Are you prepared for the resurgence? Knowing drivers and navigating the opportunities*, New York, June [online] https://www.jpmorgan.com/jpmpdf/1320694341265.pdf.

La Porta, R. and others (1997), "Legal determinants of external finance", *Journal of Finance*, vol. 52, No. 3.

Mercados y Tendencias (2015), "Honduras destaca a nivel mundial en inversión de energías renovables", 1 December [online] http://revistamyt.com/honduras-destaca-a-nivel-mundial-en-inversion-de-energias-renovables/.

Mining Council of Chile (2015), "Catastro del Consejo Minero", Santiago [online] http://www.consejominero.cl/wp-content/uploads/2016/01/Catastro-proyectos-CM-December-2015.pdf.

Ministry of Mining of Chile (2016), "Reporte CIFES: energías renovables en el mercado eléctrico chileno" Santiago, Centro Nacional para la Innovación y Fomento de las Energías Sustentables (CIFES) [online] http://cifes.gob.cl/documentos/home-destacado/reporte-cifes-January-2016/.

Mitsubishi Corporation (2015), "Final Investment Decision Reached on Trinidad and Tobago Methanol/Dimethyl Ether Plant", 3 September [online] http://www.mitsubishicorp.com/jp/en/pr/archive/2015/html/0000028457.html.

Núñez, G. and A. Oneto (coords.) (2015), "Corporate governance in Brazil, Chile, Colombia, Mexico and Peru: The determinants of risk in corporate debt issuance", *Project Documents* (LC/W.654), Santiago, Economic Commission for Latin America and the Caribbean (ECLAC).

OECD (Organization for Economic Cooperation and Development) (2016), *FDI in Figures*, Paris, April [online] http://www.oecd.org/daf/inv/investment-policy/FDI-in-Figures-April-2016.pdf.

___(2015), *G20/OECD Principles of Corporate Governance*, Paris, OECD Publishing.

___(2014), *Implementing the latest International Standards for Compiling Foreign Direct investment Statistics*, Paris, December [online] https://www.oecd.org/daf/inv/FDI-statistics-asset-liability-vs-directional-presentation.pdf.

Pv Magazine (2015), "Chile's new 600km long transmission line can boost renewable", 11 December [online] http://www.pv-magazine.com/news/details/beitrag/chiles-new-600km-long-transmission-line-can-boost-renewables_100022420/#axzz40MqjMuTs.

Rossi, S. and P. F. Volpin (2004), "Cross-country determinants of mergers and acquisitions", *Journal of Financial Economics*, vol. 74, No. 2.

Salas, V. (2002), "El gobierno de la empresa", *Colección de Estudios Económicos,* No. 29, Servicios de estudios de la Caja de Ahorros y Pensiones de Barcelona [online] https://books.google.com/books?id=5TD5pOTfN7EC&pg=PA212&dq=Salas,+V.+El+G obierno+de+la+empresa&hl=en&sa=X&ei=Hsw_VYTLJoHxggSW_YHIBw&ved=0CB QQ6AEwAA#v=onepage&q=Salas%2C%20V.%20El%20Gobierno%20de%20la%20 empresa&f=false.

Shumkov, I. (2015), "Honduras to install 460 MW of PV in 2015 – GTM" [online] http://renewables. seenews.com/news/honduras-to-install-460-mw-of-pv-in-2015-gtm-475987.

The Daily Observer (2015), "Paradise Found project to resume in 2016", 9 December [online] http://antiguaobserver.com/paradise-found-project-to-resume-in-2016/.

The Guardian (2015), "China finds an eager South American stable mate in Suriname", 23 June [online] http://www.theguardian.com/world/2015/jun/23/suriname-china-business-influence.

The Nassau Guardian (2015), "MS hinges new phases at FCP on the right tax environment", 18 December [online] http://www.thenassauguardian.com/bahamas-business/40-bahamas-business/61407-mschinges-new-phases-at-fcp-on-the-right-tax-environment.

Tribune 242 (2016), "Bran: 'I Won'T Invest Any More Because Of Crime'", January [online] http://www.tribune242.com/news/2016/jan/06/bran-i-wont-invest-any-more-because-crime/.

___(2015), "Shipping Company Signs Deal For $100m Port", 17 December [online] http://www.tribune242.com/news/2015/dec/17/shipping-company-signs-deal-100m-port/.

UNCTAD (United Nations Conference on Trade and Development) (2016a), *Global Investment Trends Monitor,* No. 23, Geneva, 3 May [online] http://unctad.org/en/PublicationsLibrary/webdiaeia2016d2_en.pdf.

(2016b), *Global Investment Trends Monitor,* No. 22, Geneva, 20 January [online] http://unctad.org/en/PublicationsLibrary/webdiaeia2016d1_en.pdf.

(2015), *World Investment Report, 2015. Reforming International Investment Governance* (UNCTAD/WIR/2015), Geneva. United Nations publication, Sales No. E.15.II.D.5 [online] http://unctad.org/en/PublicationsLibrary/wir2015_en.pdf.

World Bank (2015), "Dominica Lost Almost All its GDP due to Climate Change", 1 December [online] http://www.worldbank.org/en/news/feature/2015/12/01/dominica-lost-almost-all-gdp-climate-change.

Annex I.A1

The fifth and sixth editions of the IMF *Balance of Payments Manual*: implications for foreign direct investment statistics

The sixth edition of the *Balance of Payments and International Investment Position Manual* (BPM6) of the International Monetary Fund (IMF) has brought many changes for institutions responsible for compiling and systemizing information, especially for central banks. The sixth edition is a revision of the fifth edition of the *Balance of Payments Manual* (BPM5), which was first published in 1993. The changes were the outcome of intensive collaboration between the different multilateral and national institutions, involving different aspects of balance-of-payments statistics. There follows a description of the main changes affecting statistics on foreign direct investment.

The main change concerns the way data are presented, which has shifted from a directional presentation to an asset/liability basis. Under BPM5, FDI statistics were constructed on the directional principle, according to which direct investment was shown as "direct investment abroad" or "direct investment in the reporting economy". The directional principle is a net construction, to which operations with affiliate companies and reverse investments (where a directly investing company acquires a capital share in its immediate direct or indirect investor) are added or subtracted. That is, once the direction of influence or control is established, the value of the operations by the direct investor in respect of the receiving firm is subtracted from investments this latter firm makes in its parent (the direct investor) (see diagram I.A1.1). Analytically speaking, the sixth edition of the IMF *Balance of Payments Manual* notes that data presented according to the directional principle helps to understand the motivation behind direct investment.

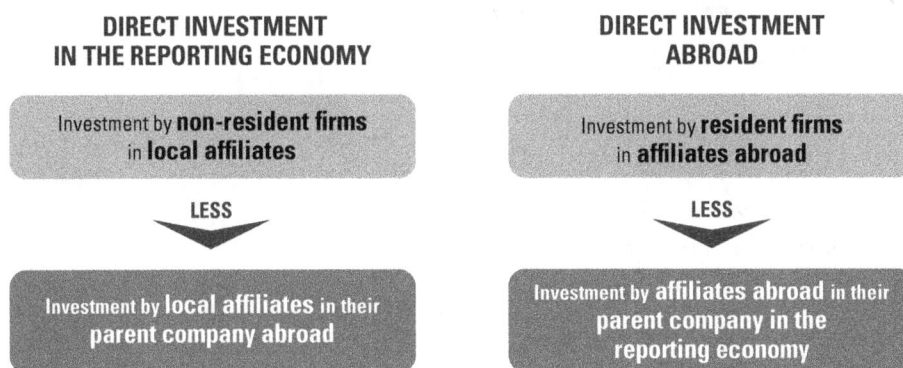

Diagram I.A1.1
Directional principle for foreign investment according to the fifth edition of the *Balance of Payments Manual* of the International Monetary Fund (IMF)

DIRECT INVESTMENT IN THE REPORTING ECONOMY

Investment by **non-resident firms** in **local affiliates**

LESS

Investment by **local affiliates** in their **parent company abroad**

DIRECT INVESTMENT ABROAD

Investment by **resident firms** in **affiliates abroad**

LESS

Investment by **affiliates abroad** in their **parent company in the reporting economy**

Source: Economic Commission for Latin America and the Caribbean (ECLAC), on the basis of Organization for Economic Cooperation and Development (OECD), *Implementing the latest International Standards for Compiling Foreign Direct investment Statistics*, December 2014 [online] https://www.oecd.org/daf/inv/FDI-statistics-asset-liability-vs-directional-presentation.pdf.

Under the new presentation, the same elements are organized on the basis of assets and liabilities. Here, transfers by local affiliates of non-resident firms to their parent companies are presented as an asset from the point of view of the reporting economy (and transfers in the opposite direction as a liability) (see diagram I.A1.2). For this reason, for the reporting economy, total FDI stock will not be equal to total foreign investment abroad, and total FDI liabilities will differ from total foreign direction investment.

Diagram I.A1.2
Asset and liability
presentation of foreign
investment according
to the sixth edition of
the *Balance of Payments
Manual* of the International
Monetary Fund (IMF)

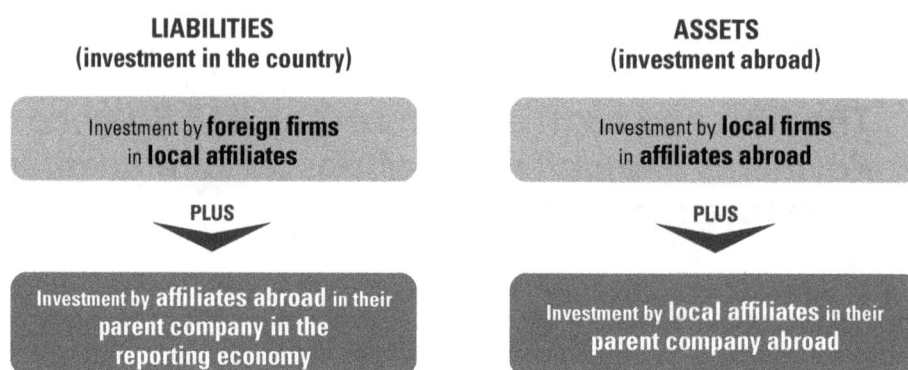

LIABILITIES (investment in the country)	ASSETS (investment abroad)
Investment by **foreign firms** in **local affiliates**	Investment by **local firms** in **affiliates abroad**
PLUS	PLUS
Investment by **affiliates abroad** in their **parent company in the reporting economy**	Investment by **local affiliates** in their **parent company abroad**

Source: Economic Commission for Latin America and the Caribbean (ECLAC), on the basis of Organization for Economic Cooperation and Development (OECD), *Implementing the latest International Standards for Compiling Foreign Direct investment Statistics,* December 2014 [online] https://www.oecd.org/daf/inv/FDI-statistics-asset-liability-vs-directional-presentation.pdf.

These differences in presentation can have major impacts on foreign direct investment statistics. Intracompany loans are very significant in the case of Brazil, for example, producing large differences between the two forms of presentation and, thus, in FDI statistics (see table I.A1.1)

Table I.A1.1
Brazil: comparison between
directional and asset/
liability presentation of
foreign direct investment
(FDI) data, 2015
(Millions of dollars)

FDI inflows	
Equity investments made by parent companies abroad	49 276
Reinvested earnings by parents abroad	7 145
Lending by foreign parents to local affiliates	7 673
Lending by foreign affiliates to resident parents	10 981
FDI flow on the basis of assets and liabilities	**75 075**
Less: lending by foreign affiliates to resident parent companies	-10 981
Less: lending by local affiliates to parent companies abroad	397
FDI flow on a directional basis	**64 491**

FDI outflows	
Equity investments in affiliates abroad	9 832
Reinvested earnings in affiliates abroad	4 506
Lending by resident parents to foreign affiliates	-443
Lending by resident affiliates to parent company abroad	-397
FDI flow on the basis of assets and liabilities	**13 498**
Less: borrowing by resident parents from foreign affiliates	-10 981
Less: lending by resident affiliates to the foreign parent	397
FDI flow on a directional basis	**2 914**

Source: Economic Commission for Latin America and the Caribbean (ECLAC).

The absolute difference between the two presentations is the same for both inflows and outflows. For Brazil in 2015, presentation by assets and liabilities gives a value of US$ 10.584 billion more than the figure obtained using the directional approach, for both investment abroad and foreign direct investment in the reporting economy. In 2014, the difference between the two approaches was US$ 24 billion.

IMF has recommended the change in methodology to better harmonize the various components of the balance of payments and to make them more comparable with other macroeconomic variables. However, from the perspective of this publication, the changes proposed do not appear to progress in that direction. In fact, for analysis of FDI by sector and by origin, the Organization for Economic Cooperation and Development (OECD) recommends a directional presentation for constructing statistics. This has meant some countries publishing their statistics in different ways and to both methodologies being used, which throws up differences in total figures and in the breakdowns by origin and branch of economic activity.

Annex I.A2

Table I.A2.1
Latin America and the Caribbean: inward foreign direct investment by country, 2002-2015
(Millions of dollars)

	2002	2003	2004	2005	2006	2007	2008	2009	2010	2011	2012	2013	2014	2015
Antigua and Barbuda[a]	80	179	95	238	361	341	161	85	101	68	138	101	155	154
Argentina	2 149	1 652	4 125	5 265	5 537	6 473	9 726	4 017	11 333	10 840	15 324	9 822	5 065	11 655
Bahamas	354	713	804	1 054	1 492	1 623	1 512	873	1 148	1 533	1 073	1 111	1 596	385
Barbados	228	185	228	390	342	476	615	255	446	362	313	-35	486	254
Belize	25	-11	111	127	109	143	170	109	97	95	189	95	133	59
Bolivia (Plurinational State of)	677	197	85	-288	281	366	513	423	643	859	1 060	1 750	648	503
Brazil[b]	16 587	10 123	18 161	15 460	19 418	44 579	50 716	31 481	88 452	101 158	86 607	69 181	96 895	75 075
Chile[c]	2 550	4 334	7 241	7 482	8 798	13 178	16 604	13 392	15 510	23 309	28 493	19 362	22 342	20 457
Colombia[a]	2 134	1 720	3 116	10 235	6 751	8 886	10 565	8 035	6 430	14 648	15 039	16 209	16 325	12 108
Costa Rica[d]	659	575	794	861	1 469	1 896	2 078	1 615	1 907	2 733	2 696	3 555	3 064	3 094
Dominica[a]	21	32	27	32	29	48	57	58	43	35	59	25	35	36
Dominican Republic[e]	917	613	909	1 123	1 085	1 667	2 870	2 165	2 024	2 277	3 142	1 991	2 209	2 222
Ecuador[a]	783	872	837	493	271	194	1 057	308	165	644	567	727	773	1 060
El Salvador	470	142	363	511	241	1 551	903	366	-230	218	482	179	311	429
Grenada[a]	57	91	66	73	96	172	141	104	64	45	34	114	38	61
Guatemala[f]	205	263	296	508	592	745	754	600	806	1 026	1 244	1 295	1 389	1 209
Guyana	44	26	30	77	102	152	178	164	198	247	294	214	255	122
Haiti	6	14	6	26	161	75	29	55	178	119	156	160	99	104
Honduras	275	403	547	600	669	928	1 006	509	969	1 014	1 059	1 060	1 144	1 204
Jamaica	481	721	602	682	882	866	1 437	541	228	218	413	595	591	794
Mexico	24 048	18 221	24 914	25 971	21 110	32 407	29 078	17 900	26 431	23 649	20 437	45 855	25 675	30 285
Nicaragua	204	201	250	241	287	382	627	434	490	936	768	816	884	835
Panama	78	771	1 012	1 027	2 498	1 777	2 402	1 259	2 363	3 132	2 980	3 943	4 309	5 039
Paraguay	6	25	28	36	114	202	209	95	216	557	738	72	346	283
Peru	2 156	1 335	1 599	2 579	3 467	5 491	6 924	6 431	8 455	7 665	11 918	9 298	7 885	6 861
Saint Kitts and Nevis[a]	81	78	63	104	115	141	184	136	119	112	110	139	120	78
Saint Lucia[a]	57	112	81	82	238	277	166	152	127	100	78	95	93	95
Saint Vincent and the Grenadines[a]	34	55	66	41	110	121	159	111	97	86	115	160	110	121
Suriname	-74	-76	-37	28	-163	-247	-231	-93	-248	70	174	188	163	276
Trinidad and Tobago[g]	791	808	998	940	883	830	2 801	709	549	1 831	2 453	1 995	2 488	1 214
Uruguay	194	416	332	847	1 493	1 329	2 106	1 529	2 289	2 504	2 536	3 032	2 188	1 647
Venezuela (Bolivarian Republic of)[g]	782	2 040	1 483	2 589	-508	3 288	2 627	-983	1 574	5 740	5 973	2 680	320	1 383

Source: Economic Commission for Latin America and the Caribbean (ECLAC), on the basis of estimates and official figures as of 27 May 2016.

[a] The data are standardized according to the methodology of the sixth edition of the Balance of Payments Manual of the International Monetary Fund (IMF).
[b] The data are standardized according to the methodology of the sixth edition of the IMF Balance of Payments Manual and include reinvested earnings from 2010.
[c] From 2003 to 2015 the data are standardized according to the methodology of the sixth edition of the IMF Balance of Payments Manual.
[d] From 2009 to 2015 the data are standardized according to the methodology of the sixth edition of the IMF Balance of Payments Manual.
[e] From 2010 to 2015 the data are standardized according to the methodology of the sixth edition of the IMF Balance of Payments Manual.
[f] From 2008 to 2015 the data are standardized according to the methodology of the sixth edition of the IMF Balance of Payments Manual.
[g] The 2015 data correspond to the first three quarters only.

Table I.A2.2
Latin America and the Caribbean: inward foreign direct investment by destination sector, 2007-2015[a]
(Millions of dollars)

	2007	2008	2009	2010	2011	2012	2013	2014	2015
Argentina[b]									
Natural resources	2 474	2 647	1 418	2 559	790	2 415	4 781	3 148	...
Manufactures	3 058	5 219	414	4 797	5 257	5 414	3 949	5 807	...
Services	1 990	2 387	2 173	2 558	4 495	4 789	3 687	4 490	...
Belize									
Natural resources	9	37	7	13	29	100	22	16	...
Manufactures	0	0	0	0	0	0	0	0	...
Services	101	117	93	79	59	90	64	116	...
Other	34	16	9	5	5	6	9	9	...
Bolivia (Plurinational State of)[c]									
Natural resources	486	859	420	530	622	1 166	1 550	1 558	...
Manufactures	164	154	74	274	240	119	317	390	...
Services	303	290	193	132	171	220	162	164	...
Brazil									
Natural resources	4 751	12 995	4 597	16 261	10 297	6 528	9 990	5 621	8 310
Manufactures	13 481	14 013	13 481	21 273	26 837	22 206	15 218	16 922	20 967
Services	16 103	17 449	13 601	14 702	31 987	31 444	23 880	33 357	28 409
Other	...	...	...	347	409	364	258	199	221
Chile									
Natural resources	6 495	4 599	7 144	5 217	18 222	13 881	3 822	7 264	...
Manufactures	-657	1 570	441	637	942	2 602	1 615	1 820	...
Services	6 481	8 725	4 113	6 838	4 876	8 999	9 144	8 822	...
Other	215	256	1 693	2 817	-732	2 975	4 683	4 096	...
Colombia									
Natural resources	4 452	5 176	5 672	4 976	7 336	7 970	8 385	6 517	3 816
Manufactures	1 760	1 696	1 364	210	1 214	1 985	2 481	2 837	2 412
Services	2 673	3 693	1 000	1 244	6 098	5 084	5 343	6 971	5 880
Costa Rica									
Natural resources	33	467	73	31	38	-15	-9	97	442
Manufactures	689	555	407	966	737	600	382	503	799
Services	1 170	1 031	845	446	1 401	1 674	2 717	2 148	1 609
Other	4	26	22	23	2	0	0	0	0
Dominican Republic									
Natural resources	30	357	758	240	1 060	1 169	93	-39	6
Manufactures	184	574	280	566	355	1 257	404	607	368
Services	1 453	1 938	1 128	1 218	862	716	1 494	1 640	1 848
Ecuador									
Natural resources	-77	265	58	189	380	243	274	725	408
Manufactures	99	198	118	120	122	136	138	108	261
Services	173	594	132	-144	142	189	315	-59	390
El Salvador									
Natural resources	109	31	9	1	-1	-3	6	1	1
Manufactures	23	28	92	-65	149	-47	285	88	263
Services	1 315	479	243	-225	66	502	-147	245	140
Other (maquila)	103	365	21	59	4	29	35	-23	24
Guatemala									
Natural resources	70	174	139	120	325	418	335	201	140
Manufactures	210	175	51	299	150	145	186	179	189
Services	437	369	401	363	544	636	707	951	749
Other	28	36	9	23	7	46	67	58	131

Table I.A2.2 (concluded)

	2007	2008	2009	2010	2011	2012	2013	2014	2015
Honduras									
Natural resources	30	4	10	84	62	41	70	65	65
Manufactures	384	267	98	341	392	438	325	347	395
Services	513	736	402	545	560	579	665	733	744
Other	0	0	0	0	0	0	0	0	0
Mexico									
Natural resources	1 872	4 582	1 326	1 609	747	3 126	5 700	2 451	871
Manufactures	13 158	8 862	6 706	13 984	10 293	8 947	30 065	14 764	15 156
Services	17 378	15 635	9 868	10 838	12 609	8 364	10 089	8 460	14 258
Nicaragua									
Natural resources	11	57	47	77	191	123	272	109	39
Manufactures	121	122	70	108	226	302	234	233	158
Services	250	447	318	323	550	347	350	394	545
Other	0	0	0	0	0	22	125	149	94
Panama									
Natural resources	-59	-59	-34	77	94	1 164	476	520	...
Manufactures	161	161	104	-114	298	520	326	357	...
Services	2 106	2 106	1 190	2 760	2 761	1 526	3 141	3 432	...
Other	-11	-11	0	0	0	0	0	0	...
Paraguay									
Natural resources	-2	3	8	-6	14	35	43	5	0
Manufactures	8	149	-109	53	105	290	-36	76	0
Services	196	56	195	163	500	413	65	155	0
Uruguay									
Natural resources	338	604	253	329	383	220	378	136	...
Manufactures	263	261	242	131	190	340	240	290	...
Services	592	1 003	962	1 010	1 360	1 536	1 642	1 274	...
Other	136	238	71	820	572	440	772	487	...

Source: Economic Commission for Latin America and the Caribbean (ECLAC), on the basis of estimates and official figures as of 27 May 2016.

[a] Data may not correspond to those reported in the balance of payments.

[b] Data from the Central Bank of the Republic of Argentina.

[c] Gross foreign direct investment flows, excluding divestments.

Table I.A2.3
Latin America and the Caribbean: inward foreign direct investment by country of origin, 2007-2015
(Millions of dollars)

	2007	2008	2009	2010	2011	2012	2013	2014	2015
Argentina[a]									
United States	780	2 581	1 755	2 071	2 875	3 301	2 937	4 923	...
Netherlands	615	1 074	-106	57	433	2 067	1 863	1 978	...
Spain	1 181	-2 643	1 237	1 258	-433	-868	1 583	1 370	...
Germany	845	281	47	164	154	473	661	1 076	...
Canada	320	279	388	678	233	681	1 046	692	...
Brazil	-46	766	216	383	1 018	1 174	341	654	...
France	545	547	95	313	403	633	-50	647	...
Italy	227	525	131	-1 914	258	291	395	492	...
Bolivia (Plurinational State of)[b]									
Spain	50	25	145	271	246	364	676	537	...
United Kingdom	24	48	70	11	2	111	309	442	...
Peru	35	26	40	82	12	56	102	442	...
France	13	36	22	89	55	73	220	200	...
United States	322	295	162	85	76	89	61	140	...
Brazil									
Netherlands	8 129	4 639	6 515	6 702	17 582	12 213	10 511	8 791	11 573
United States	6 073	7 047	4 902	6 144	8 909	12 310	9 024	8 580	6 647
Luxembourg	2 857	5 937	537	8 819	1 867	5 965	5 067	6 659	6 599
Spain	2 202	3 851	3 424	1 524	8 593	2 523	2 246	5 962	6 570
Germany	1 801	1 086	2 473	538	1 125	826	1 011	1 574	3 453
Japan	501	4 099	1 673	2 502	7 536	1 471	2 516	3 780	2 878
France	1 233	2 880	2 141	3 479	3 086	2 155	1 489	2 945	2 841
Norway	284	207	671	1 540	1 073	936	405	554	2 445
Chile									
United States	0	0	469	2 902	4 749	8 162	1 808	6 804	...
Spain	0	0	1 886	1 529	2 087	144	3 092	3 197	...
Canada	0	0	763	2 962	2 746	4 573	5 466	1 876	...
Japan	0	0	1 014	128	1 152	1 478	-75	1 054	...
Netherlands	0	0	112	388	2 483	970	1 276	786	...
Colombia									
Switzerland	2 697	2 874	2 343	1 593	2 155	2 476	2 839	2 267	2 121
Panama	839	1 141	789	1 368	3 508	2 395	2 040	2 446	1 603
United States	572	1 040	830	113	1 164	628	884	2 219	1 402
Spain	82	404	645	624	924	367	848	1 009	1 283
United Kingdom	122	140	166	180	994	698	2 096	2 817	1 078
Bermuda	-660	60	197	1	1 072	-1 792	632	490	957
Costa Rica									
United States	962	1 328	1 022	1 036	1 376	1 015	1 392	1 182	1 503
Spain	51	24	27	7	30	32	109	-59	471
Mexico	1	5	3	13	7	1	18	3	171
Panama	30	50	6	98	152	106	79	109	141
Canada	71	20	7	40	183	336	172	237	123
Colombia	57	141	79	28	247	311	247	291	120
Dominican Republic									
United States	536	360	455	1 055	499	252	374	321	404
Mexico	113	383	773	696	1 126	851	143	158	63
Canada	2	8	8	9	-1	4	1	0	50
Netherlands	53	11	31	208	70	55	47	44	31
Venezuela (Bolivarian Republic of)	605	181	151	203	137	128	33	7	27
Ecuador									
Canada	50	-29	-607	-535	12	94	42	10	186
China	3	32	14	13	7	13	12	7	170
Spain	85	47	56	45	80	86	94	79	94
Netherlands	12	5	19	7	16	16	24	18	78
Uruguay	8	-8	-4	11	7	11	48	76	77
Switzerland	49	58	65	105	252	59	28	229	74

Table I.A2.3 (concluded)

	2007	2008	2009	2010	2011	2012	2013	2014	2015
El Salvador									
Luxembourg	499	129	74	-124	23	6	-72	111	203
Spain	841	321	80	206	27	-480	323	2	180
United States	0	0	0	-41	-0	18	170	149	160
Guatemala									
United States	326	229	151	343	127	227	221	441	348
Canada	3	15	21	22	155	48	155	142	182
Mexico	76	76	50	97	81	96	143	105	98
Colombia	25	54	74	114	305	290	156	109	63
United Kingdom	42	66	64	50	2	49	74	43	60
Russian Federation	0	0	0	0	13	134	185	86	57
Spain	37	37	21	6	0	0	25	39	45
Honduras									
Mexico	22	16	1	14	16	22	63	109	195
United States	139	51	-39	159	187	132	114	115	164
Luxembourg	460	449	92	185	141	173	128	154	137
Canada	92	30	168	124	154	192	266	201	134
Panama	0	0	0	0	20	22	31	64	127
Guatemala	103	72	-88	109	85	94	97	34	125
Mexico									
United States	13 118	11 761	7 483	7 032	12 218	9 592	13 749	7 747	15 798
Spain	5 493	5 018	3 032	4 206	3 539	-438	181	4 447	2 804
Canada	453	554	385	573	927	1 805	1 911	1 330	1 386
Germany	649	667	-15	449	397	1 087	1 713	1 621	1 268
Netherlands	880	3 454	1 840	2 023	1 432	1 849	4 522	2 982	1 090
Japan	25	93	151	409	230	443	39	542	1 003
Belgium	231	351	393	60	232	488	280	1 046	804
Nicaragua									
United States	84	126	88	88	159	121	244	...	...
Mexico	128	164	48	90	115	149	125	...	...
Venezuela (Bolivarian Republic of)	47	132	147	29	45	210	108	...	...
Panama	5	4	1	1	34	78	77	...	...
Spain	45	59	25	33	116	-19	74	...	...
Panama									
Colombia	134	60	135	82	486	533	305	912	...
United States	163	224	-19	1 120	652	28	715	612	...
Belgium	18	35	16	9	48	1 097	505	408	...
Switzerland	60	69	154	-9	171	-51	367	297	...
Japan	28	126	15	130	114	12	111	261	...
South Africa	19	26	20	13	115	52	320	258	...
Mexico	13	19	26	879	191	612	246	199	...
Paraguay									
United States	107	190	111	255	354	59	-128	141	...
Brazil	41	42	-26	29	90	177	83	135	...
Netherlands	-30	20	-28	4	11	34	79	25	...
United Kingdom	1	-2	3	2	19	50	25	20	...
Spain	19	11	16	19	-10	63	-9	17	...
Trinidad and Tobago									
United States	574	403	469	363	488	560	1 272	361	...
India	21	16	17	13	2	1	2	348	...
Canada	3	2194	4	3	994	1 586	357	248	...
United Kingdom	159	146	152	118	64	25	21	31	...
Uruguay									
Argentina	373	534	432	588	809	975	672	616	...
Brazil	153	232	55	75	194	136	132	370	...
Netherlands	86	183	110	108	170	178	255	253	...
Spain	25	17	23	35	-132	4	118	102	...
France	43	144	167	-36	77	88	87	96	...
United States	0	3	39	0	0	0	19	80	...

Source: Economic Commission for Latin America and the Caribbean (ECLAC), on the basis of estimates and official figures as of 27 May 2016.
a Data from the Central Bank of the Republic of Argentina.
b Gross foreign direct investment flows, excluding divestments.

Table I.A2.4
Latin America and the Caribbean: inward foreign direct investment by component, 2007-2015
(Millions of dollars)

	2007	2008	2009	2010	2011	2012	2013	2014	2015
Antigua and Barbuda									
Capital contributions	328	149	79	96	61	110	65	106	143
Intracompany loans	0	0	1	1	2	6	29	41	3
Reinvested earnings	12	12	5	5	5	22	7	7	7
Argentina									
Capital contributions	2 578	4 552	2 133	2 504	4 508	4 861	2 784	-112	...
Intracompany loans	1 846	4 777	-1 010	3 507	2 600	3 120	-783	-945	...
Reinvested earnings	2 050	396	2 894	5 322	3 732	7 343	7 821	6 121	...
Bahamas									
Capital contributions	887	1 032	753	960	971	575	410	374	104
Intracompany loans	736	481	120	187	563	498	701	1 222	281
Reinvested earnings	0	0	0	0	0	0	0	0	0
Barbados									
Capital contributions	420	340	140	393	218	225	112	293	210
Intracompany loans	24	231	103	41	165	-32	-87	-73	-64
Reinvested earnings	32	45	13	13	-21	120	-61	266	108
Belize									
Capital contributions	100	141	80	80	103	193	98	134	...
Intracompany loans	13	8	6	2	1	0	0	0	...
Reinvested earnings	30	21	23	15	-8	-4	-6	7	...
Bolivia (Plurinational State of)[a]									
Capital contributions	27	45	1	1	5	19	17	313	20
Intracompany loans	654	850	177	141	130	282	331	889	638
Reinvested earnings	272	407	509	793	899	1 204	1 682	910	402
Brazil									
Capital contributions	26 074	30 064	19 906	40 117	54 782	52 836	41 648	47 220	49 276
Intracompany loans	18 505	20 652	11 575	13 470	16 451	22 541	38 346	38 977	18 653
Reinvested earnings	...	...	...	34 865	29 925	11 230	-10 813	10 698	7 145
Chile									
Capital contributions	2 622	7 775	1 905	4 662	10 921	8 532	4 806	10 685	6 438
Intracompany loans	374	2 232	967	2 985	3 162	10 876	8 584	8 423	10 045
Reinvested earnings	10 182	6 597	10 519	7 863	9 226	9 085	5 973	3 234	3 974
Colombia									
Capital contributions	7 024	7 861	4 907	3 741	8 282	9 088	9 749	9 176	7 355
Intracompany loans	-121	47	731	-635	1 872	1 239	2 368	2 493	2 006
Reinvested earnings	1 983	2 657	2 396	3 325	4 494	4 712	4 091	4 656	2 746
Costa Rica									
Capital contributions	1 377	1 594	1 050	818	959	852	2 054	1 286	1 313
Intracompany loans	-2	39	-174	150	711	1 136	714	912	817
Reinvested earnings	521	446	471	497	509	708	788	866	964
Dominica									
Capital contributions	28	39	39	28	25	45	16	28	29
Intracompany loans	9	9	13	13	7	9	4	4	4
Reinvested earnings	10	9	6	3	2	4	5	4	4
Dominican Republic									
Capital contributions	1 616	2 199	704	985	1 153	2 414	195	965	...
Intracompany loans	-446	278	1096	204	79	-274	391	-177	...
Reinvested earnings	498	394	365	835	1 044	1 002	1 405	1 420	...
Ecuador									
Capital contributions	151	229	278	265	252	227	424	848	985
Intracompany loans	-368	530	-226	-312	64	39	-7	-389	-211
Reinvested earnings	411	298	256	213	328	301	310	314	287

Table I.A2.4 (concluded)

	2007	2008	2009	2010	2011	2012	2013	2014	2015
Grenada									
Capital contributions	140	128	97	56	39	29	109	33	55
Intracompany loans	17	1	2	3	1	0	0	0	0
Reinvested earnings	15	12	5	5	5	5	5	5	6
Guatemala									
Capital contributions	260	198	94	265	198	446	208	137	702
Intracompany loans	-30	75	19	-102	58	219	416	431	-497
Reinvested earnings	515	482	488	643	770	580	672	820	1 004
Honduras									
Capital contributions	220	568	84	29	284	310	174	174	137
Intracompany loans	203	-40	65	378	56	52	240	355	229
Reinvested earnings	505	479	360	562	674	697	645	615	838
Mexico									
Capital contributions	18 082	12 783	11 389	15 351	9 430	4 488	22 220	5 415	11 521
Intracompany loans	5 862	7 245	1 379	5 902	4 800	6 312	7 454	6 436	9 620
Reinvested earnings	8 463	9 050	5 132	5 178	9 420	9 637	16 181	13 825	9 143
Panama									
Capital contributions	719	918	898	948	759	1 561	1 614	1 534	1 196
Intracompany loans	178	136	105	540	1 224	682	550	329	951
Reinvested earnings	879	1348	257	874	1 150	737	1 779	2 447	2 891
Paraguay									
Capital contributions	43	20	173	-9	366	439	242	254	121
Intracompany loans	129	132	-102	129	280	61	-322	-138	-69
Reinvested earnings	31	57	24	96	-90	238	151	230	230
Peru									
Capital contributions	733	2 981	1 828	2 445	896	5 393	2 460	1 487	3 058
Intracompany loans	924	656	-782	693	2 117	-508	3 075	2 420	854
Reinvested earnings	3 835	3 287	5 385	5 317	4 652	7 033	3 764	3 978	2 949
Saint Kitts and Nevis									
Capital contributions	135	178	132	116	107	106	137	118	76
Intracompany loans	3	3	1	1	1	2	0	0	1
Reinvested earnings	2	2	2	2	4	1	1	1	2
Saint Lucia									
Capital contributions	254	135	135	109	80	54	76	71	72
Intracompany loans	8	21	13	13	15	16	10	11	12
Reinvested earnings	15	11	3	4	5	8	9	11	11
Saint Vincent and the Grenadines									
Capital contributions	102	142	100	91	79	112	157	101	118
Intracompany loans	8	8	8	2	2	2	2	2	2
Reinvested earnings	11	9	2	4	4	1	1	7	1
Suriname									
Capital contributions	0	0	0	0	0	0	0	0	...
Intracompany loans	-247	-231	-93	-248	-51	113	71	-21	...
Reinvested earnings	...	...	...	...	121	11	69	27	...
Trinidad and Tobago									
Capital contributions	554	2 322	426	309	0	1	0	1 175	...
Intracompany loans	-21	-16	-12	-11	136	698	1 040	667	...
Reinvested earnings	297	495	296	251	1 696	1 754	955	646	...
Uruguay									
Capital contributions	550	1 012	990	1 617	1 412	1 665	1 866	2 267	1 056
Intracompany loans	448	540	82	8	263	94	306	-527	39
Reinvested earnings	331	554	457	664	828	777	860	448	552
Venezuela (Bolivarian Republic of)									
Capital contributions	-806	302	-3348	-1 319	-495	-307	-79	139	...
Intracompany loans	773	-11	367	1 457	2 752	3 292	1 784	-967	...
Reinvested earnings	3 321	2 336	1 998	1 436	3 483	2 988	975	1 148	...

Source: Economic Commission for Latin America and the Caribbean (ECLAC), on the basis of estimates and official figures as of 27 May 2016.
ᵃ Gross foreign direct investment flows, excluding divestments.

Table I.A2.5
Latin America and the Caribbean: inward foreign direct investment stock by country, 2001-2015
(Millions of dollars and percentages of GDP)

	Millions of dollars							Percentages of GDP						
	2001	2005	2011	2012	2013	2014	2015	2001	2005	2011	2012	2013	2014	2015
Argentina	79 504	55 139	93 199	100 821	91 557	82 739	93 853	25	25	17	17	15	15	17
Bolivia (Plurinational State of)	5 893	4 905	7 749	8 809	10 558	11 206	11 710	72	51	32	33	34	34	33
Brazil	121 949	181 344	695 505	742 144	741 436	739 201	614 975	22	20	27	30	30	31	36
Chile	0	78 993	175 753	206 041	213 129	223 113	229 229	0	63	70	78	77	86	95
Colombia	15 377	36 987	97 364	112 926	128 191	141 942	149 692	16	25	29	31	34	38	51
Costa Rica	0	0	20 310	20 310	24 627	28 223	31 854	0	0	49	45	50	57	62
Dominican Republic	...	...	21 740	25 143	26 660	29 035	31 326	...	...	37	42	44	45	47
Ecuador	6 876	9 861	12 500	13 067	13 794	14 567	15 627	28	24	16	15	15	14	15
El Salvador	2 252	4 167	8 120	8 789	8 918	9 392	10 108	16	24	35	37	37	37	39
Guatemala	0	3 319	7 751	8 938	10 255	11 977	13 176	0	12	16	18	19	20	21
Haiti	99	150	784	963	...	...	...	3	4	10	12	...	...	...
Honduras	1 585	2 870	7 965	9 024	10 084	11 228	12 431	21	29	45	50	55	59	64
Jamaica	3 931	6 919	11 110	11 988	12 457	13 159	13 606	43	62	77	81	87	94	99
Mexico	156 583	233 710	338 995	376 348	394 727	389 672	354 996	23	27	29	32	31	30	31
Nicaragua	1 565	2 461	5 617	6 385	7 200	8 084	8 919	29	39	58	61	66	69	70
Panama	7 314	10 167	23 875	26 762	31 413	35 917	40 314	59	62	69	67	70	73	77
Paraguay	1 016	1 127	3 877	5 288	5 077	5 492	5 774	13	13	15	21	18	18	21
Peru	11 835	15 889	50 641	62 559	71 857	79 707	86 114	23	21	29	32	36	39	45
Suriname	...	...	859	1 035	1 232	1 397	1 676	...	...	19	21	24	27	33
Uruguay	2 406	2 844	15 147	17 407	19 564	21 240	...	12	16	32	34	34	37	...
Venezuela (Bolivarian Republic of)	39 074	44 518	40 206	40 180	33 018	30 139	...	32	31	13	11	9	5	...

Source: Economic Commission for Latin America and the Caribbean (ECLAC), on the basis of estimates and official figures as of 27 May 2016.

Table I.A2.6
Latin America and the Caribbean: outward foreign direct investment flows by country, 2001-2015
(Millions of dollars)

	2001	2002	2003	2004	2005	2006	2007	2008	2009	2010	2011	2012	2013	2014	2015
Antigua and Barbuda	13	14	13	15	17	2	2	2	4	5	3	4	6	6	0
Argentina	161	-627	774	676	1 311	2 439	1 504	1 391	712	965	1 488	1 055	890	1 921	1 139
Bahamas	94	40	72	169	143	333	459	410	216	150	524	132	277	397	158
Barbados	25	24	24	52	153	43	69	59	16	342	186	-123	28	133	81
Belize	0	0	0	0	0	1	1	3	0	1	1	1	1	3	0
Bolivia (Plurinational State of)	3	3	3	3	3	3	4	5	-4	-29	0	77	-255	55	5
Brazil	-1 489	2 479	229	9 822	2 910	28 798	17 061	26 115	-4 552	26 763	16 067	5 208	14 942	26 040	13 498
Chile		0	1 709	2 145	2 135	2 212	4 852	9 151	7 233	9 461	20 252	20 555	9 872	12 915	15 794
Colombia	16	857	938	192	4 796	1 268	1 279	3 085	3 505	5 483	8 420	-606	7 652	3 899	4 218
Costa Rica	0	0	0	0	0	0	0	0	274	318	405	894	772	398	386
Dominica	4	1	0	1	13	3	7	0	1	1	0	0	0	0	0
El Salvador	0	0	19	0	113	0	95	80	0	5	-0	-2	3	1	0
Grenada	2	3	1	1	3	6	16	6	1	3	3	3	3	3	3
Guatemala	0	0	0	0	0	0	0	16	26	24	17	39	34	106	93
Honduras	3	7	12	-6	1	1	2		4	-1	2	208	68	24	91
Jamaica	89	74	116	60	101	85	115	76	61	58	75	24	73	...	0
Mexico	4 404	891	1 253	4 432	6 474	5 758	8 256	1 157	9 604	15 050	12 636	22 470	13 138	7 463	12 126
Paraguay	0	0	0	0	0	0	0	0	0	0	0	0	0	0	0
Peru	74	0	60	0	0	0	66	736	411	266	147	78	137	96	127
Saint Kitts and Nevis	2	1	2	7	11	4	6	6	5	3	2	2	2	2	2
Saint Lucia	4	5	5	5	4	4	6	5	6	5	4	4	4	4	4
Saint Vincent and the Grenadines	0	0	0	0	1	1	2	0	1	1	0	0	0	0	0
Suriname	0	0	0	0	0	0	0	0	0	0	3	-1	0	0	0
Trinidad and Tobago [a]	58	106	225	25	341	370	0	700	0	0	1 060	1 681	2 061	1 275	716
Uruguay	6	14	15	18	36	-1	89	-11	16	-60	-7	-3	5	39	33
Venezuela (Bolivarian Republic of) [a]	204	1 026	1 318	619	1 167	1 524	-495	1 311	2 630	2 492	-370	4 294	752	1 024	-1 112

Source: Economic Commission for Latin America and the Caribbean (ECLAC), on the basis of estimates and official figures as of 27 May 2016.
[a] The 2015 data correspond to the first three quarters only.

Foreign investment in metal mining

A. Disruptive market changes

This chapter looks at key aspects of the processes that have transformed global metal markets and examines their relationship with foreign investment in Latin American and Caribbean economies. Considering that several of the region's countries are major producers of metallic minerals, the study focuses on those that are of greatest significance for international exports, notably precious metals (such as gold and silver), base metals (such as bauxite, zinc, copper, tin, nickel and lead) and ferrous metals (chiefly iron ore).

Section A analyses the changes that have occurred in markets and the geographical distribution of activities, with special emphasis on China and the capacity of Latin America and the Caribbean to maintain its leading position. Section B considers the role and strategies of the principal economic agents in the sector, namely transnational corporations. Section C addresses the radical shifts in the metal mining sector in the past 15 years, and their consequences for foreign direct investment (FDI) in Latin America and the Caribbean. Section D reflects on the changes of recent years and their impact on FDI in the region and, lastly, section E considers the challenges associated with the sector's potential to make a greater contribution to capacity-building and production diversification in the region.

1. China: the engine of demand

The metal mining sector presents certain characteristics that are key to understanding its dynamics and its close relationship with FDI. One the one hand, it is highly concentrated, both in terms of international demand and production; on the other, the specificities of the investment and production process mean that the vast majority of leading firms are transnational.

After a period of stagnation, international prices for the main products enjoyed a strong growth cycle between 2003 and 2011, but since then have suffered a sharp decline.

Understanding these dynamics requires some consideration of the fluctuations that have occurred in international demand, and of changes in the characteristics and strategies of transnational corporations. These aspects are fundamental not only for explaining the transformations in the sector at the international level, but also for comprehending the consequences for FDI in Latin America and its outlook for the coming years.

International demand has seen strong shifts in the past 15 years, with China's rise to prominence a key factor.

China's exceptional growth and it industrialization strategy caused its consumption of iron ore and base metals to outstrip the increase in its domestic production. This gap, which began to open up in the 1990s, widened further during the 2000s. In 2005, China's consumption of iron ore was three times its national output, while base metal consumption was twice the level of domestic production. This situation led to a surge in mineral imports, especially from Latin American countries, which were experiencing the reverse trend; extraction of base and ferrous metals at around seven times the level of consumption (Rogich and Matos 2008). The high volume of imports from China altered the structure of the international market: in 2000 China imported 70 million metric tons of iron ore, equivalent to 14.4% of global imports by volume and 14.3% by value. By 2014, these figures had risen to 932 million metric tons, equivalent to 68.4% of the volume and 64.6% of the value of total global imports. Countries that historically had carried greater weight therefore lost market share: these included Germany, the Republic of Korea and above all Japan, which until 2001 was the world's largest importer of iron ore.

A similar pattern was observed for copper concentrate (albeit to a lesser extent, given that China's imports rose from 12.6% of the total in 2000 to 40.1% in 2014), and bauxite and aluminium.

China's imports of copper concentrate began to increase in 1995, and by 2000 the country had already overtaken most of the world's top importers, such as Germany, India, the Republic of Korea and Spain. China became the largest importer in 2009, overtaking Japan, whose market share has been in constant decline (see figure II.1).

Figure II.1
Selected countries: share of global imports of iron, copper, and bauxite and alumina, by value, 1992-2014
(Percentages)

China becomes the world's leading importer of metallic minerals

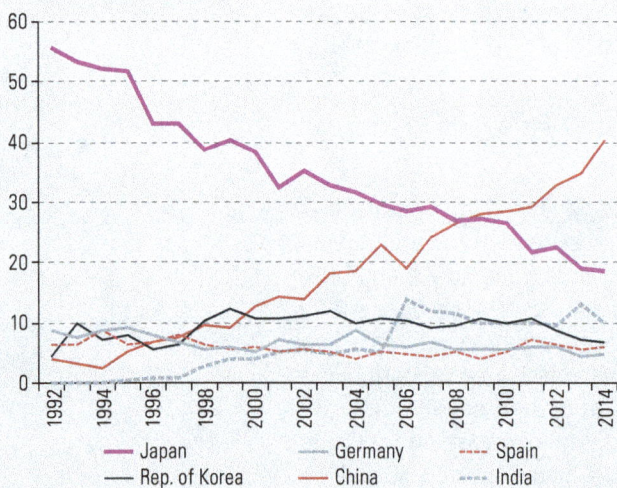

A. Iron

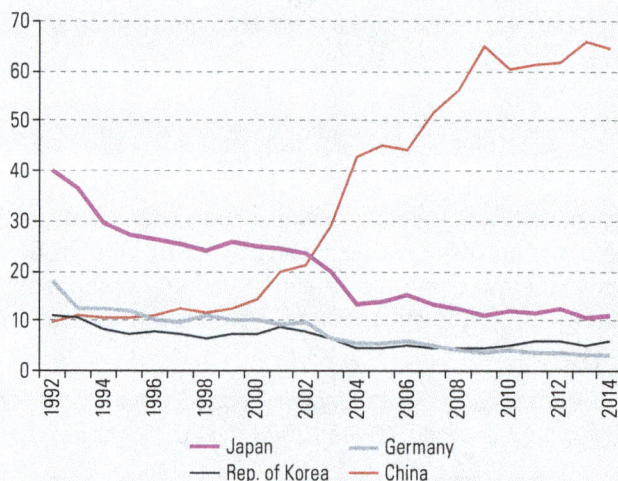

B. Copper concentrates

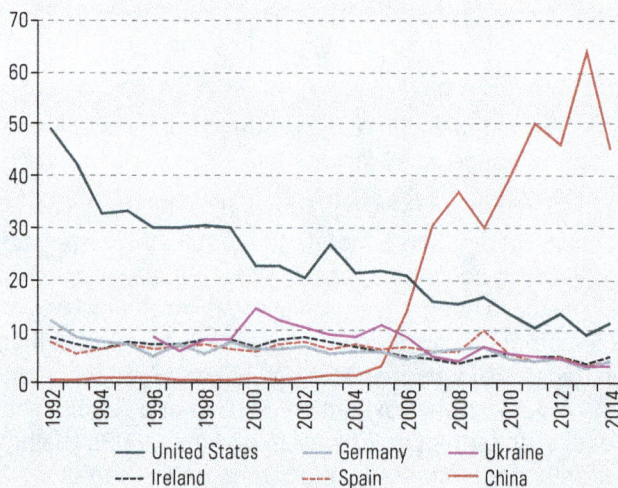

C. Bauxite and alumina

Source: Economic Commission for Latin America and the Caribbean (ECLAC), on the basis of United Nations Commodity Trade Statistics Database (COMTRADE) and TradeMap.

Similarly strong growth in aluminium and bauxite imports meant that China was to overtake the United States' share of the international market in 2007, consolidating itself as the top importer with a market share of about 40%.

China's growth and industrialization strategy had further consequences. Not only did the country import metallic minerals to supply its domestic market, but these imports also allowed it to satisfy international demand for metals and metal manufactures. Traditionally, Germany and Japan were the main exporters of basic iron and steel manufactures, but in 2004 China began to consolidate its position and by 2014 had assumed leadership of this export market, accounting for 13.6% of exports by value (see figure II.2). A similar situation was observed in aluminium and aluminium manufactures, with China's share of total exports rising from 5.7% in 2004 to 13.4% in 2014, overtaking Germany which had led the market since 1995.

> Not only did China import metallic minerals to supply its domestic market, but these imports also allowed it to satisfy international demand for metals and metal manufactures.

Figure II.2

Selected countries: share of global exports of iron, steel and aluminium manufactures, by value, 1992-2014
(Percentages)

China overtakes traditional exporters of metal manufactures

A. Iron and steel manufactures

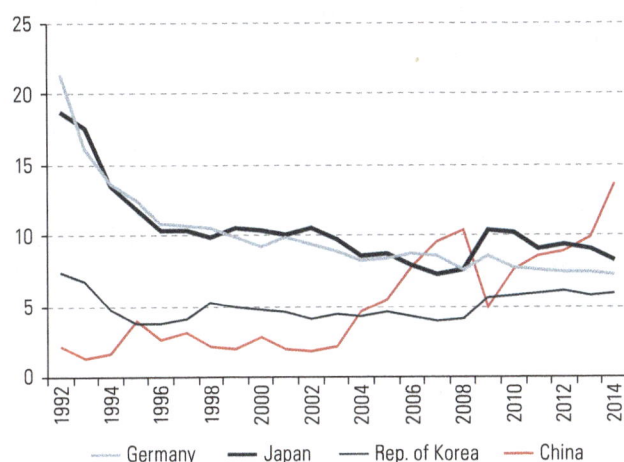

Legend: Germany — Japan — Rep. of Korea — China

B. Aluminium and aluminium manufactures

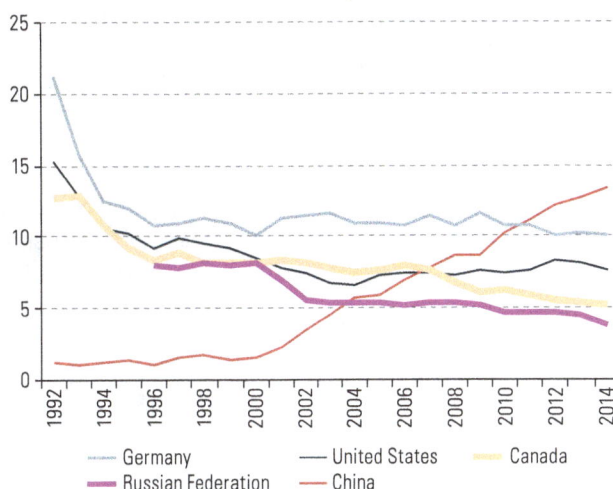

Legend: Germany — United States — Canada — Russian Federation — China

Source: Economic Commission for Latin America and the Caribbean (ECLAC), on the basis of United Nations Commodity Trade Statistics Database (COMTRADE) and TradeMap.

China's aluminium exports mainly went to other Asian countries (49.2% of the total value on average for the period 2011-2015), 27 countries of the European Union (14.3%), and the United States (12.7%). This pattern was mirrored by exports of iron and steel manufactures; 44.4% of the average value of exports between 2011 and 2015 went to other Asian countries, 15.7% to the United States and 13.7% to the European Union (27 countries).

Changes in demand, together with China's new position in the world economy, created a cycle of extremely high prices, especially for iron, during the 2000s. By 2011, the price of iron had soared to 14 times its level during the 1980s, while that of copper had risen five-fold. Gold prices quadrupled and aluminium prices doubled over the same period (see figure II.3).

Figure II.3
Main metallic mineral prices, 2000-2015
(Index 1980=100)

Increasing demand causes a price boom

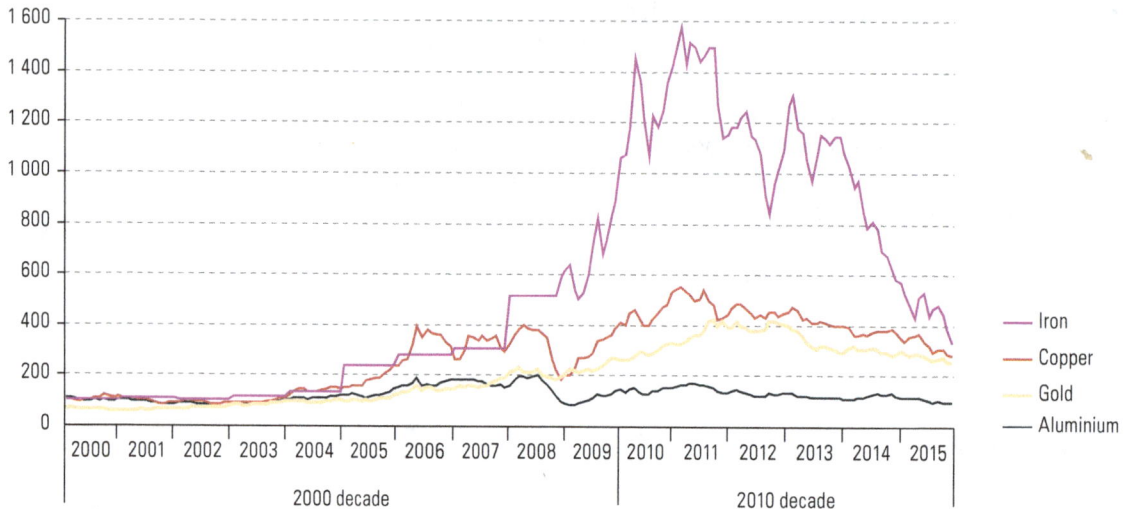

Source: Economic Commission for Latin America and the Caribbean (ECLAC), on the basis of information provided by the International Monetary Fund (IMF) and the United Nations Conference on Trade and Development (UNCTAD).

ᵃ Index of current prices for Chinese imports of iron ore fines 62% Fe (in dollars per ton), the cash price of grade A electrolytic copper bars/cathodes on the London Metal Exchange (LME) (in pounds sterling per ton), the London fix price of 99.5% pure gold (in dollars per ounce), and the cash price of high grade primary aluminium listed on the LME.

A downtrend in metal prices commenced in 2012 and continues today. As will be discussed below, this marked trend shift is chiefly due to slower growth in China and weak demand from developed countries, together with increased global production capacity for minerals and mineral products.

2.　The region remains a major player

The shifting global scenario during the 2000s coincided with changes in international production, as rising prices fuelled a steady increase in metallic mineral production from 2003 onwards (see figure II.4). Global iron ore production tripled, while other minerals posted smaller but still significant increases in output: bauxite by more than 80%, copper by 40.7%, and gold by 18.0%.[1]

The global geography of production has also shifted. Chinese iron production leapt by 570% between 2000 and 2014, and accounted for half of worldwide output by the end of that period (see table II.1). In absolute terms (metric tons), sizeable increases also occurred in Australia (which boosted its share of the world market), Brazil and India (whose relative share declined). In 2000, 62% of world production was concentrated in these four countries, a figure that rose to 82% in 2014. Output in the four countries grew at markedly different rates. Apart from the surge in China —almost certainly the most significant change in the sector— it is striking that in 2000 Brazil's mineral production was 16% higher than Australia's, but by 2014 it had fallen behind, with Australia producing almost twice as much iron.

---

[1]　The drop in bauxite production in 2014 reflected lower output in Indonesia, as explained below.

Global production of metallic minerals steadily increased

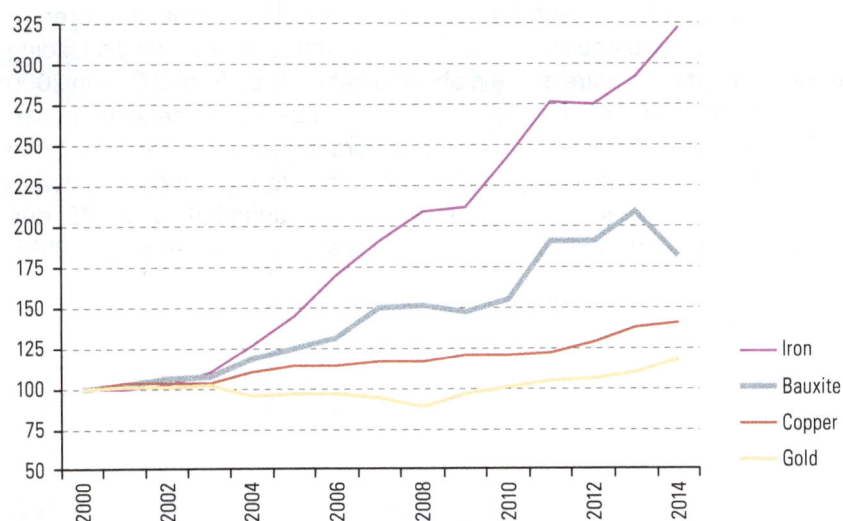

Figure II.4
Global metallic mineral
production, by volume,
2000-2014
(Index 2000=100)

Source: Economic Commission for Latin America and the Caribbean (ECLAC), on the basis of information provided by the United States Geological Survey.

Table II.1
Selected countries: iron ore production, 2000 and 2014
(Millions of metric tons and percentages)

Brazil was one of the world's main iron ore producers

Country	2000		2014		Growth	
China	224	21.1	1 510	44.1	1 286	54.5
Australia	168	15.8	774	22.6	606	25.7
Brazil	195	18.3	411	12.0	216	9.2
India	75	7.1	129	3.8	54	2.3
South Africa	34	3.2	81	2.4	47	2.0
Islamic Republic of Iran	...	...	33	1.0	33	1.4
Sweden	21	2.0	37	1.1	16	0.7
Russian Federation	87	8.2	102	3.0	15	0.6
Ukraine	56	5.3	68	2.0	12	0.5
Kazakhstan	16	1.5	25	0.7	9	0.4
Canada	35	3.3	44	1.3	9	0.4
United States	63	5.9	56	1.6	-7	-0.3
Other countries	89	8.4	153	4.5	64	2.7
Total	**1 063**	**100.0**	**3 423**	**100.0**	**2 360**	**100.0**

Source: Economic Commission for Latin America and the Caribbean (ECLAC), on the basis of information provided by the United States Geological Survey.

Note: The source only identifies production by the world's largest producing countries. Data is not provided for years in which production did not reach the minimum level necessary to be included in the list of the world's largest producers.

Increasing production and rising prices coincided with the rapid expansion of international trade in iron ore; the value of exports peaked at US$ 148 billion in 2011 (nine times the total figure for 2004).[2]

The changes in production observed in Australia and Brazil were mirrored in the external sector. These two countries retained their status as the world's leading exporters, but while Australia's share of the global market climbed from 27.8% in 2000 to 52.9% in 2014, Brazil's share contracted from 33.1% to 22.7% in the same period (see figure II.5). Meanwhile India, which was the third-largest exporter during the 2000s (accounting for 15% of global exports in 2005), saw its exports decline owing to a government ban on mining operations in several states during 2011 and 2012, due to legal and environmental concerns. Some of these measures were revoked in 2015.

Figure II.5
Selected countries: share of global iron ore exports, by value, 1992-2014 *(Percentages)*

Australia's iron exports overtake those of Brazil

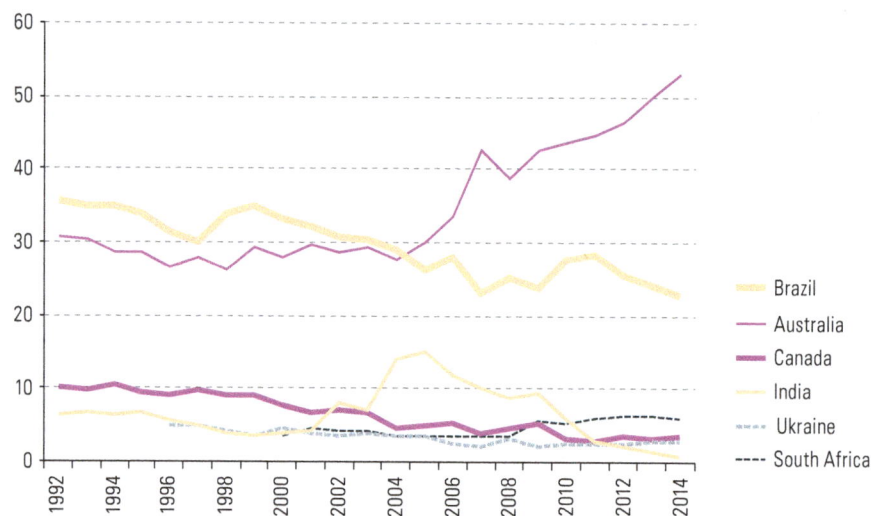

Source: Economic Commission for Latin America and the Caribbean (ECLAC), on the basis of United Nations Commodity Trade Statistics Database (COMTRADE) and TradeMap.

The copper market is less concentrated, with the four largest producers taking a 53.1% market share in 2014 (see table II.2). Contrary to iron production, in which Brazil was the region's only significant market presence, several Latin American and Caribbean countries recorded high levels of mined copper production.[3] Chile retained its position as the world's leading producer, albeit with a share that fell from 34.8% in 2000 to 31.0% in 2014, and together with Argentina, Brazil, Colombia, Mexico, Peru and the Plurinational State of Bolivia, accounted for 43.5% of global production in 2014. All the copper-producing countries of the region, with the exception of Argentina, have boosted output in the past 15 years.

---

[2]   The price of iron ore also peaked in 2011.
[3]   Figures refer to mined copper to differentiate the copper obtained through mining from that recovered in recycling processes.

Chile and Peru are among the world's leading producers of mined copper

Table II.2
Selected countries: mined
copper production,
2000 and 2014
*(Thousands of metric tons
and percentages)*

Country	2000		2014		Growth	
Chile	4 600	34.8	5 750	31.0	1 150	21.4
Democratic Republic of the Congo	...	...	1 030	5.5	1 030	19.2
China	590	4.5	1 760	9.5	1 170	21.8
Peru	554	4.2	1 380	7.4	826	15.4
Zambia	240	1.8	708	3.8	468	8.7
Russian Federation	570	4.3	742	4.0	172	3.2
Australia	829	6.3	970	5.2	141	2.6
Mexico	365	2.8	515	2.8	150	2.8
Canada	634	4.8	696	3.7	62	1.2
Kazakhstan	430	3.3	430	2.3	0	0.0
Poland	456	3.5	425	2.3	-31	-0.6
United States	1 440	10.9	1360	7.3	-80	-1.5
Indonesia	1 012	7.7	400	2.2	-612	-11.4
Other countries	1 480	11.2	2400	12.9	920	17.1
Total	**13 200**	**100.0**	**18 566**	**100.0**	**5 366**	**100.0**

Source: Economic Commission for Latin America and the Caribbean (ECLAC), on the basis of information provided by the United States Geological Survey.

Note: The source only identifies production by the world's largest producing countries. Data is not provided for years in which production did not reach the minimum level necessary to be included in the list of the world's largest producers.

Chile, China, the Democratic Republic of the Congo (where production recovered after 2010) and Peru were the main drivers of increased production. Mined copper output in Australia and Canada expanded more slowly, and decreased in the United States.

In 2014, the main international supplier of copper concentrates and refined copper was Chile, which accounted for 33.5% of global concentrate exports and 29.9% of refined copper exports.

Peru's copper concentrate exports leapt after 2003, whereas Indonesia, historically one of the largest exporters, has lost much of its market share in recent years (see figure II.6). The value of global exports amounted to US$ 50.0 billion in 2014, of which Australia, Canada, Chile and Peru together accounted for 63.6%. The drop in copper concentrate exports from Indonesia is partly due to the Mineral and Coal Mining Law of 2009, which stipulated that minerals extracted in the country must be processed and refined domestically before export. Accordingly, a regulation prohibiting the export of concentrates was adopted in 2012; this was subsequently postponed and eventually partly implemented in 2014. It is expected that the value of mineral exports will more than double by 2017 as a result of this policy (Sujatmiko, 2015), although an adjustment period is needed in which to make the required investments in smelting and refining. Provided there is sufficient incentive, the loss of share in world copper concentrate trade due to the application of industrialization policies may actually be beneficial if the period of lower exports subsequently leads to growth of refined mineral exports, such as grade A copper cathodes, whose prices are known and listed on the world's metal markets.

Exports of refined copper were less concentrated. In 2014, the four main exporters (Australia, Chile, Japan and Zambia) together accounted for 50.2% of the market, with exports valued at US$ 64.0 billion. Chile's relative weight has declined as exports from the Democratic Republic of the Congo and Zambia have made steady inroads into this market.

The main international supplier of copper concentrates and refined copper has been Chile.

Figure II.6
Selected countries: share of global copper concentrate and refined copper exports,
by value, 1992-2014
(Percentages)

Chile remains the world's largest copper exporter, despite losing market share

A. Copper concentrates

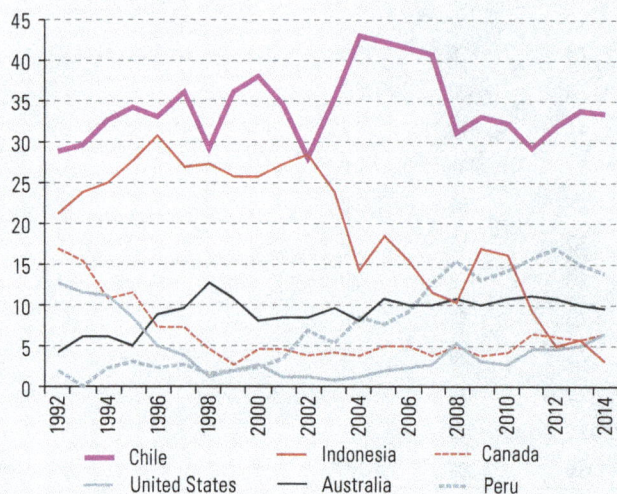

B. Refined copper

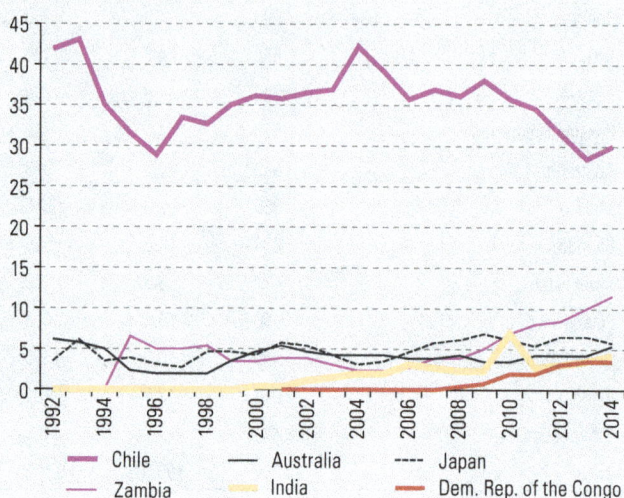

Chile — Indonesia — Canada
United States — Australia — Peru

Chile — Australia — Japan
Zambia — India — Dem. Rep. of the Congo

Source: Economic Commission for Latin America and the Caribbean (ECLAC), on the basis of United Nations Commodity Trade Statistics Database (COMTRADE) and TradeMap.

Regulatory change in Indonesia also had an impact on the production and export of bauxite, the raw material from which alumina and subsequently aluminium are obtained.[4] Global alumina and bauxite production almost doubled between 2000 and 2014, owing to booming production in Australia, Brazil and China. Indonesia was one of the largest producers in 2013 (20% of the total), however the regulatory impact saw production levels plummet in 2014. This market was highly concentrated, with 84% of global output originating in Australia, Brazil and China, three countries whose production rose substantially. By contrast, the Bolivarian Republic of Venezuela and Jamaica, countries that in 2000 had held a strong market position, suffered a steep decline during the period to 2014 (see table II.3).

Export trends show that the international market has become less concentrated as Guinea's share of exports has fallen, from 65.5% in 1995 to 26.4% in 2014, during a period in which that country's export growth was surpassed by that of other countries (see figure II.7). Exports from Australia and Brazil increased steadily during the period, so that Australia, Brazil, Guinea and India together accounted for 73.8% of the value of world exports in 2014. Jamaica's share declined amid relatively weak export growth, while Indonesia's exports plummeted and were partially replaced by those from Malaysia, whose share expanded from around zero to 4.8% of the total in 2014.

---

4   Bauxite is an aluminium ore, processed to obtain alumina, which in turns gives aluminium via electrolysis.

Brazil was the only country in the region to boost bauxite production

Table II.3
Selected countries: bauxite production, 2000 and 2014
(Thousands of metric tons and percentages)

Country	2000		2014		Growth	
China	9 000	6.6	55 000	22.5	46 000	25.1
Australia	53 800	39.7	78 600	32.1	24 800	18.5
Brazil	14 000	10.3	34 800	14.2	20 800	12.5
India	7 370	5.4	16 500	6.7	9 130	5.4
Kazakhstan	...	...	5 200	2.1	5 200	3.7
Indonesia	...	...	2 550	1.0	2 550	37.7
Guinea	15 000	11.1	17 300	7.1	2 300	2.6
Greece	...	...	1 900	0.8	1 900	1.4
Russian Federation	4 200	3.1	5 590	2.3	1 390	0.8
Viet Nam	...	...	1090	0.4	1 090	0.2
Suriname	3 610	2.7	3 000	1.2	-610	-0.6
Guyana	2 400	1.8	1 600	0.7	-800	-0.5
Jamaica	11 100	8.2	9 680	4.0	-1 420	-1.1
Venezuela (Bolivarian Republic of)	4 200	3.1	1 500	0.6	-2 700	-1.4
Other countries	10 800	8.0	10 460	4.3	-340	-4.2
Total	**135 480**	**100.0**	**244 770**	**100.0**	**109 290**	**100.0**

Source: Economic Commission for Latin America and the Caribbean (ECLAC), on the basis of information provided by the United States Geological Survey.

Note: The source only identifies production by the world's largest producing countries. Data is not provided for years in which production did not reach the minimum level necessary to be included in the list of the world's largest producers.

The region's bauxite exporters lost share to Australia and Indonesia

Figure II.7
Selected countries: share of world alumina and bauxite exports, by value, 1995-2014
(Percentages)

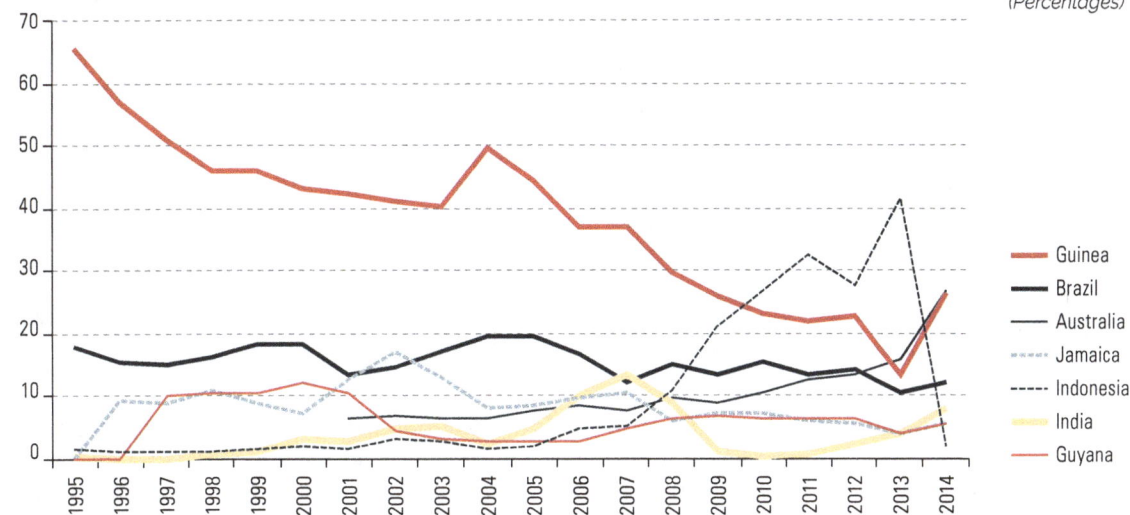

Guinea
Brazil
Australia
Jamaica
Indonesia
India
Guyana

Source: Economic Commission for Latin America and the Caribbean (ECLAC), on the basis of United Nations Commodity Trade Statistics Database (COMTRADE) and TradeMap.

For gold, international trade and production patterns differ from those of the base and ferrous metals examined above, reflecting its different end use as a precious metal. While base and ferrous metals are extracted for mass use in construction, infrastructure, manufacturing and consumer goods, gold is used as an industrial input, in final goods, and also as a store of value alternative to currency.

Gold production has risen more slowly than that of other metals, driven by increased output in traditional gold-producing countries and the emergence of some new players —especially after 2007—, thus helping to reduce its geographical concentration. In 2000, a group of 8 countries was responsible for 71.1% of global production, whereas 14 countries accounted for a similar percentage of output in 2014 (see table II.4). China managed to double its market share during that period, consolidating its presence as the world's leading producer followed by Australia, the Russian Federation, the United States and Canada. Gold production fell sharply in the United States and South Africa, but held steady in the Russian Federation. In Latin America and the Caribbean, Peru was the world's seventh-largest gold producer in 2014, while output increased in Mexico, Brazil and, to a lesser extent, Chile.

Table II.4
Selected countries: gold production, 2000 and 2014
(Thousands of metric tons and percentages)

Peru, Mexico and Brazil are the region's main gold producers

Country	2000		2014		Growth	
China	180	7.1	450	15.0	270	58.6
Russian Federation	126	5.0	247	8.2	121	26.2
Mexico	...	...	118	3.9	118	25.6
Uzbekistan	...	...	100	3.3	100	21.7
Ghana	...	...	91	3.0	91	19.7
Brazil	...	...	80	2.7	80	17.4
Papua New Guinea	...	...	53	1.8	53	11.5
Chile	...	...	50	1.7	50	10.8
Peru	133	5.3	140	4.7	7	1.5
Canada	154	6.1	152	5.1	-2	-0.4
Australia	296	11.7	274	9.2	-22	-4.8
Indonesia	125	4.9	69	2.3	-56	-12.1
United States	353	13.9	210	7.0	-143	-31.0
South Africa	431	17.0	152	5.1	-279	-60.5
Other countries	735	29.0	808	27.0	73	15.8
Total	**2 533**	**100.0**	**2 994**	**100.0**	**461**	**100.0**

Source: Economic Commission for Latin America and the Caribbean (ECLAC), on the basis of information provided by the United States Geological Survey.
Note: The source only identifies production by the world's largest producing countries. Data is not provided for years in which production did not reach the minimum level necessary to be included in the list of the world's largest producers.

In international markets, gold tends to be traded directly as a metal, processed to varying degrees, in manufactured goods, and often alloyed with other metals, rather than as unprocessed ore. Accordingly, the international gold trade refers to non-monetary gold, whose production includes mining and part of the manufacturing activity (ore refining and metal processing).[5]

---

[5]   Harmonized Commodity Description and Coding System, codes 710811, 710812 and 710813.

The above characteristics make it more difficult to discern patterns in international trade. Switzerland included the gold trade in its official statistics in 2012, emerging as the world's main importer and exporter of this metal in 2014. Besides Switzerland, the main importers of non-monetary gold were Hong Kong Special Administrative Region of China, India, where gold is used primarily as jewellery or for personal reserves, and the United Kingdom. These four countries accounted for 72.4% of international imports, overtaking countries that had formerly exhibited most demand, such as Italy, Japan and the United States (see figure II.8). International supply was less intensely concentrated, with the three main exporters, Switzerland, Hong Kong SAR and the United Kingdom, responsible for 64.6% of the total. These countries increased their share of gold exports in recent years, at the expense of countries such as Australia, Canada and the United States, which had dominated exports in the 1990s.

Figure II.8
Selected countries: share of international gold trade, by value, 1992-2014
(Percentages)

International gold trade concentrated in non-producing countries

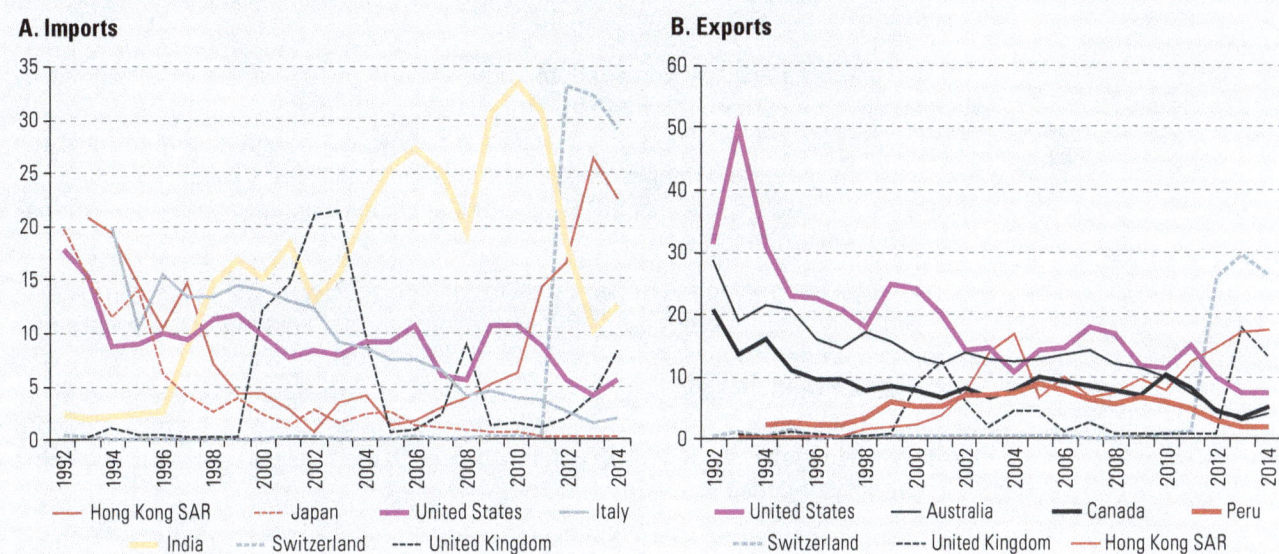

A. Imports

B. Exports

Source: Economic Commission for Latin America and the Caribbean (ECLAC), on the basis of United Nations Commodity Trade Statistics Database (COMTRADE) and TradeMap.

Latin American and Caribbean countries accounted for 7.8% of the total value of non-monetary gold exports in 2014, and were led by Peru (the world's seventh-largest exporter in 2014, with 2.0% of the market) and Mexico (with 1.7% of total exports). Brazil (0.8%), Argentina, Colombia and the Dominican Republic (each around 0.6%) enjoyed smaller shares of this export market.

In summary, Latin America has maintained a solid position in the new international production and trade scenario for the minerals in question, with marked increases in output and exports. However, it should be noted that new actors have emerged (the Democratic Republic of the Congo and Zambia in the case of copper, and Kazakhstan in respect of alumina and bauxite), while Australia has boosted its share of iron production and China had steadily expanded its extractive capacity for all minerals. This has translated into a loss of market share for some countries: certainly Brazil in the case of iron production, Jamaica in alumina and bauxite, and to some extent, Chile in copper (although the country remains the world's leading producer).[6]

B.   The lead actor: transnational corporations

1.   Competitive advantages: scale, markets and technology

Mining is traditionally characterized by an uneven geographical distribution of production and consumption. Some developing countries are among the main producers and net exporters, while developed countries are the major consumers and importers (UNCTAD 2007). The growth of China and India and the development of the Republic of Korea have brought new actors into this system; however, since mining requires the exploitation of natural resources associated with a particular territory, the uneven pattern continues to prevail. In that context, transnational corporations have played a key role in business development, investing in areas with natural resources and catering to demand via the international market.

Transnational corporations have played a key role in business development, investing in areas with natural resources and catering to demand via the international market.

The predominance of transnational corporations in this sector is explained by several factors, not least the need for large investments over lengthy time periods, it being estimated that on average 10 years are needed to identify and determine the feasibility of a greenfield mining project, and an additional 6 years before investors can expect returns (Behre Dolbear, 2015). An additional factor is that mining is a high-risk activity (see diagram II.1).

The exploration stage is fundamental for mining activity. In the industry, reserves refer to that portion of a territory's mineral resources that is identified as feasible for exploitation under certain legal, economic and technical conditions; in other words, resources with known conditions of economic viability. Exploration is either undertaken by transnational firms themselves, or performed by "junior companies", which are listed firms that, although not conducting mining operations themselves, sell extraction rights to larger firms if finds are made.

It should not be forgotten that mining is a risky business. The exploitation of these resources usually takes place in hard-to-reach geographical locations, under hazardous conditions for the personnel involved, and with profound environmental impacts both for natural resources and the communities residing in the affected areas. Safety and respect for the environment are therefore core aspects of mining investment, and are among the most frequent sources of conflict in cases of planned expansion.

Mining corporations operate on a huge scale. In 2014, the assets of the leading firms topped US$ 100 billion, with transnationals clearly in the vanguard (see table II.5).[7] The four largest mining corporations appeared in the Fortune Global 500 ranking, an annual compilation of the world's 500 largest companies by market value.

---

[6]   Latin America as a whole maintained its relative importance thanks to the rapid growth of natural resource extraction in Peru.
[7]   For illustrative purposes, in 2014 the GDP of Uruguay (population 3.4 million) was US$ 57.5 billion at current prices, according to data from CEPALSTAT.

Diagram II.1
Factors explaining the predominance of transnational corporations in the mining sector

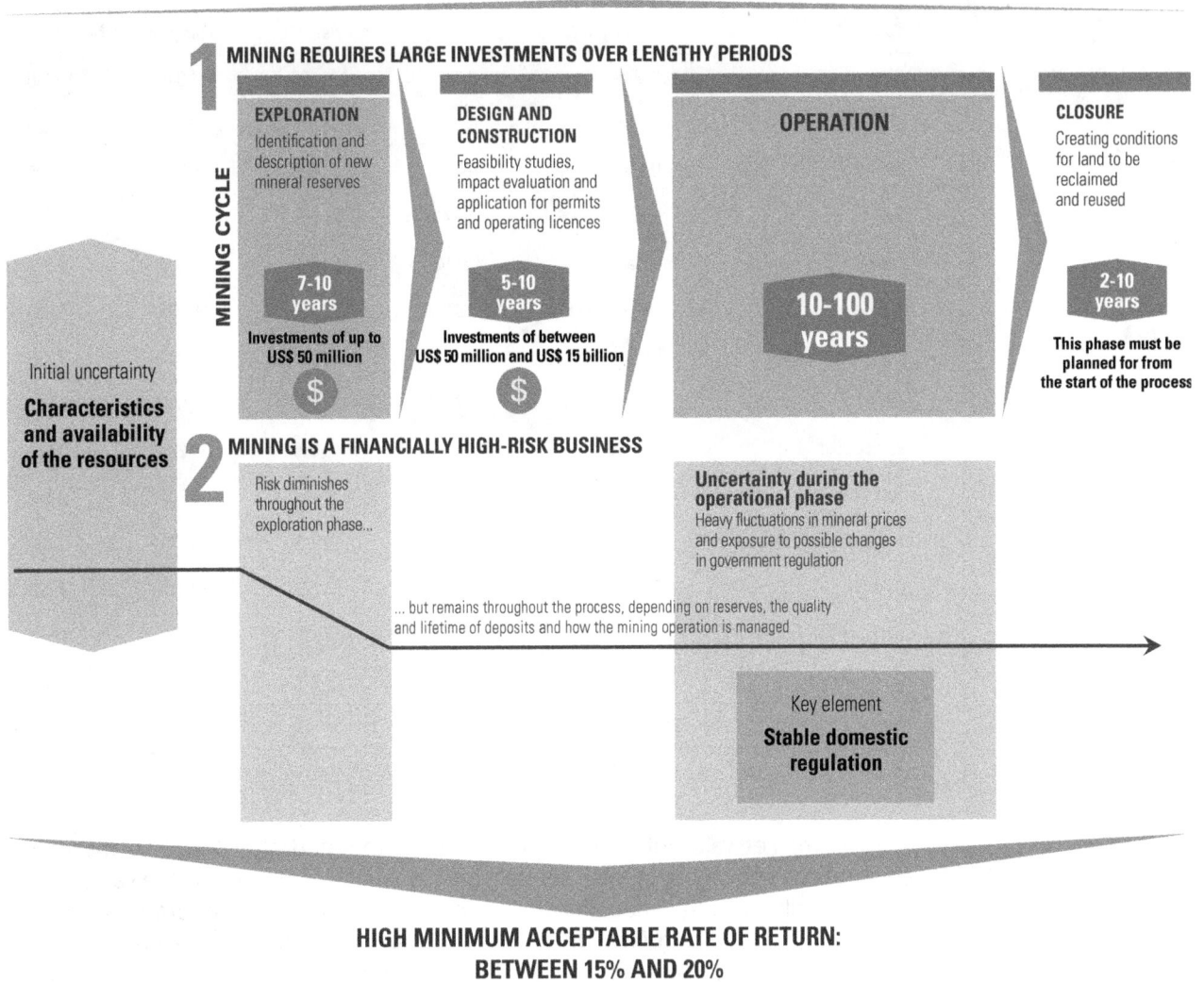

1 MINING REQUIRES LARGE INVESTMENTS OVER LENGTHY PERIODS

MINING CYCLE

EXPLORATION
Identification and description of new mineral reserves

7-10 years

Investments of up to US$ 50 million

$

DESIGN AND CONSTRUCTION
Feasibility studies, impact evaluation and application for permits and operating licences

5-10 years

Investments of between US$ 50 million and US$ 15 billion

$

OPERATION

10-100 years

CLOSURE
Creating conditions for land to be reclaimed and reused

2-10 years

This phase must be planned for from the start of the process

Initial uncertainty

Characteristics and availability of the resources

2 MINING IS A FINANCIALLY HIGH-RISK BUSINESS

Risk diminishes throughout the exploration phase...

Uncertainty during the operational phase
Heavy fluctuations in mineral prices and exposure to possible changes in government regulation

... but remains throughout the process, depending on reserves, the quality and lifetime of deposits and how the mining operation is managed

Key element
Stable domestic regulation

**HIGH MINIMUM ACCEPTABLE RATE OF RETURN:
BETWEEN 15% AND 20%**

Source: Economic Commission for Latin America and the Caribbean (ECLAC), on the basis of H. Halland, M. Lokanc and A. Nair, *The Extractive Industries Sector: Essentials for Economists, Public Finance Professionals, and Policy Makers,* Washington, D.C., World Bank, 2015.

Table II.5
The world's leading metal mining corporations, by assets, 2014[a]
(Millions of dollars and employees)

The sector is led by large transnationals whose market values are highly sensitive to prices

Corporation	Country of origin	Assets	Sales	Employees	Market value
Glencore PLC	Switzerland	152 205	170 497	181 349	19 190
BHP Billiton	Australia	124 580	44 636	72 499	65 454
Rio Tinto	United Kingdom	107 827	34 829	59 775	53 908
Vale	Brazil	99 424	26 051	76 531	15 830
Vedanta	India	67 527	24 938	34 928	4 997
AngloAmerican	United Kingdom	66 010	20 455	95 000	5 690
Freeport-McMoran	United States	58 795	15 877	35 000	7 825
Alcoa Inc.	United States	37 399	22 534	59 000	12 931
Barrick Gold	Canada	33 879	9 029	17 260	8 626
Teck Resources	Canada	31 717	6 467	10 200	2 242
Aluminum Corp. of China	China	31 033	19 648	75 749	9 704
Goldcorp	Canada	27 866	4 375	18 217	9 600
Newmont	United States	24 916	7 729	13 700	9 519
Grupo México	Mexico	20 605	8 175	29 998	16 624

Source: Economic Commission for Latin America and the Caribbean (ECLAC), on the basis of information provided by Bloomberg.
[a] Market value at 31 December 2015, a date which marked a new low for many firms. Only listed companies are included; accordingly Chile's National Copper Corporation (CODELCO), which holds US$ 35.0 billion in assets, is not shown.

The market value of most mining firms plummeted after 2011, so the mining corporations shown in the table above were selected and classed by the value of their assets. While most transnational mining corporations are headquartered in developed countries; metal mining firms from Brazil, China, India and Mexico all posted strong sales and built up considerable assets during the boom period. Notable Latin American corporations include Brazil's Vale, which has operations in Australia, Canada, China, Indonesia and Japan, and the somewhat smaller Grupo México, which operates in Chile, Peru and the United States.

Some of these firms have far-reaching geographical presence and diversified production, including metallic minerals, energy minerals and mineral fertilizers, while others carry out more specialized operations with a narrower geographical scope (see table II.6).

While most corporations are in private hands, State-owned enterprises have also played a significant role. The need to secure raw materials for strategic purposes, and to appropriate natural resource rents, led to various forms of State intervention, from direct participation in business activities to more traditional instruments such as charges for subsoil use, royalties, corporate income tax, and others.

Table II.6
Geographical presence and specialization of the world's major metal mining corporations

Location and mineral type as sources of competitive advantage

	Corporation	Country of origin	Number of countries present	Production	Location
Global diversified firms	Glencore plc	Switzerland	50	Copper, zinc, nickel, ferro-alloys, aluminium, iron. Oil and coal	Global, diversified
	Rio Tinto	United Kingdom	40	Aluminium, iron, copper. Diamonds. Coal	Global, diversified
	Vale	Brazil	26	Iron, nickel, copper, ferro-alloys. Coal. Fertilizers	Concentrated in Brazil, Canada, Africa and South-East Asia
	Aluminum Corp. of China [a]	China	20	Bauxite, alumina, aluminium, copper, rare earths. Energy	Australia, China, Democratic Republic of the Congo, Guinea, Indonesia, Laos and Peru
	Alcoa Inc.	United States	30	Global Primary Products Unit: bauxite, aluminium. Energy	Bauxite/aluminium: Australia, Brazil, Europe, Guinea, Jamaica, Suriname and United States
Diversified firms with less extensive global scope	BHP Billiton [b]	Australia	10	Iron, copper, nickel, zinc. Oil, potash, coal	Copper and iron in Australia, Brazil, Chile and Peru
	Vedanta [c]	India	7	Aluminium, coal, iron, zinc. Oil and gas. Power	Africa, Australia, India. Zinc mine in Ireland
	Anglo American	United Kingdom	9	Copper, iron, diamonds, platinum group metals, nickel, niobium. Coal	Africa, Australia, Brazil, Canada and Colombia
	Freeport-McMoRan	United States	5	Cobalt, copper, molybdenum, gold. Oil and gas	Chile, Democratic Republic of the Congo, Indonesia, Peru and United States
	Teck Resources	Canada	4	Copper, zinc. Coal. Energy	Canada, Chile, Peru and United States
More specialized firms	Barrick Gold	Canada	10	Gold (87% of sales in 2015), copper	Americas, Australia, Papua New Guinea, Saudi Arabia, Zambia
	Newmont	United States	6	Gold (84% of sales in 2015), copper	Australia, Ghana, Indonesia, Peru, Suriname, United States
	Goldcorp	Canada	6	Gold, with lesser production of copper, silver, lead and zinc	Argentina, Canada, Chile, Dominican Republic, Guatemala and Mexico
	Grupo México	Mexico	4	Copper (64% of sales in 2014), silver, lead, zinc and gold. Coal	Chile, Peru, Mexico and United States

Source: Economic Commission for Latin America and the Caribbean (ECLAC), on the basis of information from the websites of the respective companies.
[a] Data include the subsidiaries Chinalco Mining Corporation and Yunnan Copper.
[b] In 2015, BHP Billiton spun off its aluminium, nickel, manganese and silver businesses to form the company South32.
[c] Vedanta Resources and Vedanta Limited.

After the Second World War, and even in the 1990s, many developed countries such as Finland, France and Sweden invested in State-owned mining companies. Mining activity was nationalized in several developing countries in the 1960s and 1970s, while governments took control of copper mines in Chile, Peru, Zaire (now the Democratic Republic of the Congo) and Zambia and promoted State ownership of bauxite mines in Guinea and Jamaica. Governments also took over iron ore production in the Bolivarian Republic of Venezuela, Brazil and India, and tin production in Indonesia and the Plurinational State of Bolivia (UNCTAD, 2007). In Mexico, the Mexicanization of Mining Law was enacted, stipulating a mandatory minimum 51% national ownership of mining projects and strengthening direct ownership by the State (Wise and Del Pozo, 2001).

Since the 1990s, many of these nationalizations have been reversed amid low metal prices and shifts in the global political climate, with the prevailing trend being for less State involvement in the economy. In 1997, Brazil's privatization policy led to one of the world's largest miners, Vale do Rio Doce, being sold to a consortium of

Brazilian and foreign investors. Nevertheless, the Government of Brazil retained control of the company though holdings known as golden shares, which give it considerable influence over decision-making. It also holds a 5.3% stake in the company through the National Bank for Economic and Social Development (BNDES). In Peru, all State-owned mining corporations were sold, mostly to foreign investors, as part of a privatization programme that commenced in 1991. Before then, most mining in the country was done by publicly owned operators, with the exception of a single foreign private firm (Campodónico 1999). Mexico's State-owned enterprises were acquired by the same domestic groups that had been operating since 1960, and therefore no new actors entered the market (Wise and Del Pozo, 2001).

> Nevertheless, State-owned firms continue to operate in several countries.

Nevertheless, State-owned firms continue to operate in several countries. In Chile, the National Copper Corporation (CODELCO) remains a key actor, while State-owned enterprises remain in charge of iron ore production in India and Sweden (NDMC Limited and LKAB, respectively). In China too, mining corporations are government owned (the five largest are listed on stock exchanges but the State retains control). These companies have stepped up their international investments, chiefly because deposits located in China are of low grade, meaning that the country looks overseas to meet its demand for better quality natural resources (World Bank, 2011).

In summary, excluding China, the State share of global metallic mineral production stood at 10.6% in 2008, compared with 42.3% in 1984.[8] Including China, where State-owned firms are in the ascendancy, the figure rises, but at 23.8% is still smaller than in previous decades (World Bank, 2011). Despite nationalizations in mineral-producing countries such as the Plurinational State of Bolivia during the 2000s, and the resurgence of debate over nationalization in countries such as South Africa (a proposal that was ultimately rejected), metal mining remains dominated by private corporations.

2.   The emergence of new actors

The business structure of the metal mining sector changed somewhat during the recent growth cycle, with existing actors expanding and newcomers entering the market. The number of listed metal mining firms (not including steelmakers) rose from roughly 900 in 2000 to about 2,400 in 2015. The companies that were operating at the beginning of the decade continued their activity and in 2015 held assets worth 66% of the total. With the exception of Switzerland's Glencore, most of the major corporations that have consolidated their presence since the mid-2000s are based in emerging economies, notably Brazil (Vale), China (Aluminum Corporation of China Limited), the Russian Federation (United Company Rusal) and India (Vedanta).

Between 2000 and 2015, some 7,400 cross-border mergers and acquisitions were registered in the metal mining sector, worth US$ 620 billion in total. Rising prices in the early 2000s invigorated the market as the largest corporations sought to consolidate their leadership through mergers, acquiring companies that would allow them to diversify their product portfolio or improve their position in segments with existing operations. Meanwhile, firms in developing countries consolidated their position in the international market through acquisitions. The mergers and acquisitions market was at its most buoyant between 2006 and 2013, with about 600 transactions concluded each year (see figure II.9); this figure halved in 2014 and 2015.

---

[8]   Figures refer to the production of bauxite, copper, gold, iron ore, lead, manganese, nickel, tin and zinc.

Booming investment in mergers and acquisitions

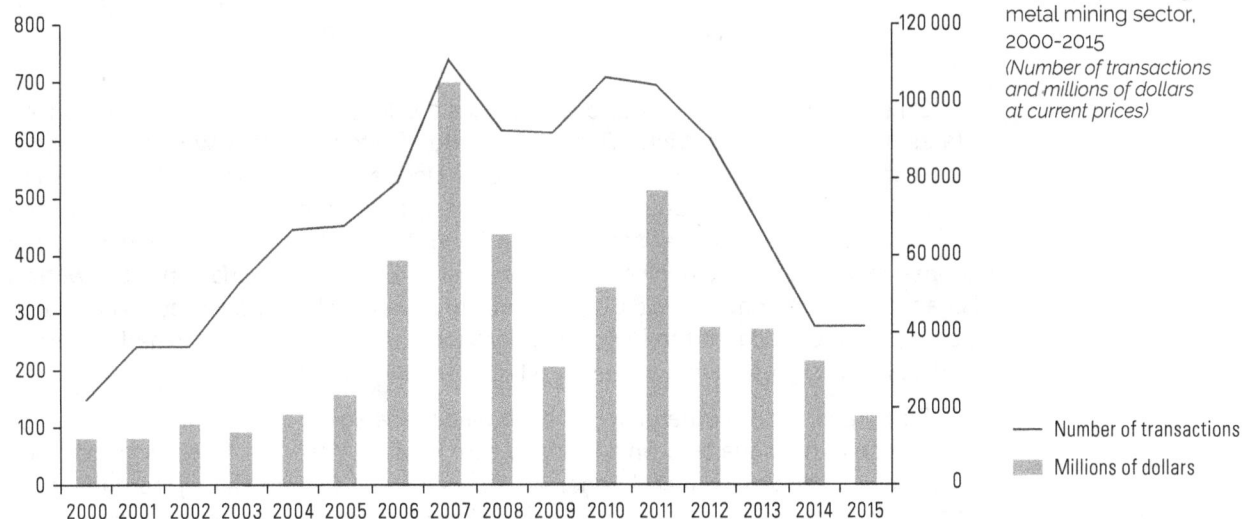

Figure II.9
Cross-border mergers and acquisitions in the global metal mining sector, 2000-2015
(Number of transactions and millions of dollars at current prices)

— Number of transactions

▨ Millions of dollars

Source: Economic Commission for Latin America and the Caribbean (ECLAC), on the basis of information provided by Bloomberg.

A number of record-breaking transactions took place in the metal mining sector between 2000 and 2015. The 10 largest mergers and acquisitions, representing 22% of the total value for the period, were nearly all concluded between 2006 and 2013 (see table II.7). The most significant of these was Glencore's purchase of Xstrata Ltd for US$ 43.4 billion: the largest transaction in the history of the metal mining sector. According to analysts, the merger of these Swiss-based firms combined Glencore's strengths in selling of energy products, metals and agricultural products with Xstrata's coal, copper and zinc mining capacity.

Table II.7
Mergers and acquisitions in the global metal mining sector valued above US$ 10 billion, 2000-2015
(Millions of dollars)

Corporations from developed countries concluded most of the largest transactions

Year	Corporation	Country of origin	Corporation acquired	Country of origin	Amount
2013	Glencore plc	Switzerland	Xstrata Ltd (65.92% stake not already owned)	Switzerland	43 424
2007	Rio Tinto plc	United Kingdom	Alcan Inc. (100%)	Canada	42 934
2007	Freeport-McMoRan Inc.	United States	Phelps Dodge (100%)	United States	22 908
2006	Xstrata Ltd	Switzerland	Falconbridge (80.2% stake not already owned)	Canada	18 049
2007	Vale SA	Brazil	Inco (100%)	Canada	16 727
2006	Polyus Gold	Russian Federation	Spin-off of MMC Norilsk Nickel	Russian Federation	14 439
2008	Alcoa Inc. and Aluminum Corp. of China	United States and China	Rio Tinto plc (12%)	United Kingdom	14 135
2001	BHP Limited	Australia	Billiton plc (100%)	Australia	13 242
2010	JX Nippon Oil & Energy Corp.	Japan	JX Nippon Mining & Metals Corp. (100%)	Japan	11 766
2006	Barrick Gold Corp.	Canada	Placer Dome Inc. (100%)	Canada	10 179

Source: Economic Commission for Latin America and the Caribbean (ECLAC), on the basis of information provided by Bloomberg.

The second largest transaction was the acquisition of Canada's Alcan Inc. by Rio Tinto, for US$ 42.9 billion in 2007. With a financial structure based in the Australia and the United Kingdom, Rio Tinto specializes in the mining, exploration, extraction and processing of aluminium, copper, diamonds, energy minerals (coal and uranium), gold, base metals and iron ore. The purchase of Alcan Inc. gives the firm a solid position in the aluminium market.

Other major transactions involved companies headquartered in Canada and the United States. In 2007, Freeport-McMoRan Inc., a United States company whose main asset was a gold mine in Indonesia, acquired Phelps Dodge —an established United States mining firm that had been operating since the early twentieth century— to become one of the world's largest copper producers. In 2006, Xstrata Ltd of Switzerland absorbed another long-established mining corporation, Falconbridge of Canada, while the world's largest gold miner, Barrick Gold Corporation, purchased its fellow gold specialist, Placer Dome Inc. of Canada. In the Russian Federation, 2006 also saw the spin-off of MMC Norilsk Nickel's gold mining assets into the company Polyus Gold.

Corporations from emerging countries also made some significant acquisitions of transnationals headquartered in developed countries. In 2007, Brazil's Vale acquired Inco of Canada, a specialized nickel miner with Canadian operations dating from the early twentieth century. Together with the sale of Falconbridge, this transaction placed two of Canada's biggest mining firms under foreign ownership. And in 2008, Aluminum Corporation of China (Chinalco) and Alcoa of the United States acquired a 12% stake in the United Kingdom's Rio Tinto plc, for US$ 14.1 billion. This was the first major transnational operation involving a Chinese mining firm.

The 2001 merger of Australia's BHP Limited and the United Kingdom's Billiton plc created one of the world's largest mining companies, while in 2010 Japan's JX Nippon Oil & Energy Corporation and JX Nippon Mining & Metals Corporation merged to form the conglomerate JX Holdings Inc.

Most cross-border transactions in metal mining targeted businesses based in North America and Asia and the Pacific, two regions that between 2000 and 2015 accounted for 30% and 29%, respectively, of the value of mergers and acquisitions in the sector (see figure II.10). Transactions targeting European companies accounted for 18.6% of the total, while the value of transactions targeting Latin American and Caribbean and African and Middle Eastern companies, respectively, amounted to 12.6% and 9.8% of the total. While firms from developing countries improved their position, those of developed countries still dominate the sector.

Approximately 16% of mergers and acquisitions targeted companies based in Latin America and the Caribbean, with transactions between 2000 and 2015 amounting to US$ 78 billion. Ninety-two per cent this total was distributed among target companies in eight countries, led by Brazil, Chile, Mexico and Peru (see figure II.11).

Transaction participants were more sparsely concentrated in terms of their origins, with firms in Canada, China, the United Kingdom and the United States all making significant contributions to the value of mergers and acquisitions. Australia, Canada, the United Kingdom and the United States accounted for the bulk of transactions (74% of the total number); however, China concluded a large transaction that accounted for 9% of the total value of mergers and acquisitions in the region during the study period.

Besides investing in other Latin American and Caribbean countries, leading firms in Brazil, Chile, Mexico and Peru have sought to expand through mergers and acquisitions in other regions, particularly North America, where 6.75% of the value of mergers and acquisitions originated in Latin American corporations. The region's companies were less active in Europe, Asia and the Pacific, and Africa and the Middle East, although some notable transactions were carried out in Australia by Chile's Antofagasta plc and Vale of Brazil, while in 2006 Mexico's Alfa S.A.B. de C.V. acquired a high-tech aluminium business unit from Norway's Norsk Hydro.

Asia and the Pacific and North America were fertile ground for mergers and acquisition

Figure II.10
Cross-border mergers and acquisitions in the metal mining sector, by region of investment destination, 2000-2015
(Percentages)

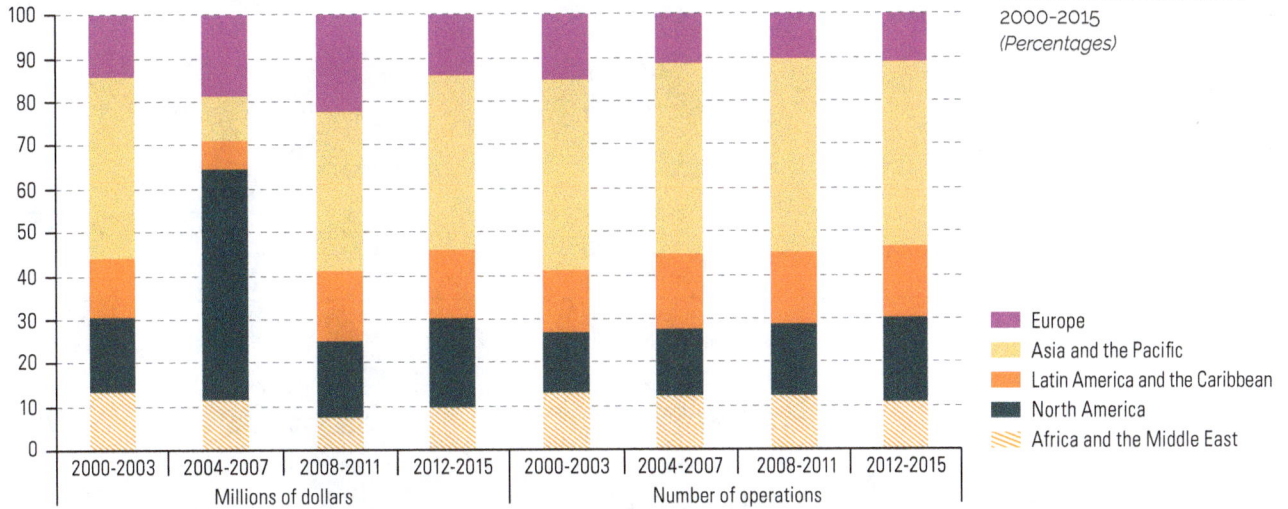

Legend:
- Europe
- Asia and the Pacific
- Latin America and the Caribbean
- North America
- Africa and the Middle East

Source: Economic Commission for Latin America and the Caribbean (ECLAC), on the basis of information provided by Bloomberg.

Figure II.11
Latin America and the Caribbean: countries of origin and destination in cross-border mergers and acquisitions in metal mining, 2000-2015
(Percentage share of cumulative value)

Canada was the largest investor in the region, with Brazil, Chile, Mexico and Peru attracting the most capital

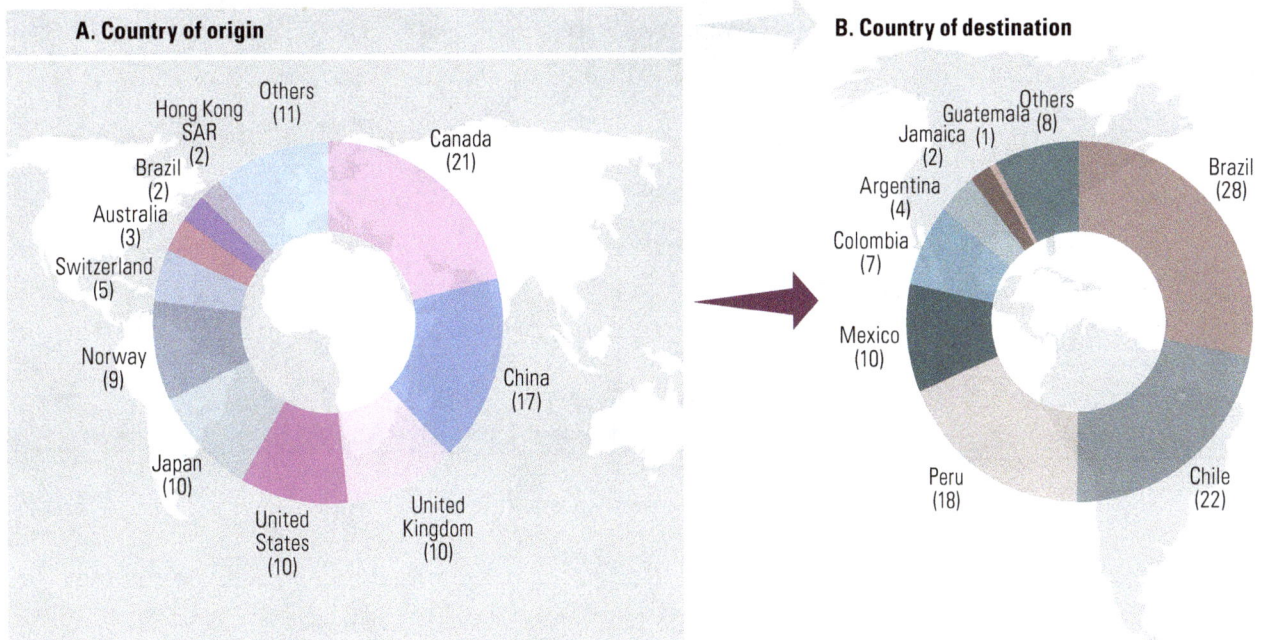

A. Country of origin

- Canada (21)
- China (17)
- United Kingdom (10)
- United States (10)
- Japan (10)
- Norway (9)
- Switzerland (5)
- Australia (3)
- Brazil (2)
- Hong Kong SAR (2)
- Others (11)

B. Country of destination

- Brazil (28)
- Chile (22)
- Peru (18)
- Mexico (10)
- Colombia (7)
- Argentina (4)
- Jamaica (2)
- Guatemala (1)
- Others (8)

Source: Economic Commission for Latin America and the Caribbean (ECLAC), on the basis of information provided by Bloomberg.

The region's largest transaction took place in 2014, when China's MMG Ltd and partners acquired the Las Bambas copper deposit from Glencore for US$ 7.005 billion. Another important operation took place in 2011, when Norsk Hydro purchased a number of bauxite extraction and alumina production assets from Vale for US$ 5.27 billion (see table II.8).

Table II.8
Latin America and the Caribbean: 20 largest cross-border mergers and acquisitions in metal mining, 2010-2015

Most large transactions in the region dealt in copper mining

Year	Company	Country of origin	Assets acquired	Asset location	Vendor location	Subsector	Amount (millions of dollars)
2014	MMG Limited and partners	China	Glencore Las Bambas copper deposit	Peru	Switzerland	Copper	7 005
2011	Norsk Hydro	Norway	Vale S.A. bauxite and alumina	Brazil	Brazil	Aluminium	5 270
2011	CITIC Group Corporation and partners	China	Companhia Brasileira de Metalurgia e Mineração (15%)	Brazil	Brazil	Niobium	1 950
2014	Lundin Mining Corporation	Canada	Candelaria and Ojos del Salado mines (80%)	Chile	United States	Copper	1 800
2011	Nippon Steel, Sumitomo Metal Corporation and partners	Japan	Companhia Brasileira de Metalurgia e Mineração (10%)	Brazil	Brazil	Niobium	1 300
2010	East China Mineral Exploration	China	Itaminas Comércio de Minérios	Brazil	Brazil	Iron	1 220
2012	Mitsui & Co Ltd	Japan	Inversiones Mineras Acrux Spa (17%)	Chile	Chile	Copper	1 100
2014	Franco-Nevada Corporation	Canada	La Candelaria - gold and silver (80%)	Chile	Canada	Gold and silver	648
2012	Marubeni Corporation	Japan	Antucoya Project (30%)	Chile	United Kingdom	Copper	541
2010	Primero Mining Corp.	Canada	San Dimas gold mines, from Goldcorp	Mexico	Canada	Gold	510
2012	Silver Wheaton Corp.	Canada	Constancia - silver	Peru	Canada	Silver	500
2010	Goldcorp Inc.	Canada	SCM El Morro (70%)	Chile	United Kingdom	Copper and gold	495
2010	Barrick Gold Corporation	Canada	Cerro Casale project (25%)	Chile	Canada	Copper and gold	454
2010	Votorantim Participações S.A.	Brazil	Compañía Minera Milpo (16%)	Peru	Peru	Zinc, lead, copper	420
2012	Gold Fields Ltd	South Africa	Gold Fields La Cima S.A.	Peru	Peru	Copper and gold	419
2010	Mitsubishi Corporation	Japan	Compañía Minera del Pacifico, S.A. (9%) (previously 16%)	Chile	Chile	Iron	401
2010	Honbridge Holdings Ltd	Hong Kong SAR	Sul Americana de Metais S.A.	Brazil	Brazil	Iron	390
2015	Audley Capital Advisors and Orion Mine Finance	United Kingdom, United States	Anglo American Norte S.A.	Chile	United Kingdom	Copper	300
2011	Sierra Metals Inc.	Canada	Sociedad Minera Corona S.A. (82%)	Peru	Peru	Copper, silver, lead, zinc	292
2010	Royal Gold Inc.	United States	Carmen de Andalloco - gold	Chile	Canada	Gold	270

Source: Economic Commission for Latin America and the Caribbean (ECLAC), on the basis of information provided by Bloomberg.

It was also observed that Chinese and Japanese firms purchased assets from Companhia Brasileira de Metalurgia e Mineração (CBMM) for the extraction of niobium, a mineral used in steel alloys. These investments suggest an effort to gain a strategic position in access to raw materials, since Brazil and Canada are the countries with the largest niobium reserves, with Brazil accounting for 90% of production in 2013, according to the United States Geological Survey. Similarly, in 2011 the Republic of Korea acquired a stake in CBMM for US$ 650 million (although at less than 5% of that company's share capital, it is not counted as FDI).

C.   A strategic sector for foreign direct investment in the region

A high percentage of the world's metallic mineral reserves is concentrated in Latin America and the Caribbean: 66% of its lithium, 47% of its copper, 45% of its silver, 25% of its tin, 23% of its bauxite, 23% of its nickel and 14% of its iron, among others (see map II.1).

This wealth has traditionally attracted the attention of foreign capital in search of natural resources, and inward FDI in the region's mining sector intensified throughout the recent commodity price boom. In the *Where to Invest 2015* ranking of countries for mining investment compiled by Behre Dolbear, Chile and Mexico occupied fourth and fifth places behind Canada, Australia and the United States. Peru ranked sixth, having improved its standing of previous years, while Colombia occupied ninth and Brazil eleventh place, respectively.[9]

In the past 15 years, the natural resources sector has expanded its share of foreign investment inflows to Latin America and the Caribbean. The relative weight of natural resources in total FDI flows increased from 16.6% and 17.1% on average for the 1990s and 2000s, respectively, to 22.3% in 2010-2014. During this recent period, the region's natural resource sectors attracted US$ 170.555 billion in FDI, with mining accounting for the vast majority of FDI in natural resources in several recipient countries (see table II.9).[10]

In most countries with metallic mineral reserves, the mining sector's percentage of total inward FDI has increased in recent years (see figure II.12). This was the case in Chile, the Dominican Republic, Mexico, Nicaragua and Peru; albeit official information was unavailable for the latter country.

In the past 15 years, the natural resources sector has expanded its share of foreign investment inflows to Latin America and the Caribbean.

---

[9]   This ranking surveys 25 countries and expresses the opinions of 200 experts. It is based on seven criteria: political system, economic system, currency stability, social licence issues, permitting, competitive taxation and corruption.

[10]   One of the main recipients of FDI in metal mining, Peru, does not publish official data disaggregated by sector. In Brazil, in 2015 the central bank changed its data collection methodology to that used in the sixth edition of the *Balance of Payments Manual*, published by the International Monetary Fund. The estimates included in this analysis use the previous methodology, which enables comparison with earlier years.

Mexico

Copper	Gold	Silver
6.4	2.5	6.5

Lead	Zinc
6.3	7.4

Map II.1

Latin America and the Caribbean (13 countries):
metallic mineral reserves, by country, 2015
(Percentages of world total)

The region possesses sizeable metallic mineral reserves capable of attracting foreign direct investment

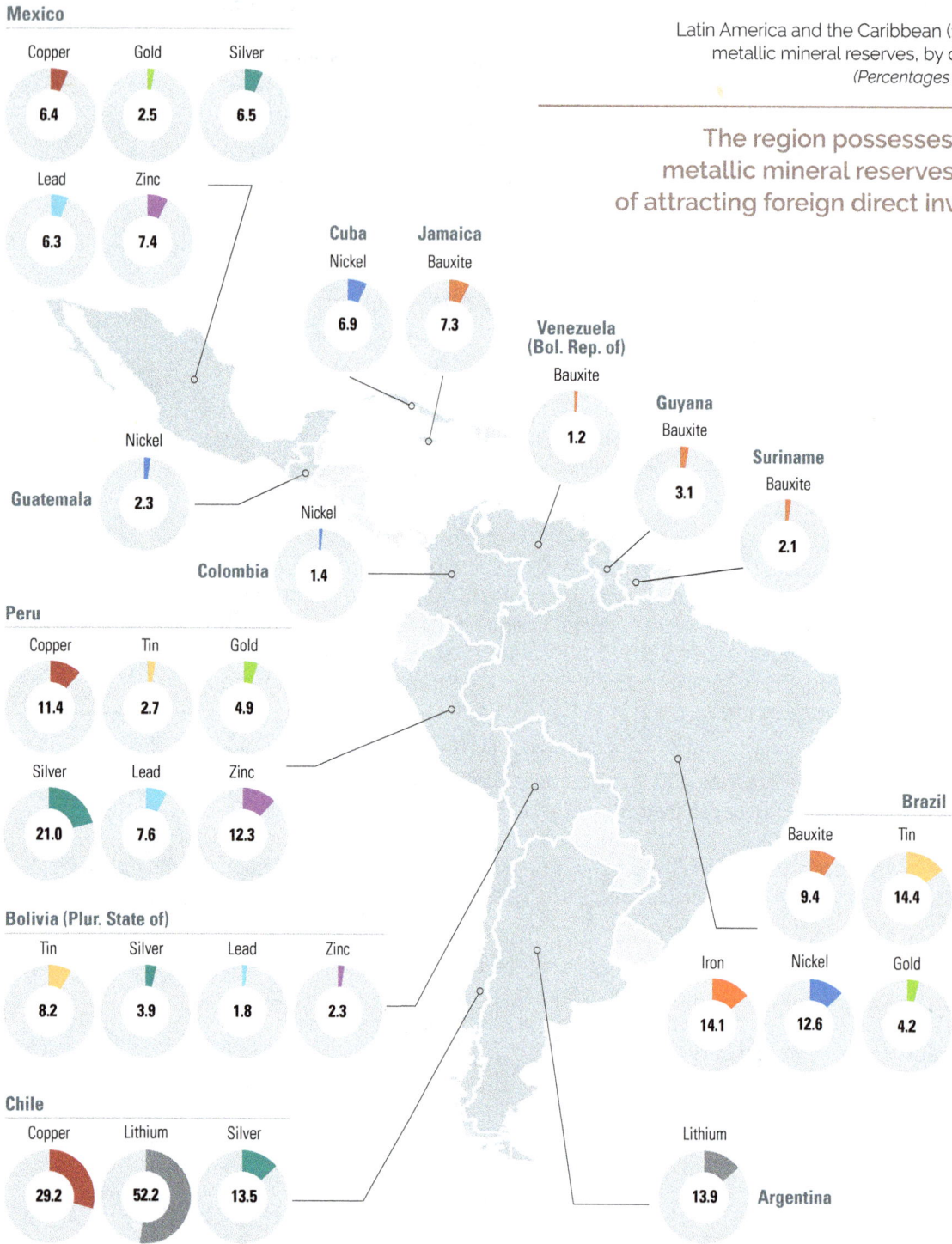

Cuba — Nickel — 6.9

Jamaica — Bauxite — 7.3

Venezuela (Bol. Rep. of) — Bauxite — 1.2

Guyana — Bauxite — 3.1

Suriname — Bauxite — 2.1

Guatemala — Nickel — 2.3

Colombia — Nickel — 1.4

Peru

Copper	Tin	Gold
11.4	2.7	4.9

Silver	Lead	Zinc
21.0	7.6	12.3

Brazil

Bauxite	Tin
9.4	14.4

Iron	Nickel	Gold
14.1	12.6	4.2

Bolivia (Plur. State of)

Tin	Silver	Lead	Zinc
8.2	3.9	1.8	2.3

Chile

Copper	Lithium	Silver
29.2	52.2	13.5

Argentina — Lithium — 13.9

Total de los países seleccionados

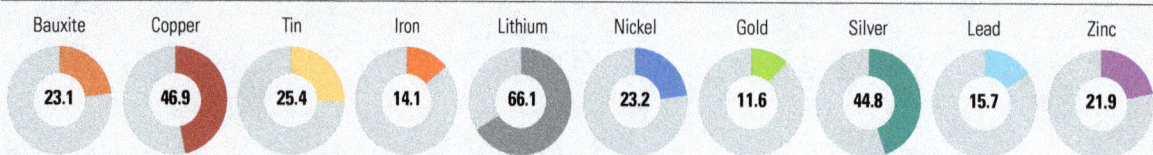

Bauxite	Copper	Tin	Iron	Lithium	Nickel	Gold	Silver	Lead	Zinc
23.1	46.9	25.4	14.1	66.1	23.2	11.6	44.8	15.7	21.9

Source: Economic Commission for Latin America and the Caribbean (ECLAC), on the basis of information provided by the United States Geological Survey.
Note: In keeping with the source, only countries with more than 1% of total world reserves, and only reserves rather than identified resources, were included. This accounts for the absence of lithium resources in the Plurinational State of Bolivia, for example.

A high proportion of the region's inward foreign direct investment went to metal mining

Table II.9
Latin America and the
Caribbean (11 countries):
foreign direct investment in
natural resources, 2010-2014
*(Millions of dollars
and percentages)*

Country	FDI in natural resources	FDI in natural resources, share of total FDI	FDI in mining, share of FDI in natural resources
Brazil	57 526	18.7	36.8
Chile	38 277	43.5	99.8
Colombia	35 286	51.6	32.2
Mexico	13 047	9.6	96.2
Dominican Republic	2 523	21.7	100.0
Panama	1 366	10.1	87.7
Uruguay	1 309	12.6	1.9
Nicaragua	862	21.1	77.8
Honduras	322	6.1	70.6
Paraguay	91	4.9	43.2
El Salvador	5	0.6	100.0

Source: Economic Commission for Latin America and the Caribbean (ECLAC), on the basis of official figures and estimates at 18 May 2015.
Note: Data for Chile, Panama and Uruguay are for 2010-2013. Data for Brazil, Colombia and Mexico exclude hydrocarbons.

The boom precipitated a relative increase in inward foreign direct investment in metal mining

Figure II.12
Selected countries: foreign
direct investment in mining
as a proportion of total
foreign direct investment,
2000-2014
(Percentages)

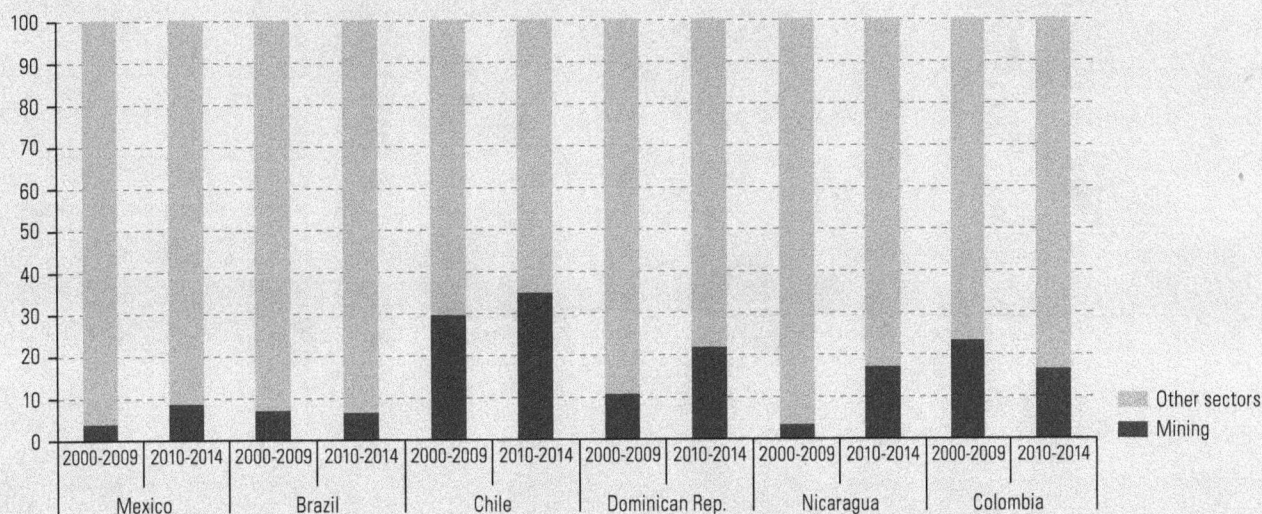

Source: Economic Commission for Latin America and the Caribbean (ECLAC), on the basis of official figures and estimates at 18 May 2015.

A more detailed analysis of metal mining investment can be carried out using the information on announced investment projects published in fDi Markets (by the Financial Times), which allows the breakdown of projects by country of origin, country of destination and mineral extracted. This information is an approximation, since investment may be cancelled or may differ from the amount given in the announcement.

According to this source, between 2003 and 2015, investment announcements in metal mining totalled US$ 445.7 billion and were mostly associated with projects in developing countries. Investment announcements for Latin America and the Caribbean, Asia and the Pacific and Africa accounted for 84.6% of the total (33.8%, 29.7% and 21.1%, respectively).

Copper, nickel, lead and zinc was the segment that accounted for the largest share of announced investment in metal mining (see figure II.13), equivalent to 28.1% of the total for 2003-2015, ahead of gold and silver (27.6% of total announced investment), bauxite and aluminium (27.1%), and iron (11.8%).[11] The composition of investment varied from one region to the next according to the type of mineral exploited. In Latin America and the Caribbean, the bulk of investment was earmarked for the exploitation of precious metals (53.7%), and copper, nickel, lead and zinc (44.9%). Asia-Pacific countries were leaders in aluminium and iron (41.4% and 37.0% of investment, respectively). Within the Asian and Pacific region, Australia, India and Indonesia attracted most investment, while in Africa the largest investment announcements were those recorded in Algeria, the Democratic Republic of the Congo and South Africa.

Figure II.13
Investment announcements in metal mining, by regions, 2003-2015
(Millions of dollars)

The region conformed to the global trend, with the majority of investment announcements in metal mining concentrated in developing countries

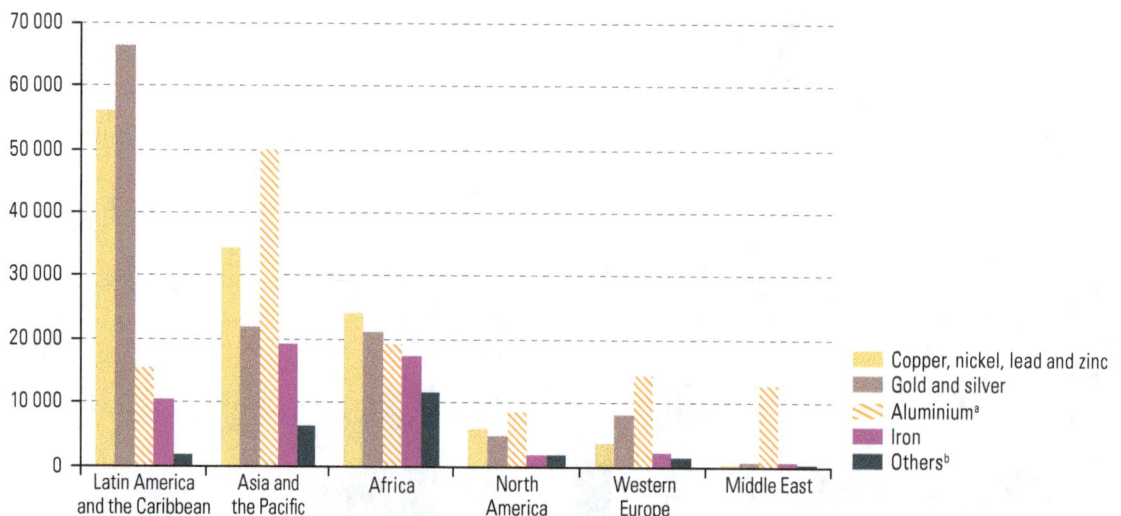

Source: Economic Commission for Latin America and the Caribbean (ECLAC), on the basis of Financial Times, *fDi Markets*. Data updated on 28 January 2016.
[a] Includes bauxite mining, aluminium extraction and aluminium products.
[b] Investment projects announced for unidentified metals.

---

[11]   The data do not allow for further disaggregation by metal.

Investment in exploration for non-ferrous metals matched the rapid growth trend, multiplying tenfold between 2003 and 2012 and peaking at US$ 21.5 billion in 2012 (albeit subsequently dropping to US$ 11.4 billion in 2014). Latin America and the Caribbean accounted for the largest share of investment in exploration between 2004 and 2014, attracting 27% of global spending in 2014. Base metals were the top exploration target (42% of overall budgets), followed by gold (41%) (SNL Metals & Mining, 2015). Australia and Canada, which had attracted the largest exploration budgets before the boom, held shares of 12% and 14% respectively, while 16% of worldwide budgets were allocated to Africa. The privatizations undertaken by Latin America and the Caribbean in 1990s, together with the higher cost of mining in traditional countries such as Australia, Canada and the United States, helped the region consolidate its status as the most popular destination for investments in mineral exploration during the past decade (ECLAC, 2013b).

Between 2003 and 2015, some 510 metal mining investment projects were announced for Latin America and the Caribbean, worth an estimated US$ 150.54 billion and equivalent to 12.2% of total investment announcements for the region. The average announcement was for US$ 300 million, although this figure was dwarfed by a number of mega-projects, for example a US$ 8.0 billion gold project in Chile in 2003, and a US$ 6.4 billion copper project in Panama in 2014. There were 25 projects with announced capital investment in excess of US$ 1.0 billion, which together represented 40% of total investment during the study period.

Most projects announced in the region were associated with gold and silver mining (44.0% of announced investment), followed by projects for the extraction of copper, nickel, lead and zinc (37.3%). Brazil, Chile and Peru were the countries with the most announcements and together accounted for 75.6% of total investment in the region (see table II.10). In both Chile and Peru, metal mining accounted for approximately 40% of total investment announced in the country, a share that was smaller in Brazil and Mexico. Gold and silver mining was the segment that attracted most widespread investment across the region, with projects announced for 19 countries. Copper, nickel, lead and zinc mining projects were more concentrated, with Chile, Panama and Peru jointly accounting for 88.4% of announced investment. Brazil attracted the bulk of investment in iron ore mining (69.0%), followed by Peru (27.2%). The aluminium segment followed a similar pattern, with Brazil receiving 72.1% of total investment and Guyana and Jamaica also enjoying a significant share thanks to their sizeable bauxite deposits.

Latin America and the Caribbean accounted for the largest share of investment in exploration between 2004 and 2014, attracting 27% of global spending in 2014.

Metal mining is positioned as a strategic sector for foreign direct investment in Chile and Peru

Table II.10
Latin America and the Caribbean (9 countries): investment announcements in metal mining, 2003-2015
(Percentages of investment value)

Country	Share of total investment in the region	Metal mining share of total announced investment in the country
Chile	32.3	39.4
Peru	22.8	42.5
Brazil	20.5	8.7
Mexico	5.0	2.8
Panama	4.6	25.2
Dominican Republic	3.5	24.6
Argentina	1.8	3.9
Bolivia (Plurinational State of)	1.4	14.3
Guyana	1.2	73.5
Other countries	7.0	3.8
Latin America and the Caribbean	**100.0**	**12.2**

Source: Economic Commission for Latin America and the Caribbean (ECLAC), on the basis of Financial Times, *fDi Markets*. Data updated on 21 January 2016.

The transnational mining corporations that have invested in the region are largely headquartered in developed countries, notably Australia, Canada, the United Kingdom and the United States. Half of announced investment in metal mining between 2003 and 2015 originated in Canadian firms (50.6%), which also accounted for 83.0% of total investment in gold and silver mining. United Kingdom-based companies made up the next largest source, representing 52.2% of investment in iron ore mining and 21.3% of investment in copper, nickel, lead and zinc mining. The United States was the main source of investment in aluminium and the second-largest investor in iron ore extraction.

While developed countries have led the way in mining investment, China has strengthened its presence as an investor since 2007, chiefly through participation in copper and iron mining projects in Peru, and bauxite mining and aluminium production projects in Guyana and Trinidad and Tobago. Estimates by the Ministry of Energy and Mines of Peru indicated that in October 2015 some 34.0% of the country's mining investment portfolio was in Chinese hands, while 17.0% was owned by United States companies and 14.8% by Canadian firms.[12] Peruvian enterprises accounted for just 6.5%, a figure that demonstrates the predominance of foreign capital in Peru's mining industry. Copper projects accounted for the bulk of the portfolio (64.7%), followed by gold and iron operations (12.6% and 9.4%, respectively).

In Chile too, mining activity mostly targeted copper and, to a lesser extent, gold and silver. Although the existence of two State-owned enterprises explains a higher share of domestic capital in the industry, foreign firms retained a substantial presence. For example, 42.1% of copper production was in the hands of Chilean companies (with 32.9% belonging to State-owned enterprises), while the remaining producers were transnational firms based in Australia, Canada, Japan, Poland, Switzerland, the United Kingdom and the United States. However, foreign firms were the pre-eminent gold producers. In 2014, 76% of production was owned by Canadian corporations, 9% by Japanese firms, and 15% by Chilean companies (Correa, 2016).

> While developed countries have led the way in mining investment, China has strengthened its presence as an investor since 2007.

D.   Uncertainty in a new scenario

1.   Prices, profitability and investment are falling

A sharp fall in prices has brought about remarkable reductions in the profits and the market values of mining firms. The combined market value of the top 40 mining companies, as listed in the PricewaterhouseCoopers ranking, halved from US$ 1.6 trillion in 2010 to US$ 791 billion in 2014, including a loss of 16% in 2014 (PwC, 2015). This meant that the 40 leading firms in the mining sector barely topped the market value of Apple Inc., which was valued at US$ 725 billion in 2014. The combined market value of the main metal mining enterprises listed in Table II.5 rose from US$ 280 billion in 2005 to US$ 723 billion in 2010, before declining to a new low of US$ 242 billion at the end of 2015.

There is a strong positive correlation between investments in exploration and price trends. One of the first impacts of falling prices was that mining corporations cut their exploration budgets, which fell steadily after 2012 to US$ 9.2 billion in 2015 (SNL Metals & Mining, 2015). This context also affected the exploration operations of junior companies. Traditionally these firms raise capital by listing on the stock exchange, meaning that their access to capital hinges on the evolution of prices and market expectations.

---

[12]   This portfolio includes mining unit expansion projects, projects in an advanced exploration phase and projects with environmental impact studies approved or under evaluation. Projects are discounted from the portfolio upon entry into operation.

Junior miners began to experience difficulties in raising capital for exploration in 2012, and it is now predicted that the only funds available for such projects will come from specialized investors that are focused on a longer term investment horizon that looks beyond the current price fluctuations, and which are able to leverage their greater mining expertise (PwC, 2015).

In a sector in which the minimum required rates of return have topped 15%, in 2014 the average return on assets employed among the world's 40 leading mining companies fell to 9% in 2014, a 10-year low (PwC, 2015). The situation is no better for the companies operating in Latin America and the Caribbean. The publication *América Economía* produces an annual list of the 500 largest companies in the region, ranked by sales the previous year. Between 1998 and 2015, a total of 70 mining firms appeared in the ranking, 20 of which were included for more than 10 consecutive years (see annex II.A1). Rising commodity prices boosted the value of sales and, consequently, the number of mining corporations included in the ranking. During the 1990s, fewer than 20 firms were included in the list, but this figure stood at about 40 in the late 2000s, with companies from Argentina, the Bolivarian Republic of Venezuela, Brazil, Chile, Colombia, Mexico and Peru. According to this information, private foreign firms dominated the market, except in Chile, where hegemony was shared with State-owned enterprises, and Mexico, where domestically owned companies had the highest turnover.

The *América Economía* rankings are indicative of trends in companies' returns, which reflected the commodity price upcycle and downcycle, respectively (see figure II.14).

Figure II.14
Latin America: sales and return on assets of major mining corporations
(Millions of dollars and percentages)

The price downcycle has caused the profitability of the sector to fall below expectations

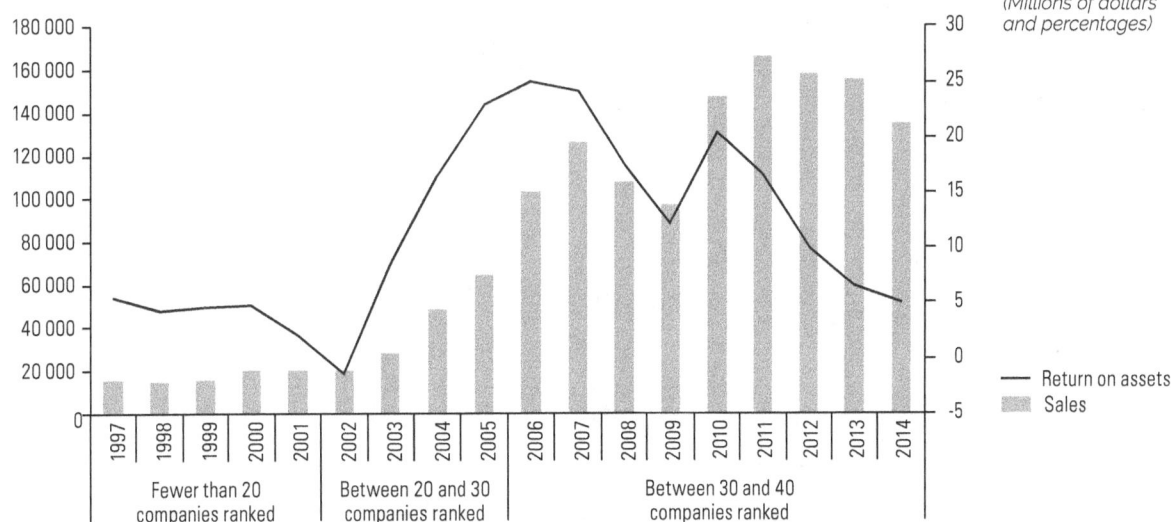

Fewer than 20 companies ranked | Between 20 and 30 companies ranked | Between 30 and 40 companies ranked

— Return on assets
▨ Sales

Source: Economic Commission for Latin America and the Caribbean (ECLAC), on the basis of *América Economía*.

The average return on assets began to rise in the early 2000s, peaking at 24.9% in 2006, before entering a decline after 2010 and reaching a new low of 4.9% in 2014. This rate is far below expectations for the mining sector, and is strongly influenced by the profitability of Brazil's Vale, which in 2014 secured a return on assets of just 0.3%. Given that this company's assets make up 45% of the entire sector, excluding them gives an average return of 8.7% for the region's largest mining firms, a figure in line with the global average.

Despite the steep drop in profitability in the sector, average returns remained higher than those of the largest 500 firms in Latin America, whose average return on assets in 2014 stood at 2.2%.

Falling profitability, both in the world and in Latin America, had repercussions for investment announcements in the metal mining sector. Between 2003 and 2011, the average annual sum of metal mining investments announcements in the world was US$ 42.2 billion, a figure that dropped to US$ 16.4 billion between 2012 and 2015 (see figure II.15). Latin America was no exception to this trend. Metal mining investment announcements in the region for 2015 marked a new low of eight projects, amounting to US$ 674 million, equivalent to just 1.1% of announced investment in the region, compared with the 12.2% that the sector attracted on average between 2003 and 2015.

The importance of metal mining for foreign direct investment income in many Latin American and Caribbean countries, such as Chile, Colombia and Peru, was reflected in the falling FDI flows presented in chapter I.

Figure II.15
Latin America and the Caribbean and the rest of the world: investment announcements in metal mining, 2003-2015
(Millions of dollars and number of projects)

Investment announcements declined more steeply
in the region than in the world

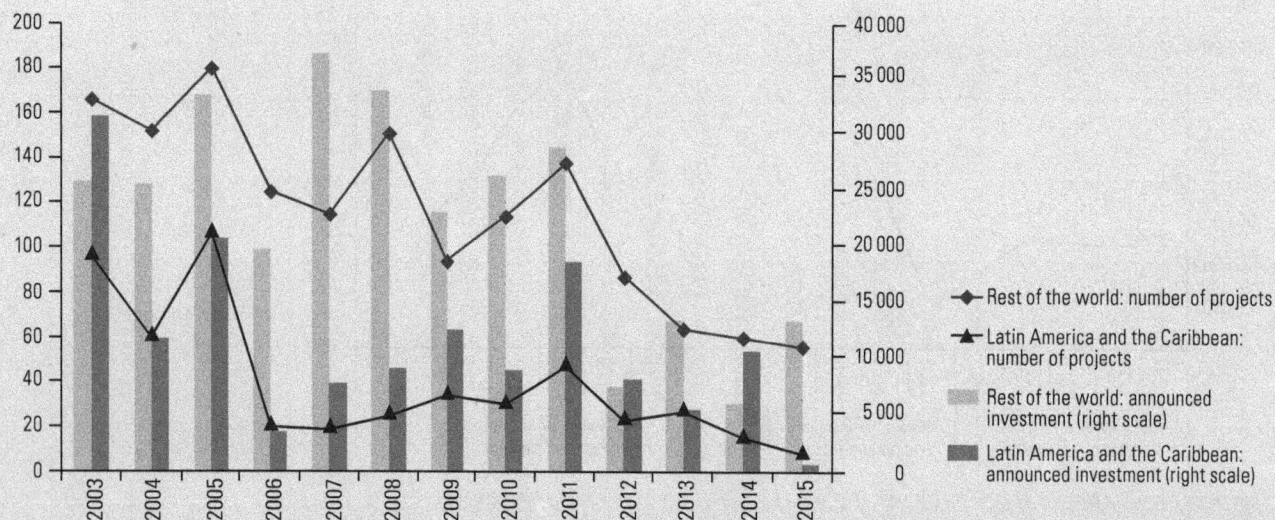

Source: Economic Commission for Latin America and the Caribbean (ECLAC), on the basis of Financial Times, *fDi Markets*. Data updated on 28 January 2016.

2.   Companies are adjusting to the downcycle

Forecasts suggest that the mining sector faces a complex short- and medium-term scenario. Much of the sector's growth was based on meeting demand from the Chinese economy, whose growth over the past decade has coincided with intense infrastructure development. China's growth prospects and future development pattern are now uncertain, and therefore it is not known whether the country will trigger a resurgence in global demand for metals. The current outlook of reduced infrastructure development is of deep concern for iron ore production, but there may be better news for other metals used in mass consumer goods such as copper and nickel (used in cars and computers, for example) (PwC 2015). According to Deloitte (2015), most experts agree that a downcycle is in progress and are expecting demand from emerging countries and regions such as India, South-East Asia and even Africa, to eventually rebound to the point where it once again outstrips supply. However, this is still some way off, and firms will continue to retrench until the revival takes effect.

In this context, the sector's largest companies have reduced their exploration expenditure and capital investment. According to their reports they expect to maintain this strategy until 2017, generally targeting cost reduction, productivity improvements and asset rationalization. Moreover, many corporations took on high levels of debt during the boom period. The subsequent price downcycle, compounded by the strength of the dollar, caused a deterioration of their financial position that also contributed to asset sales and the focus on strategic products.

To concentrate on its key assets of iron ore, copper and energy products, BHP Billiton committed to the divestment of non-strategic assets valued at US$ 7.0 billion between 2013 and 2015 (BHP Billiton, 2015). In May 2015 the company also approved the demerger of South32 Ltd. in a transaction valued at US$ 4.4 billion, with the spin-off company retaining alumina, aluminium, coal, manganese, nickel, silver, lead and zinc assets in Australia, Colombia and South Africa. Meanwhile, Rio Tinto sold various assets for US$ 2.5 billion in 2013 (Rio Tinto, 2015), while in 2014 it divested its 50.1% stake in Australia's Clermont coal mine to a joint venture (in equal shares) of Sumitomo Corporation and Glencore for US$ 1.005 billion. Switzerland's Glencore also carried out a significant asset divestment in 2014, selling the Las Bambas copper deposit in Peru for US$ 7.005 billion. Anglo American responded to the prospect of lower prices and a slow recovery in demand by concentrating on its strategic diamond, platinum and copper mines, specializing in minerals required at more advanced stages of economic development, rather than during the urbanization phase (Anglo American, 2015). In 2015, the company divested assets worth US$ 2.1 billion and is following a strategy that aims to divest US$ 5.0 billion to US$ 6.0 billion by 2016. Vale also focused on cost reduction and enhanced productivity. In 2015, it divested US$ 3.0 billion in non-strategic assets, notably through the sale of 12 iron ore carrier ships to China for US$ 1.3 billion, as well as a 36.4% stake in Minerações Brasileiras Reunidas S.A. for US$ 1.089 billion.

Leading consultants suggest that mining firms must innovate to survive in the industry. McKinsey & Company believes that the mining industry is at an inflection point in which the traditional form of production needs to be modified to enhance productivity. This consulting firm advocates a new form of production based on the adoption of digital technologies, both in production and in the planning and analysis of information, which could unlock a new productive model that utilizes the available information in a more efficient way. In this way, the industry would seek to optimize processes, automate the most hazardous operations and, ultimately, improve productivity by better managing volatility, external conditions, and the risks that companies face owing to the nature of their activity (Durrant-Whyte and others, 2015).

Companies operating in the region have already made significant technological changes. The first large-scale iron-ore mining project to incorporate an automated mineral transport system will enter operation in 2016 in Brazil, having been installed by a transnational specializing in automation and technological solutions. This Vale project (known as Carajás S11D) required a US$ 14.4 billion investment, and includes the mine, a processing plant and logistics. The 30-kilometre automated transport system is able to move the equivalent of 100 240-ton truckloads of mineral with a 70% saving on fuel, thus reducing costs and greenhouse gas emissions. Other technological innovations, such as a 93% reduction in water use at the iron-ore treatment plant (a saving equivalent to the water consumption of a city of 400,000 inhabitants) and a modular plant design mean that the facility is at the cutting edge of iron ore production.

Lastly, during the study period some Latin American firms purchased operational mines in the region from foreign-owned companies, but this was not a widespread pattern. In 2012, a joint venture between CODELCO of Chile (67.8%) and Mitsui of Japan (32.2%) acquired a 29.5% stake in the mining company Anglo American Sur for US$ 2.8 billion, while in 2015 Antofagasta plc, also Chilean-owned, purchased 50% of the Zaldívar copper mine from Barrick Gold for US$ 1.005 billion (see table II.11).

Table II.11
Latin America and the Caribbean: largest divestments in metal mining, 2010-2015

Few foreign firms sold assets to domestic investors

Year	Vendor	Country of vendor	Assets sold	Purchaser	Country of purchaser	Sector	Monto (millions of dollars)
2012	Anglo American plc	United Kingdom	Anglo American Sur (29.5%)	CODELCO (67.8%) Mitsui (32,2%)	Chile, Japan	Copper	2 800
2015	Barrick Gold	Canada	Zaldívar copper mine (50%)	Antofagasta plc	Chile	Copper	1 005
2012	AuRico Gold	Canada	Ocampo gold and silver mine	Minera Frisco	Mexico	Gold	766
2010	Mitsubishi	Japan	Compañía Minera Huasco S.A. (50%)	CAP S.A.	Chile	Gold	523
2012	CST Mining	Hong Kong SAR	Marcobre S.A.C. (70%)	Minsur S.A.	Peru	Copper	505
2014	Newmont	United States	Penmont joint venture (44%)	Fresnillo plc	Mexico	Gold	450
2014	Gold Fields	South Africa	Canteras del Hallazgo (51%)	Compañía de Minas Buenaventura	Peru	Gold	81

Source: Economic Commission for Latin America and the Caribbean (ECLAC), on the basis of information provided by Bloomberg.

3.   The region has fallen behind in value chains

China was the central protagonist in the expansion of metal mining during the 2000s. In 2004, two Chinese firms (China Shenhua Energy Company Limited and Yanzhou Coal Mining Company Limited) entered the PricewaterhouseCoopers ranking of the top 40 mining companies by market capitalization for the first time. Ten years later China had nine firms in the top 40, overtaking Canada and the United Kingdom, which both had seven companies in the 2015 edition.

During the mining boom, Chinese companies stepped up mineral extraction and demanded more minerals on the international market, as well as investing in smelting and refining and thus moving up the mining/metallurgy value chain. The first link in this chain is mining, which comprises the extraction of ore from deposits and its concentration. The second step in adding value is ore processing to obtain the metal (or metal compounds), while the third link refers to the utilization of that metal to manufacture intermediate inputs or final goods. In China, the development of the sector included at least the first two stages.

In the first stage of the copper value chain (from copper concentrate to refined or smelted copper), China's production outstripped that of Latin American and Caribbean countries, although Chile remains the leading exporter of refined and smelted copper. Data on the global market share of refined copper production indicates that China steadily increased its industrial copper processing capacity between 2005 and 2014 (see figure II.16). In 2014, the region's countries produced 43.6% of the world's mined copper and less than 20% of its refined or smelted copper, whereas China produced 8.8% of mined copper and 34.8% and 25.8% of refined and smelted copper, respectively.

Figure II.16
Latin America and the Caribbean and China: share of mined,
refined and smelted copper production, 2005-2014
(Index and percentage of world total)

China outperformed the region in smelted and refined copper production

A. Copper production, index 2005=100

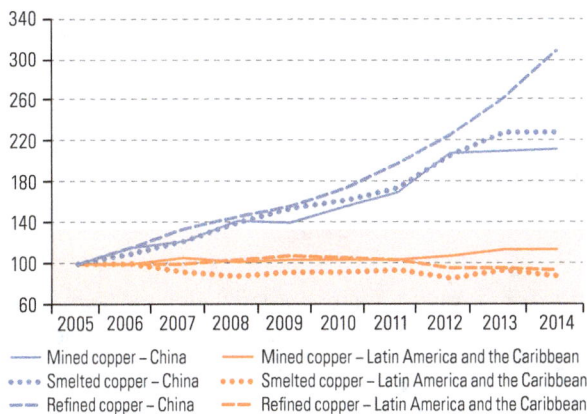

Legend:
— Mined copper – China
— Mined copper – Latin America and the Caribbean
•••• Smelted copper – China
•••• Smelted copper – Latin America and the Caribbean
– – Refined copper – China
– – Refined copper – Latin America and the Caribbean

B. Share of copper production, by stages, 2014

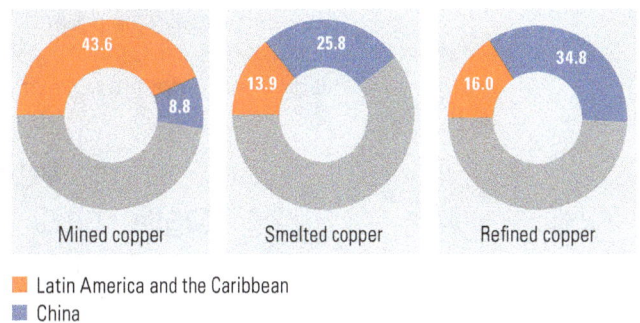

Mined copper: 43.6 / 8.8
Smelted copper: 25.8 / 13.9
Refined copper: 34.8 / 16.0

■ Latin America and the Caribbean
■ China

Source: Economic Commission for Latin America and the Caribbean (ECLAC), on the basis of information provided by the Chilean Copper Commission (COCHILCO).

It may therefore be discerned that China is following an industrialization strategy in which minerals are imported at an early stage of production and subsequently processed and exported as base or finished metals, with the consequent addition of value in the local market.

This imbalance in the production of ore concentrate and refined copper may extend to the other minerals produced in Latin America and the Caribbean. Mineral exports from the region increased after 2003, but this growth largely corresponded to minerals at early stages of the production process. Refining and smelting capacity in Latin American and Caribbean countries did not keep pace with rising mineral production, which helped create a pattern of growth in exports of mined minerals rather than refined metals. A similar trend was observed in Australia, which also tended to export minerals at the early stages of processing, rather than finished metals or manufactured metal products (ECLAC, 2013b).

This does not mean that metal production is currently absent from the region's countries. There are cases where it exists, but the present trend in copper refinery and smelter production may be of concern if China manages to satisfy its domestic consumption and increase its competitiveness in the international market. In any case, the further processing of concentrates prior to export would deliver benefits both in sales and in the development of forward linkages, consequently expanding the production matrix.

E. Mining for production diversification

The exploitation of natural resources for inclusive economic development entails huge challenges: from the essential requirement that the sector's development is compatible with safeguarding the environment and the rights of peoples and communities, and the creation of production linkages and synergies with other sectors, to fiscal and monetary issues and infrastructure investment.

Considering the abundance of metallic mineral resources in the region and the impact of transnational strategies in territories, it is imperative to build governments' capacities to leverage metal mining in support of structural change, so that the growth of this sector makes a strong contribution to enhancing technological innovation and capabilities.

As it attempts to harness the mining sector as a driver of diversification, the State has a key role to play in appropriating and utilizing rents and in promoting synergies between metal mining and other production sectors, a process that the Economic Commission for Latin America and the Caribbean (ECLAC) is promoting through its vision for the governance of non-renewable natural resources (ECLAC, 2014).

1. Strong growth improved the availability of resources

Foreign direct investment inflows to the metal mining sector surged during the favourable price cycle of the 2000s, boosting production and exports, which in turn helped deliver higher foreign exchange earnings and fiscal revenues.

Between 2001 and 2003, inflows averaged almost US$ 20 billion a year from metallic mineral and metal exports from Latin American and Caribbean countries. In 2004, an uptrend commenced that eventually saw annual export revenues top US$ 100 billion after 2010.[13] Exports from Brazil, Chile, Mexico and Peru, chiefly those of copper, iron and gold, accounted for 89.8% of the total between 2005 and 2014. However, the impact of mining as a source of foreign exchange differed greatly between countries. In Chile and Peru, mining accounted for 60% of income during the past 10 years (see table II.12) and made a substantial contribution to the trade surplus.

---

[13]   Based on data provided by TradeMap. Minerals and metals included in accordance with the Harmonized Commodity Description and Coding System: copper (codes 2600, 7401, 7402 and 7403), iron ores (2601), gold (7108), zinc (2608, 7901), lead (2607, 7801), silver (7106), gold and silver ores (2616), molybdenum (2613), aluminium (2606, 7601), tin (2609, 8001), Nickel (2604, 7501 and 7502).

Table II.12
Latin America and the Caribbean (12 countries): value of metallic mineral exports
and proportion of total exports, 2001-2014
(Millions of dollars and percentages)

Surge in revenues from metallic mineral exports

Country	2001		2005		2010		2014	
	Value	Proportion of total	Value	Proportion of total	Value	Proportion of total	Value	Proportion of total
Chile	7 549	40.3	23 280	55.5	44 097	62.0	41 755	54.5
Brazil	4 424	7.6	10 217	8.6	34 452	17.5	31 889	14.2
Peru	3 133	45.9	9 633	56.3	21 468	60.0	19 661	51.1
Mexico	1 031	0.7	2 485	1.2	11 776	3.9	12 964	3.3
Argentina	803	3.0	1 294	3.2	4 735	6.9	3 873	5.7
Bolivia (Plurinational State of)	325	24.0	505	18.1	2 309	33.2	3 799	29.6
Colombia	9	0.1	555	2.6	2 154	5.4	1 622	3.0
Cuba	463	27.8	1 075	46.4	465	16.8	221	9.6
Guatemala	1	0.1	16	0.3	505	6.0	853	7.8
Guyana	179	37.2	113	20.9	459	51.0	420	35.8
Dominican Republic	0	0.0	6	0.1	66	1.4	1 730	17.4
Jamaica	94	7.7	98	6.5	138	10.4	131	9.1

Source: Economic Commission for Latin America and the Caribbean (ECLAC), on the basis of TradeMap.
Note: Metals included in accordance with the Harmonized Commodity Description and Coding System: copper (2600, 7401, 7402 and 7403), iron orse (2601), gold (7108), zinc (2608, 7901), lead (2607, 7801), silver (7106), gold and silver ores (2616), molybdenum (2613), aluminium (2606, 7601), tin (2609, 8001), nickel (2604, 7501 and 7502).

Latin American and Caribbean countries accounted for about a quarter of world trade in metals and metallic minerals between 2005 and 2011 (24.1%), clearly surpassing the region's share of total global trade (5.7%) and demonstrating the comparative advantage it holds in the sector. The region's share of metallic mineral exports remained stable during the expansion phase, and its performance was broadly in line with the world's other metallic mineral exporters until 2011, when falling prices hit the region harder and its share of global exports dropped to 18.8% on average for 2012-2014.

The high rents obtained by the mining sector had a positive impact on the fiscal revenues of the region's countries, especially between 2005 and 2008, before the international financial crisis.[14] Chile and Peru were the countries where fiscal revenues from mining made the greatest contribution to GDP and total fiscal revenues. In Chile, the mining sector went from contributing 4.0% of fiscal revenues in 2000-2003 to 28.1% in 2005-2008, while in Peru the figure rose from 1.0% to 10.6% in the same period (see table II.13). The State-owned enterprise CODELCO lent weight to the leap in fiscal revenues from mining in Chile, while revenues from private mining corporations in that country were equivalent to 10.6% of the cumulative total between 2005 and 2008, equalling the contribution of large mining firms in Peru. The slowdown in mining activity after 2011 led to a sharp reduction in the share of fiscal revenue contributed by mining, notably in Chile, Jamaica and Peru, although the figures for Chile and Peru remained higher than those recorded prior to the expansion phase.

---

[14]   See Acquatella and others (2013) and Gómez Sabaini, Jiménez and Morán (2015) for an analysis of trends in non-renewable natural resource rents in Latin America and the Caribbean and an analysis of fiscal systems and their impacts.

Table II.13
Latin America and the
Caribbean: fiscal revenues
from mining, relative to GDP
and total fiscal revenues,
2000-2014[a]
(Percentages at current prices)

Fiscal revenues rose during the expansion phase

Country	Contribution to total GDP			Contribution to total fiscal revenues[b]		
	2000-2003	2005-2008	2010-2014	2000-2003	2005-2008	2010-2014
Argentina[c]	-	0.1	0.1	-	0.4	0.4
Bolivia (Plurinational State of)	0.1	0.7	1.0	0.4	2.0	2.8
Brazil	-	0.2	0.2	0.1	0.5	0.8
Chile	0.8	6.9	3.0	4.0	28.1	13.8
CODELCO	0.7	4.3	1.4	3.2	17.5	6.5
Private mining (GMP-10)[d]	0.2	2.6	1.2	0.8	10.6	5.4
Colombia	0.2	0.5	0.4	0.5	1.5	1.3
Jamaica	0.5	0.6	0.1	2.1	2.1	0.4
Mexico	-	0.1	0.2	0.3	0.8	1.0
Peru	0.2	2.1	1.3	1.0	10.6	6.4

Source: Economic Commission for Latin America and the Caribbean (ECLAC), *Panorama Fiscal de América Latina y el Caribe 2015. Dilemas y espacios de políticas* (LC/L.3961), Santiago, 2015.
[a] Fiscal revenues includes tax revenues and non-tax resources generated by mining.
[b] Refers to total overall government fiscal revenues net of social security contributions. Information for the non-financial public sector is taken into account in the cases of Argentina and Colombia.
[c] Does not include the value of mining royalties that are not disaggregated from total royalties (which mostly originate in hydrocarbons production).
[d] GMP-10: the ten largest private mining corporations.

In most countries, the contribution of mining to fiscal revenues was obtained through corporate income tax, which accounted for 70% to 90% of revenues from the sector, with a smaller share coming from royalties and other specific forms of payment for the right to exploit State-owned natural resources. Colombia, Jamaica and the Plurinational State of Bolivia were exceptions in that royalties were the main instrument of revenue collection (Gómez Sabaini, Jiménez and Morán, 2015).

Many countries implemented reforms to ensure the sufficient appropriation of mining rents during the period. These included the introduction of a specific tax on mining activity in Chile (2006); the establishment of a special surtax applied to mining companies during periods of high prices in the Plurinational State of Bolivia (2008); the introduction of the Mining Royalties Law and the creation of a special tax and levy on mining in Peru (2011); the amendment of the General System of Royalties in Colombia (2011), and the creation of three new fees applicable to mining activity in Mexico (2013). One of the goals of these reforms was to make the system more progressive, seeking a greater appropriation of rents during periods of extraordinary prices.

In general terms, the State's involvement in the sector increased, although the growth of fiscal revenues from mining was outpaced the growth of economic rents from mining as a whole, indicating a lack of progressivity in the region's fiscal regimes (Gómez Sabaini, Jiménez and Morán, 2015). Nevertheless, in Chile, Colombia and Peru the appropriation of mining rents was put at 30% to 35% for the period 2004-2009, a broadly similar percentage to that of Australia and other countries of the Organization for Economic Cooperation and Development (OECD), although in other economies in the region, percentages stood at about 10% (Acquatella and others, 2013). In many cases, the application of new fiscal regimes was hampered by pre-existing agreements offering more lenient conditions with a view to promoting foreign investment. This shows the delicate balance between policies to attract investment to a highly capital-intensive sector, and States' capacity to appropriate rents.

The territorial distribution of rents often creates political tension between different levels of government. The regional overview is heterogeneous, with some countries presenting a high degree of distribution to subnational administrative levels, for example Peru (56.9% of fiscal revenues from mineral exploitation between 2010 and 2012), Colombia (51.5%) and the Plurinational State of Bolivia (37.3%). In Argentina and Brazil, the share allocated to subnational governments was 12.8% and 9.9%, respectively, while in Chile and Mexico the central government controlled 100% of these revenues (ECLAC, 2014). In Colombia, the new General System of Royalties changed the situation by establishing a centralized regime in which the distribution of rents to departments and municipalities gradually declined (to 9.8% in 2015). In Peru, revenue from mining activities is geographically concentrated, with 5 of the country's 24 regions accounting for 60% of income. This has caused some discussion about the need to improve the redistribution of the system; however, reforms have been impeded by certain municipalities' high dependence on mining resources.

Since the fiscal management of rents generated from natural resource extraction is important for development, governments have promoted the creation of global multilateral forums to favour greater transparency in the management of these resources. One example is the Extractive Industries Transparency Initiative (EITI); a voluntary initiative that began to take shape in the United Kingdom in 2002, with the goal of promoting the transparency of resources generated by extractive industries in developing countries, and which was implemented through the review and publication of data on companies' tax contributions and the resources received by States. Peru was the first Latin American and Caribbean country to comply with the reporting requirements for EITI membership in 2012, followed by Guatemala in 2014. As of March 2016, 31 countries had met the membership criteria and a further 20 were candidates (at some stage of the implementation process). In Latin America and the Caribbean, Honduras has been a candidate country since 2013, Colombia since 2014 and the Dominican Republic since February 2016. EITI is geared towards developing countries but has been little implemented in the most advanced economies. Of these, Norway is the only member country (since 2011), while the United Kingdom and the United States have been candidates since 2014 and Germany since March 2016. Australia and Canada have not yet signed up to the initiative.

The tax regime is a decision variable for transnational firms, which presents countries with the challenge of balancing State appropriation of rents with the need to attract foreign investment, often essential given the scale of the investment required to operate in the sector. As ECLAC (2014) proposes, coordination between countries on this issue is crucial to prevent detrimental tax competition for investment, which weakens the role of the State and its capacity to promote natural resource governance.

Conversely, from the macroeconomic perspective, the growth of FDI in mining and the high profitability of this activity may cause balance-of-payments difficulties in the current context of slowing FDI inflows to the sector.

The average return on assets of the largest mining corporations was about 20% between 2005 and 2011, compared with 6% for the 500 largest companies in Latin America. Transnational firms' profits are recorded as an outflow on the income side of the balance-of-payments current account, regardless of whether they are reinvested or repatriated to the parent company's country of origin. Profits that are reinvested in the domestic economy do not affect the balance of payments, since they are recorded as an outflow (debit) from the income account, and subsequently counted as an inflow (credit) in the financial account. However, profits that are repatriated to the parent company generate a debit, with a consequent negative effect (ECLAC, 2013b).

On average, about 50% of profits generated by transnational corporations operating in the region are repatriated (ECLAC, 2013b). In this context, the strong foreign capital flows to mining during the expansion phase and the sector's high profitability created a scenario in which a large proportion of profits could be repatriated. The squeeze on profits in the past two years may mitigate this effect, it being necessary to analyse each country to identify how rents from mining investment may affect the balance of payments position. The outcomes of such an analysis will hinge on the presence of transnationals in mining, their profitability, and their tendency to repatriate or reinvest earnings.

2.   Few production linkages were created

The expansion of metal mining in an economy has the potential to spur activity in other sectors and may therefore lend impetus to production diversification. This diversification is achieved through production linkages of various kinds: backward linkages (through firms that supply inputs for metal mining), forward linkages (through the local processing of metallic minerals prior to export or their use as inputs in other industries), fiscal linkages and linkages produced by the expansion of demand that drives growth in the sector (Hirschman, 1977).

Traditionally, extractive industries have been characterized as having substantial capacity for income generation, but limited capacity for creating jobs and local linkages (UNCTAD, 2007). Production processes in the sector are capital intensive and have high specialized technology requirements and low labour requirements, making difficult to develop backward linkages or to boost direct employment.

In Latin America and the Caribbean, direct employment creation in the metal mining sector is low compared with the sector's impact on GDP and foreign-exchange earnings, notwithstanding that the labour force employed in mining grew more quickly in most countries during the expansion phase. Chile has the highest proportion of direct employment in mining, at about 3% of the total workforce in 2014, almost double the figure posted in the early 2000s (see table II.14). The country where mining had the second-largest impact on jobs was the Plurinational State of Bolivia, accounting for 2.4% of the workforce in 2014, while in Colombia and Peru the proportion was about 1%.

Traditionally, extractive industries have been characterized as having substantial capacity for income generation, but limited capacity for creating jobs and local linkages.

Table II.14
Selected countries:[a] employment in the mining industry as a proportion of total employment, 2001-2014
(Percentages)

Employment in the sector rose, but has relatively low impact overall

Country	2001-2003	2004-2012	2013	2014
Bolivia (Plurinational State of)	1.2	1.7	2.2	2.4
Chile	1.5	2.2	2.8	3.0
Colombia	1.1	1.1	1.1	1.0
Dominican Republic	0.2	0.3	0.3	0.2
Mexico	...	0.2	...	0.5
Peru	0.7	1.2	1.2	1.2

Source: Economic Commission for Latin America and the Caribbean (ECLAC), on the basis of CEPALSTAT database and official figures.
[a] Brazil was not included, as mining employees in that country represent a negligible proportion of the workforce.

Synergies and linkages between mining and other productive activities will be crucial if the sector's growth is to help build capabilities at the local level, thus contributing to the diversification of the economies where mining is carried out.

Quantitative analysis of linkages shows the mining is generally a sector with low spillovers in terms of demand for other economic activities.[15] The multipliers for metal mining in Chile, Colombia and Mexico, and for non-ferrous metals in Brazil, were valued at less than 0.6 (backward linkages). This means, for example, that each additional US$ 100 million in mining production creates a US$ 60 million increase in other economic activities in the country as a result of the direct and indirect demand generated by the mining sector.

By comparing these coefficients with those of manufacturing sectors, it may be observed that the technical coefficients associated with mining are not very high. For example, non-ferrous metal basic industries in Chile and Mexico have output multipliers of 1.24 and 0.8, respectively, while in Chile the manufacture of wood products has a multiplier of 1.22 and in Brazil vehicle manufacturing has a multiplier of 1.18. This reduced spillover capacity is not exclusive to the countries of the region; the multiplier for metal mining in Canada was estimated at 0.4 in 2011. These estimates provide a macroeconomic indicator that reflects the interrelatedness of a given sector with other sectors of the economy, but does not provide any information on the technological intensity or the capabilities required by each activity. Moreover, high production levels such as those observed in the region's main mining countries may still deliver a substantial impact in absolute terms, despite modest multiplier values.

In Chile, the most influential sectors in backward linkages (in other words, the largest suppliers of the mining industry), are copper mining itself (16% of the multiplier), electricity (16%), architecture, engineering and scientific services (10%), legal, accounting and other business services (9%) and wholesale trade (7%), among others. In Mexico, the backward multiplier of the metal mining sector is lower than in other countries (0.3), with impacts on own consumption (48% of the indicator), oil and coal (9%), electricity (6%) and others. In Brazil, the multiplier for non-ferrous metal mining is quite high (1.2), with the sector relying on oil and coal (19%), transport and storage (14%), commerce (9%), machinery and equipment maintenance (6%) and machinery and equipment manufacturing (5%), among others.

From a quantitative viewpoint, the main effects of mining in the region are apparent in fiscal linkages and linkages related to resource availability, which matches the findings of studies carried out for other mining regions (Auty, 2005).

The greatest difficulties for developing backward linkages are presented by the characteristics of metal mining production processes. Large-scale mining uses specialized equipment, produced with economies of scale and sold in global distribution networks. This reduces the potential for using local suppliers. In most of the region's countries, mining firms imported machinery, chemical products and manufactured goods (rubber, iron and steel and metal products).

However, a qualitative overview of metal mining suppliers in the region revealed that some domestic suppliers have found niches in which to export to third markets, which according to Melitz (2003) suggests the higher productivity of these enterprises. If the expansion of metal mining in the region is conducive to the growth of high-productivity domestic firms, then it would also be contributing to greater economic diversification and would be an example of how FDI can contribute to local business development.

---

[15]   See Schuschny (2005) for methodology and detailed concepts. Linkages are calculated on the basis of coefficients of the Leontief inverse, capturing direct and indirect effects.

Such impacts are of limited magnitude in the region's countries, but progress has been achieved in some areas. Chile is emerging as the Latin American country that has made most progress in the development of sophisticated mining suppliers and exporters, albeit these firms account for a small proportion of total exports. In 2014, it was estimated that Chile had 5,000 suppliers of goods and services for the mining sector, with total sales of US$ 20 billion. Around 330 of these firms managed to sell their products and services overseas, with exports valued at US$ 540 million in 2014. However, these exports are highly concentrated, with just five firms responsible for 61% of total export value in 2014, and 87% of exporters reporting sales of under US$ 1 million (Fundación Chile, 2015). This reality, while far from ideal given the scarcity of larger firms, offers a glimpse of the possibility that local mining suppliers can secure a foothold in the international market for technologically complex goods and services.

Services accounted for 33% of total expenditure on domestic inputs for the Chilean mining industry in 2012.[16] The growth of the mining sector boosted demand for architecture, engineering and scientific services, and machinery and equipment repair and installation services. The proportion of mining suppliers that made more than 40% of their sales to the mining sector rose from 50% to 73% between 2010 and 2012 (Innovum, 2014).

From the viewpoint of building local capabilities and innovation, the establishment of specific research centres for mining is a key element for the future development of the sector. In Chile, research initiatives for mining innovation are being pursued that connect academic institutions with the private sector, creating an interesting opportunity for the generation of applied knowledge. One example is the Advanced Mining Technology Center (AMTC), set up with funding from the National Commission for Scientific and Technological Research (CONICYT) of Chile. Led by a board of directors formed of academics and representatives of mining companies, AMTC carries out basic and applied research projects with government funding, as well as applied research projects financed by corporations. Besides helping firms increase their productivity, this type of initiative may serve an important function in informing policy design, enabling the drafting of strategic guidelines for the growth of sector based on solid technical foundations.

Other Latin American and Caribbean countries have notable sectors or enterprises that supply the mining industry. In Peru, about 110 companies in the metalworking, chemical and iron and steel sectors provide goods and services to mining, with total sales of US$ 3.3 billion in 2013, and exports worth US$ 750 million. In Colombia, the growth of the mining sector benefited suppliers, especially those in the metalworking sector that produce basic components, whose sales and exports increased during the period (Perry and Palacios, 2013). In the Plurinational State of Bolivia, most domestic suppliers of the mining industry are concentrated in non-tradable, low-technology goods and services, although in some cases domestic metallurgy and construction companies have carried out highly complex projects for the mining industry.

A degree of integration has been achieved between the dynamics of the mining market and local suppliers that have greater technological prowess; however, the development of these supply industries is still incipient and faces competition from major international exporters of mining services, technologies and equipment (for example, Australian suppliers).

In the current context, company strategies aim to reduce costs and minimize environmental impacts; technological progress offers solutions to these problems. The energy and water requirements of mining mean that technological development

---

[16]   The main input was electricity. See Correa (2016) for a more detailed analysis of intermediate consumption in mining subsectors.

is fundamental for the growth of the sector, which needs cheaper sources of energy and water, along with greater sustainability. Attracting FDI for the provision of solutions in these areas may create an opportunity for growth associated with mining activity that contributes to the creation of intangible capital. In Chile, the mining industry increased the proportion of total energy consumption drawn from renewable sources (Correa, 2016); while the renewable energies sector received stronger foreign investment flows. The continuation of this trend could be central to achieving a more sustainable mining sector.

One final element relates to the territorial development of linkages. Both in Chile and Peru, suppliers of more technologically complex products and services are based in the main cities and the externalities they have generated at the local level are weak, even in traditional mining areas such as Antofagasta and Calama, and have greater impact nationally (Phelps, Atienza and Arias, 2015). In Peru, on average 3.6% of input purchases are transacted in the vicinity of the mine. These acquisitions tend to be low-technology goods and services, food and beverages and textile, agro-industrial or handicraft products, and are generally intended to strengthen relations with the local population, while specialized suppliers are located in Lima and Arequipa. The impact of employment on mining localities depends greatly on the context and the characteristics of the region in question. When starting up a new project, consideration should be given to how the regional economy can meet the requirements of modern mining (Söderholm and Svahn, 2015).

3.   New industrial policies are needed for mining

The benefits of foreign direct investment in the mining industry are far from being automatically accrued. In its study on the use of fiscal resources from extractive industries, ECLAC concluded that the commodity price boom increased the availability of financial resources, whose potential for achieving structural change was not fully leveraged (ECLAC, 2014). As mentioned previously, the inherent nature of the industry may limit spillovers into other sectors of production, added to the fact that major social and environmental impacts make regulation of these aspects an essential priority.

International market dynamics dictate that investment is attracted to locations that combine the availability of mineral resources with stable regulatory conditions for their exploitation and an adequate infrastructure for exports. The development of externalities, from the basic exploitation of natural resources to greater complexity and diversification, will depend to a large extent on local capacity (in terms of institutions, technology and access to energy, human capital and financing, among others). In this context, a policy space is emerging for countries to promote the accumulation of local capabilities linked to the development of a sustainable mining sector that drives diversification. The benefits that an economy may obtain from integration into global value chains are related to its local capabilities (Cimoli, Dosi and Stiglitz, 2009). Therefore, the benefits that can be obtained from exploiting natural resources at the local level are linked to these capabilities.

In recent decades, certain countries managed to attract investment to metal mining through a combination of active policy elements and passive market elements. Certifying mineral resources and reserves is one strategy for attracting investment. For example, in 2015 Brazil joined the Committee for Mineral Reserves International Reporting Standards (CRIRSCO), an initiative that also counts Chile as a member, and which seeks to offer greater investment guarantees. In Mexico, the Mining Development Programme 2013-2018 aims to promote diversification in mineral exploration and

> The development of externalities, from the basic exploitation of natural resources to greater complexity and diversification, will depend to a large extent on local capabilities.

exploitation, and will include extended coverage and deposit analysis by the Mexican Geological Survey.

Policies to attract investment in mining were accompanied by policies to regulate the sector, mainly in the area of property rights, taxation, environmental protection, community relations and respect for human rights. In Peru, the reforms implemented in the 1990s focused on promoting investment in the sector by providing legal and tax stability and guarantees, while recent policies also emphasize social and environmental conflict resolution (CEPLAN, 2011; MEM, 2012). In Colombia, the growth of the mining industry led to the sector's inclusion as a driver of sustainable development in the National Development Plan 2014-2018, with emphasis on social and environmental responsibility. The sector's rapid expansion, the excessive awarding of mining rights and a surge in illegal exports all created to situations of conflict, leading the Government to take steps to regulate the industry's growth; for that purpose it published the National Mining Management Plan, deciding not to explore for gold in *páramo* upland areas and to combat illegal production. At the same time, a policy to regularize the situation of informal miners was launched in 2014.

Despite the persistence of conflicts the significant risks entailed by the expansion and operation of mines, the region has made some progress in regulating the sector. However, policies to foster greater production linkages have been more limited.

One of the action lines explored by the region's countries has been the development of suppliers for the mining sector. In Brazil, the Brazilian Agency for Industrial Development (ABDI) developed a map of the mining goods and services supply chain with a view to proposing a supplier development programme (Prominer); an ongoing project established under the National Mining Plan 2030 (in turn part of the *Brasil Maior* Plan). The strategies set forth in Mexico's Mining Development Programme include promoting the development and consolidation of mining-sector suppliers through the Mining Promotion Trust (FIFOMI), an institution that has provided financing, training and technical assistance to producers and suppliers.

In Chile, one of the national strategic programmes of the Chilean Economic Development Agency (CORFO) is the Alta Ley National Mining Programme, which aims to "strengthen productivity, competitiveness and innovation in the national mining industry and its suppliers, to promote the country's economic development".[17] In 2016, this programme presented a road map with nine technological challenges for the development of mining in the country, and which included suppliers and innovation as an enabling cluster, on the understanding that they determine the industry's capacity for self-development (Fundación Chile, 2016). Another proposal is that of expanding the World Class Supplier Programme. This supplier development programme was launched by the private corporation BHP Billiton in 2008, later attracting the participation of the State-owned enterprise CODELCO. An agreement has since been signed by the Ministry of Mining and Fundación Chile to continue and expand the programme.[18]

The programme aims to develop knowledge-intensive suppliers, with technological solutions that may be transferred to other sectors and markets. The mining corporations identify and prioritize problems whose solutions are not available on the market, and which have potential economic, environmental or community benefits. Based on these requirements, they select firms with the potential to resolve problems, who then test their solutions within the corporations, thus creating capacity among local companies and resolving the miners' operational problems. The programme remains smaller in scale than originally envisaged, but it remains a valid tool for capacity-building in the

---

[17]   http://programaaltaley.cl/somos/.

[18]   Fundación Chile is a private not-for-profit organization whose partners are BHP Billiton-Minera Escondida and the Government of Chile. Its goal is to promote innovation in different sectors of the Chilean economy.

sector (100 suppliers were expected to participate by 2012; however, in 2014 there were only 87 participants; the current target is for 250 suppliers to join by 2020).

Just as in Chile an initiative that emerged in the private sector was later adopted by a State-owned enterprise and subsequently redefined as part of the national strategy, so too in Brazil the activity of Vale exerts strong influence on the sector. In 2009, Vale launched a specific supplier development programme for its operations in Brazil (Inove), with financing tools, training and business meetings. The programme is implemented in association with local credit entities, training providers and business associations. Focusing on small- and medium-sized enterprises (SMEs), Vale signed agreements within the production linkage programme of the Brazilian Micro and Small Business Support Service (SEBRAE) to train current and potential suppliers in the requirements that, according to SEBRAE, firms will have to meet in order to collaborate with Vale.[19]

Many countries with extractive industries take steps to promote local content, sometimes through compulsory requirements and sometimes through less stringent measures. In 2013, a proposal for a new regulatory regime for the mining sector was submitted to the National Congress of Brazil, and its adoption is presently under debate. Among other strategic reforms, the proposal would establish local content requirements for the signing of new mining contracts, similar to the regulations in force for the country's oil and gas sector. The hydrocarbon regulation introduced in 1999 sets forth that concessions will favour companies with more local content and requires suppliers to certify the domestic origins of the goods and services provided. Australia is another country that implements such policies, collectively known as Australian Industry Participation. Although this framework does not establish compulsory quotas in terms of contracting, it requires that a study be carried out for all projects with capital expenditure of more than 500 million Australian dollars, recognizing and communicating the economic effects in terms of jobs, knowledge transfer, strategic partnerships and territorial development. This facilitates the signing of local contracts. The aim is for local firms to have a genuine chance of competing for services contracts at all levels of the chain, while government business support agencies offer technical assistance to firms that wish to apply to be suppliers.

Technological development is crucial for mining activity, especially in the current context as corporations seek to enhance productivity, reduce costs and minimize environmental impacts. The technology road map of Chile's Alta Ley National Mining Programme makes a valuable attempt to identify and prioritize those areas in which new technologies would be useful in meeting the Programme's targets, while CONICYT promotes the strengthening of research capacity in the mining industry. In Mexico, FIFOMI grants funding for environmental conservation projects and the development of new technologies, while Brazil is planning to launch an innovation programme for mining (Inova Mineral) as part of the Inova incentive scheme, which operates with the support of the Studies and Projects Financing Entity (FINEP) and BNDES. The programme targets the development of technologies for the exploitation of two groups of strategic minerals: those defined by the Government as "future carrying" minerals (cobalt, graphite, lithium, molybdenum, the platinum group, niobium, rare earths) and those on which the country depends (phosphate and potassium). The technologies developed may also be used to minimize the environmental impact of extracting these minerals. The exploitation of rare earths and other minerals linked to the development of new technologies is highly concentrated in China, and Brazil is looking to bolster research and production in these areas to improve its position in this market.[20]

[19] See [online] http://www.agenciasebrae.com.br/sites/asn/uf/NA/sebrae-e-vale-investem-r-49-milhoes-para-qualificar-500-for necedores,e958ce6326c0a410VgnVCM1000003b74010aRCRD.
[20] See [online] http://www.brasilmineral.com.br/noticias/programa-inova-mineral-terá-recursos-de-r-12-bi.

Forward linkages from mining, through the use of mineral resources in smelting or more advanced stages of manufacturing, are becoming more significant in the region.

Forward linkages from mining, through the use of mineral resources in smelting or more advanced stages of manufacturing, are becoming more significant in the region. In general, large mining transnationals have worked according to a system whereby minerals are extracted worldwide but the bulk of concentrates are exported to smelting and refining plants in countries located close to demand markets and which have ready supply of cheap energy. For that reason, smelting and refining has been concentrated in Europe, Japan and the United States. The past decade has seen some changes in this system, with refineries and smelters opening in developing countries, most notably China, which then began to supply the international market.

In the copper market, Chile is pursuing a strategy to improve its position in refining and smelting. There are currently seven plants in the country, five of which are State-owned, which operate obsolete technology and have high running costs (Fundación Chile, 2016). The technology road map therefore sets out three challenges for this subsector —increase efficiency, reduce the environmental impact and improve working conditions— and proposes specific research and development measures to meet them.

The Plurinational State of Bolivia, through the State-owned Corporación Minera de Bolivia (CONMIBOL), is investing in developing the mining and metallurgy chain. Projects include the nationalization and modernization of a tin metallurgical company and the reactivation of a lead and silver smelting complex that had been inactive for the past 30 years. Furthermore, a project to exploit lithium in the Salar de Uyuni salt flat aims to create a whole value chain, from the extraction of the raw material (brine) and its processing to obtain basic compounds (lithium carbonate and potassium chloride), to the manufacture of intermediate goods (battery cathodes and electrolytes) and ultimately, lithium-ion batteries. The State plans to invest about US$ 1.0 billion,[21] and has signed agreements with foreign partners for the project's implementation and for the training of professionals (Córdova, 2016).

In the past 15 years, global markets for the main metallic minerals have experienced profound changes, with huge swings in demand, prices and output. This has generated significant flows of foreign direct investment, much of it to Latin American countries.

Global demand was invigorated above all by China's growth and its industrialization strategy, driving major transformations in international markets.

These changes materialized in the form of a price boom between 2003 and 2011 and the reshaping of the mining sector's worldwide production structure. Latin America has maintained a strong position, at least in the stages of raw material extraction; however, new actors have emerged during this period, particularly in Africa, while China too has significantly expanded its extractive capacity.

Changes of a similar magnitude have occurred in the manufacture of metal products (steel, aluminium and smelted copper), a sector in which China has acquired absolute leadership, displacing the United States, Japan, Germany and the Russian Federation (among others) and posing a serious threat to the industry in Latin American countries.

This period, therefore, has been one of dramatic transformation in the geographical distribution of extractive activities and the stages of industrial processing of metallic minerals.

The leading production agents in these processes are transnational firms, comprising a corporate segment that has also undergone significant changes. The jump in the number

---

[21]   The Economic and Social Development Plan 2016-2020 within the framework of Integrated Development for Living Well includes the lithium plant among the country's strategic industrial production complexes.

of large corporations was particularly remarkable, with many new companies formed in developing countries, especially Brazil, China, India and the Russian Federation. At the same time, there was a spate of mergers and acquisitions as enormous transactions were concluded by companies pursuing geographical and production diversification strategies. In recent years, however, falling prices and profitability have translated into more defensive strategies, with firms tending to concentrate their spending on key assets at the expense of exploration expenditure and capital investment. In this new context, companies have attached greater importance to cutting costs and minimizing environmental impacts.

Latin America and the Caribbean has been actively involved in these processes. In several of the region's countries, the boom in metallic mineral prices triggered strong investment flows, mainly from overseas, which in turn led to a significant expansion of exports and contributed to increased capital formation, sustained GDP growth, and greater availability of resources for the State. This pattern was conducive to the funding of more extensive and better quality social programmes, and the realization of investment in infrastructure improvements. Taken in conjunction with other factors, it may be said that this cycle of high prices contributed directly and indirectly to improving the well-being of the population.

Searching for better strategies so that mining can bolster development is a complex challenge, in which each country must balance an array of opposing interests. For that reason, the design and implementation of industrial policies to promote diversification based on mining sector linkages requires an institutional space for coordination between the public and private sectors. There is a need to identify those actions that could create the context for communities to participate in companies' processes of value creation. For companies, the acquisition of environmental and social licences should be internalized as an essential part of their operations, in addition to creating value in the communities where they operate by promoting the development of production capabilities. Corporate social responsibility initiatives appear to be insufficient in that regard, since building these capabilities will require more focused measures. This challenge is shared by more advanced economies that enjoy comparative advantages in natural resources. Canada was able to diversify its production thanks to a long history of industrial policy intervention, a critical element for natural-resource-based economies since States that do not define their policy in relation to the exploitation of resources and the comparative advantage they wish to obtain, will have foreign governments define it for them (Ciuriak, 2014).

The region enjoys comparative advantages in the exploitation of metallic minerals, and most countries have directly or indirectly encouraged FDI in the sector. How to keep step with the expansion of mining activity through policies in support of the sector, securing the maximum possible benefit for inclusive and sustainable development, remains a major challenge for Latin American and Caribbean countries. Considering the similarities between the problems they face, the countries' position could undoubtedly be improved through a regional rather than solely a national approach (ECLAC, 2014: Altomonte and Sánchez, 2016).

Bibliography

Acquatella, J. and others (2013), "Rentas de recursos naturales no renovables en América Latina y el Caribe: evolución y participación estatal, 1990-2010", *Seminarios y Conferencias series*, No. 72 (LC/L.3645), Santiago, Economic Commission for Latin America and the Caribbean (ECLAC).

Altomonte, H. y R.J. Sánchez (2016), *Hacia una nueva gobernanza de los recursos naturales en América Latina y el Caribe*, Libros de la CEPAL, No. 139 (LC/G.2679-P), Santiago, Economic Commission for Latin America and the Caribbean (ECLAC).

Anglo American (2015), *Annual Report 2015. Driving Change, Defining Our Future* [online] http://www.angloamerican.com/investors/annual-reporting.

Auty, R.M. (2005), "Maximising the positive socio-economic impact of mineral extraction on regional development in transition economies: a review of the literature", European Bank for Reconstruction and Development (EBRD).

Behre Dolbear (2015), "Where to invest in mining" [online] http://www.dolbear.com/.

BHP Billiton (2015), *Resourcing Global Growth. Annual Report 2015* [online] http://www.bhpbilliton.com/investors/annualreporting2015.

Campodónico, H. (1999), "Las reformas estructurales en el sector minero peruano y las características de la inversión 1992-2008", *Reformas Económicas series*, No. 24 (LC/L.1208), Santiago, Economic Commission for Latin America and the Caribbean (ECLAC).

CEPLAN (National Center for Strategic Planning) (2011), *Plan Bicentenario: El Perú al 2021*, Lima.

Cimoli, M., G. Dosi and J. Stiglitz (2009), *Industrial Policy and Development: The Political Economy of Capabilities Accumulation*, New York, Oxford University Press.

Ciuriak, D. (2014), "Re-reading Staples Theory in light of current trade and development theory", *The Staple Theory @ 50. Reflections on the Lasting Significance of Mel Watkins' "A Staple Theory of Economic Growth"*, J. Stanford (ed.), Canadian Center for Policy Alternatives.

CNC (National Competitiveness Council of Peru) (2013), "Elaboración de un mapeo de clusters en el Perú", prepared by Consorcio Cluster Development- Metis Gaia – Javier D'ávila Quevedo for CNC, Lima.

Córdova, H. (2016), "Encadenamientos mineros en el Estado Plurinacional de Bolivia", unpublished.

Correa, F. (2016), "Encadenamientos productivos desde la minería de Chile", *Desarrollo Productivo series*, No. 203 (LC/L.4160/Rev.1), Santiago, Economic Commission for Latin America and the Caribbean (ECLAC).

Deloitte (2015), *Tracking the Trends 2016. The top 10 issues mining companies will face in the coming year*, Canada.

Durrant-Whyte, H. and others (2015), "How digital innovation can improve mining productivity", McKinsey & Company [online] http://www.mckinsey.com/industries/metals-and-mining/our-insights/how-digital-innovation-can-improve-mining-productivity.

ECLAC (Economic Commission for Latin America and the Caribbean) (2015), *Panorama Fiscal de América Latina y el Caribe 2015. Dilemas y espacios de políticas* (LC/L.3961), Santiago.

___(2014), *Compacts for Equality: Towards a sustainable future* (LC/G.2586(SES.35/3)), Santiago.

___(2013a), *Natural resources: status and trends towards a regional development agenda in Latin America and the Caribbean Contribution of the Economic Commission for Latin America and the Caribbean to the Community of Latin American and Caribbean States* (LC/L.3748), Santiago.

___(2013b), *Foreign Direct Investment in Latin America and the Caribbean, 2012* (LC/G.2571-P), Santiago.

Fundación Chile (2016), *Desde el cobre a la innovación: Roadmap tecnológico 2015-2035*, Santiago, Programa Nacional de Minería Alta Ley.

___(2015), *Proveedores de la minería chilena. Reporte de exportaciones 2010-2014*, Santiago, Programa Nacional de Minería Alta Ley.

Gómez Sabaini, J.C., J.P. Jiménez and D. Morán (2015), "El impacto fiscal de la explotación de los recursos naturales no renovables en los países de América Latina y el Caribe", *Project Documents* (LC/W.658), Santiago, Economic Commission for Latin America and the Caribbean (ECLAC).

Halland, H., M. Lokanc and A. Nair (2015), *The Extractive Industries Sector: Essentials for Economists, Public Finance Professionals, and Policy Makers*, Washington, D.C., World Bank.

Hirschman, A.O. (1977), "A generalized linkage approach to development with special reference to staples", *Essays on Economic Development and Cultural Change in Honor of Bert F. Hoselitz*, Chicago University Press.

Innovum (2014), *Proveedores de la minería chilena. Estudio de caracterización*, Santiago, Fundación Chile.

Melitz, M. (2003), "The impact of trade on intra-industry reallocations and aggregate industry productivity", *Econometrica*, No. 71.

MEM (Ministry of Mining and Energy of Peru) (2012), *Plan Estratégico Institucional 2012-2016*, Lima.

Perry, G. and C. Palacios (2013), "Emprendimiento alrededor del sector de la minería y el petróleo en Colombia", *Documentos CEDE*, Bogota, Universidad de los Andes.

Phelps, N., M. Atienza and M. Arias (2015), "Encore for the Enclave: the changing nature of the industry enclave with illustrations from the mining industry in Chile", *Economic Geography*, vol. 91, No. 2.

PwC (PricewaterhouseCoopers) (2015), *Mine 2015. The Gloves Are off. Review of global trends in the mining industry* [online] http://www.pwc.com/gx/en/mining/publications/assets/pwc-e-and-m-mining-report.pdf.

Rio Tinto (2015), *Rio Tinto's Annual and Strategic Report* [online] www.riotinto.com/ar2015.

Rogich, D.G. and G.R. Matos (2008), *The Global Flows of Metals and Minerals. U.S. Geological Survey Open-File Report 2008–1355* [online] http://pubs.usgs.gov/of/2008/1355/.

Schuschny, A. R. (2005), "Tópicos sobre el Modelo de Insumo-Producto: teoría y aplicaciones", *Estudios Estadísticos y Prospectivos series*, No. 37 (LC/L.2444-P), Santiago, Economic Commission for Latin America and the Caribbean (ECLAC).

SNL Metals & Mining (2015), *World Exploration Trends: A special report from SNL Metals & Mining for the PDAC International Convention* [online] http://go.snl.com/rs/snlfinanciallc/images/World-Exploration-Trends-WET-Report-2015-English-USletter.pdf.

Söderholm, P. and N. Svahn (2015), "Mining, regional development and benefit-sharing in developed countries", *Resources Policy*, No. 45.

Sujatmiko, S. (2015), "Indonesia's mineral added value/beneficiation: Effort to promote sustainable growth and industrial development", presentation at the UNCTAD Gobal Commodities Forum, Geneva, 13-14 April.

UNCTAD (United Nations Conference on Trade and Development) (2007), *World Investment Report 2007. Transnational Corporations, Extractive Industries and Development* (UNCTAD/WIR/2007), Geneva.

Wise, R. and R. Del Pozo (2001), "Minería, Estado y gran capital en México", *Revista Economia e Sociedade*, vol. 10, No. 1, Campinas State University.

World Bank (2011), "Overview of State ownership in the global minerals industry", *Extractive Industries for Development series*, No. 20, Washington, D.C.

Annex II.A1

Table II.A1.1
Latin America: main mining companies, by sales, 1997-2014
(Millions of dollars)

Company	Country	Ownership	Years in ranking	Sales		
				2005	2010	2014
Vale	Brazil	Domestic	18	14 523	49 949	33 233
CODELCO	Chile	State	18	10 491	16 066	23 380
Grupo México	Mexico	Foreign	18	5 464	8 320	9 320
Escondida	Chile	Foreign	18	4 360	9 211	8 005
Industrias Peñoles	Mexico	Domestic	18	1 998	5 203	4 176
Southern Peru Copper Inc.	Peru	Foreign	18	4 113	3 154	2 482
Antofagasta	Chile	Domestic	12	2 445	4 577	5 290
Collahuasi	Chile	Foreign	13	1 707	3 929	2 980
Los Pelambres	Chile	Foreign	13	1 767	3 286	2 664
Minera Antamina	Peru	Foreign	13	1 680	2 664	2 503
Paranapanema	Brazil	Domestic	17	1 155	1 916	1 782
Samarco Mineração	Brazil	Foreign	16	1 062	3 745	2 805
Minera Yanacocha	Peru	Foreign	17	1 490	1 867	1 255
SQM	Chile	Domestic	18	896	1 829	2 014
Enami	Chile	State	18	1 080	1 721	1 598
Drummond	Colombia	Foreign	14	949	1 906	1 415
Alumbrera[a]	Argentina	Foreign	12	1 457	1 590	1 338

Source: Economic Commission for Latin America and the Caribbean (ECLAC), on the basis of information from *América Economía*. Mining companies included in the ranking of the 500 largest companies in Latin America.
[a] The sales figure provided for 2005 is from 2006.

Foreign direct investment as a driver of intangible capital accumulation

A. Only one third of foreign direct investment creates new physical capital

The positive effects of foreign direct investment (FDI) can foster development in the recipient economies; in particular, they can supplement national saving through new capital contributions and stimulate transfers of technology and improve management systems to enable productive modernization. These effects are not automatic, however, and the results obtained may not meet expectations.

In Latin America and the Caribbean, FDI has played a crucial role in the pattern of production and international engagement, owing to its importance in the exploitation of natural resources, manufacturing activity, exports and modern services. Its impact on technological progress and on research, development and innovation has been less, however; and its spillovers have had limited penetration in the economic structure. The effects of FDI depend on each country's production, technological and human resources capacities and knowledge, and also on the regulatory frameworks governing individual sectors, particularly services. Strategies that combine the attraction of FDI with policies that promote productive modernization and diversification would encourage transnational enterprises to enter sectors with greater potential for technological development and capacity-building; and this would help them to integrate into local economies and fuel socially inclusive and environmentally sustainable economic growth.

This chapter explores two important factors in ensuring those positive effects are attained. First, it quantifies the contribution made by FDI to gross fixed capital formation and demonstrates the importance of the intangible component of such capital flows for the development of host economies. Second, it proposes policy guidelines for exploiting the benefits of FDI.

Foreign direct investment inflows to the region have been broadly stable relative to GDP —maintaining a level around 3%, with fluctuations of about 0.5 percentage points since 2000, despite the major increase recorded in absolute terms (see figure III.1).

> FDI has played a crucial role in the pattern of production and international engagement, owing to its importance in the exploitation of natural resources, manufacturing activity, exports and modern services.

Over the long term, FDI inflows have represented about 3% of GDP

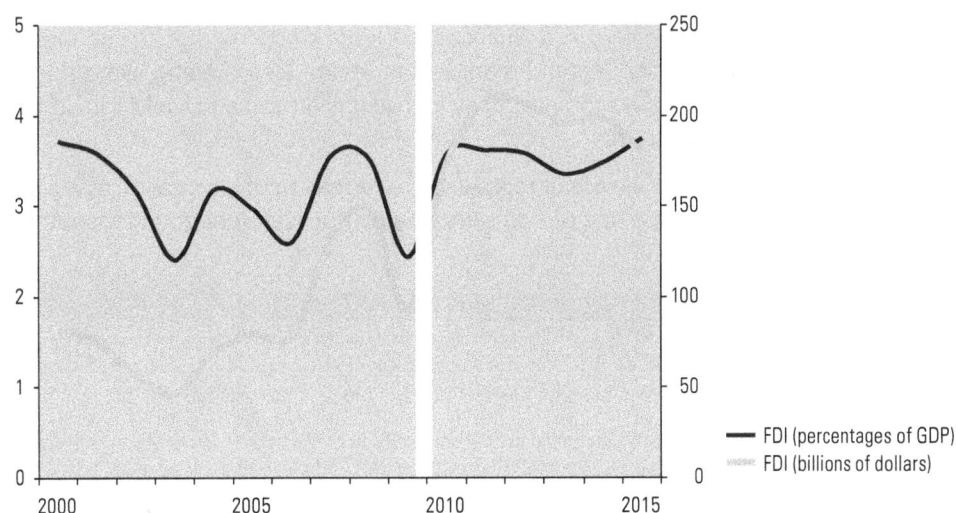

Figure III.1
Latin America and the Caribbean: foreign direct investment (FDI), 2000-2015
(Percentages of GDP and billions of dollars)

—— FDI (percentages of GDP)
—— FDI (billions of dollars)

Source: Economic Commission for Latin America and the Caribbean, on the basis of official figures as of 27 May 2016.
Note: As discussed in chapter I, the figures from 2010 onwards are not directly comparable with those of earlier years, owing to methodological changes in the collection of statistical data. The data relative to GDP exclude the Bolivarian Republic of Venezuela.

Gross fixed capital formation plays a fundamental role in development processes, along with growth of the labour force and expansion of the pool of capacities and knowledge. This is divided into fixed capital generated by domestic agents and that created by foreign firms. Foreign direct investment flows have a variety of destinations that do not always entail the creation of new fixed capital; in other words, they do not translate directly into the formation of physical capital in the receiving country (Lautier and Moreaub, 2012).[1] Mergers and acquisitions (M&A) are the best example of this since they merely involve a change in the ownership of existing assets. The M&A proportion of FDI varies widely, but it is always large and can account for as much as 60% to 80% (OECD, 2014a).[2]

On the basis of data published by the United Nations Conference on Trade and Development (UNCTAD) and Bloomberg, cross-border mergers and acquisitions are estimated to account for at least 29% of the region's FDI inflows. This figure is in line with international lower-bound estimates for that variable. The proportion differs sharply between countries: high in Peru but somewhat lower in Colombia and Mexico between 2000 and 2014. There is also considerable variation from year to year, owing to the weight of certain individual operations.

> Cross-border mergers and acquisitions are estimated to account for at least 29% of the region's FDI inflows.

The dynamic of FDI flows and the trend of fixed capital investment follow different but related paths. Data for Latin America and the Caribbean between 1990 and 2014 show a reasonably strong correlation between the two variables. However, this correlation could be spurious since both may be driven by the same underlying variables, such as GDP growth. In theory, the financial flows that contribute to the formation of gross fixed capital could come from FDI or from other sources (such as domestic financial flows). One estimate is that each additional dollar of FDI increases gross fixed capital formation by 34 cents.[3] In other words, around one third of FDI flows actually contribute to fixed capital formation in the receiving economy.

By combining information on mergers and acquisitions with the results of the direct impact of FDI on gross fixed capital formation, it is possible to identify the destination of around two thirds of the total flow. The remainder represents leakages or other types of losses:

- Crowding out of local investment: investment financed through FDI inflows may take the place of investment that would otherwise have been undertaken by national investors.

- Crowding out of financing: FDI financed on local credit markets in countries with small and imperfect capital markets can mean less funding available for local firms, which reduces their capacity to invest (Harrison and McMillan, 2003; Marín and Schnitzer, 2011).

- Investment in financial assets unrelated to the formation of physical or intangible capital (for example, the use of a country as a platform for redirecting resources to third markets).

---

[1]   Foreign firm capital formation and the FDI flow are different concepts. The first involves an increase in an economy's capital stock; the second represents a way of financing that increase, which might be supplemented with resources from the domestic or international financial systems. Although a positive relation between the two variables is hoped for, the relation is neither one-to-one nor constant over time.

[2]   There are no good data sources on mergers and acquisitions. The most widely used is the cross-border mergers and acquisitions database of the United Nations Conference on Trade and Development (UNCTAD, 2015). Nonetheless data availability is limited. Between 1990 and 2014, FDI data are available for 646 out of 850 year-country values in Latin America and the Caribbean; and UNCTAD estimates mergers and acquisitions activities for only 375 of them. While there are no estimations of mergers and acquisitions activities for eight economies (mostly from the Caribbean), only 338 cases have data for both variables.

[3]   This result is obtained by implementing Cronbach's alpha for gross fixed capital formation using a measure of FDI. Alternative estimations can be calculated by examining the slope of a scatter diagram of gross fixed capital formation and FDI, which gives 39 cents on the dollar, or by taking an average of these slopes across countries, which yields 35 cents on the dollar.

The first two can be considered negative secondary effects of FDI, whereas the third has no effect on the local economy. Thus, FDI has three main destinations: (i) creation of fixed capital; (ii) mergers and acquisitions; and (iii) leakages or losses (see figure III.2). The proportions vary widely, mainly owing to the dynamic of mergers and acquisitions; but the total rate of direct fixed capital creation through FDI remains broadly stable at around 1% of GDP.

Fixed capital creation resulting from FDI inflows represents only 1% of GDP

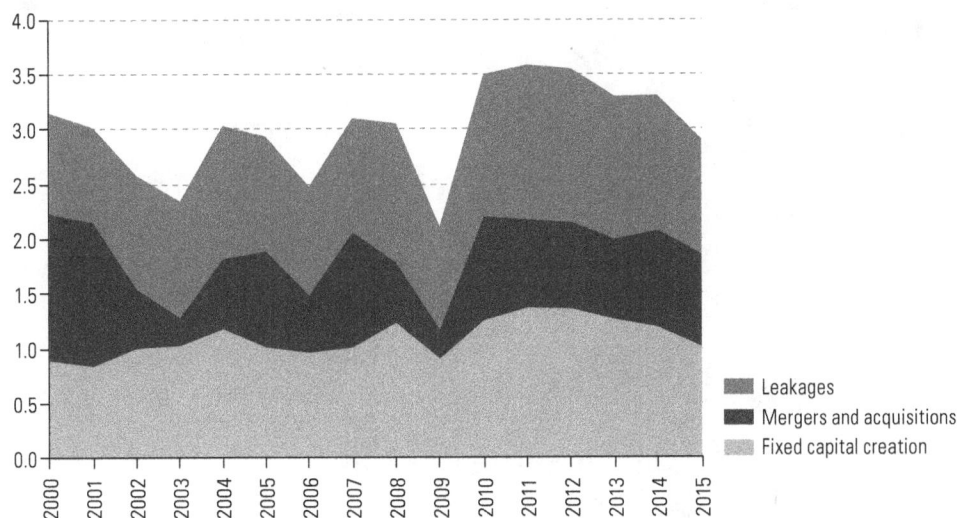

Figure III.2
Latin America and the Caribbean: estimated distribution of foreign direct investment (FDI) between fixed capital creation, mergers and acquisitions, and leakages, 2000-2015 *(Percentages of GDP)*

Source: Economic Commission for Latin America and the Caribbean (ECLAC).

A breakdown of gross fixed capital formation into non-FDI private investment, public investment and FDI shows that the capital created directly by FDI is a small proportion of the total. Non-FDI private capital formation is the largest component, and public investment also plays a significant role (see figure III.3).[4]

Between 2009 and 2013, the region's gross fixed capital formation averaged 21% of GDP per year, higher than in the European Union or the United States, and a similar rate to Africa. Rates in Asia and the Middle East were higher than in Latin America and the Caribbean (see figure III.4). The relationship between per capita GDP and the rate of fixed capital formation is not linear: both low- and high-income regions have low levels of gross fixed capital formation, albeit for different reasons. Whereas in the poorest regions income is insufficient to attain high levels of investment, in the developed regions, there is less need for investment in physical capital, owing to the greater emphasis on creating intangible capital. While not reflected in gross fixed capital formation, this second component is increasingly important, in forms such as investment in education or in technological research and development. Middle-income regions have higher rates of gross fixed capital formation.

---

[4]   In Latin America and the Caribbean, gross fixed capital formation varies greatly from one country to another. In 2014 for example, it ranged from 13% of GDP in Barbados to 30% in Saint Kitts and Nevis. The differences are greater between the smaller countries than between the medium-sized and large ones.

Figure III.3
Latin America and the Caribbean: distribution of the sources of fixed capital formation, 2000-2013
(Percentages of GDP)

FDI thus plays a minor role in gross fixed capital formation

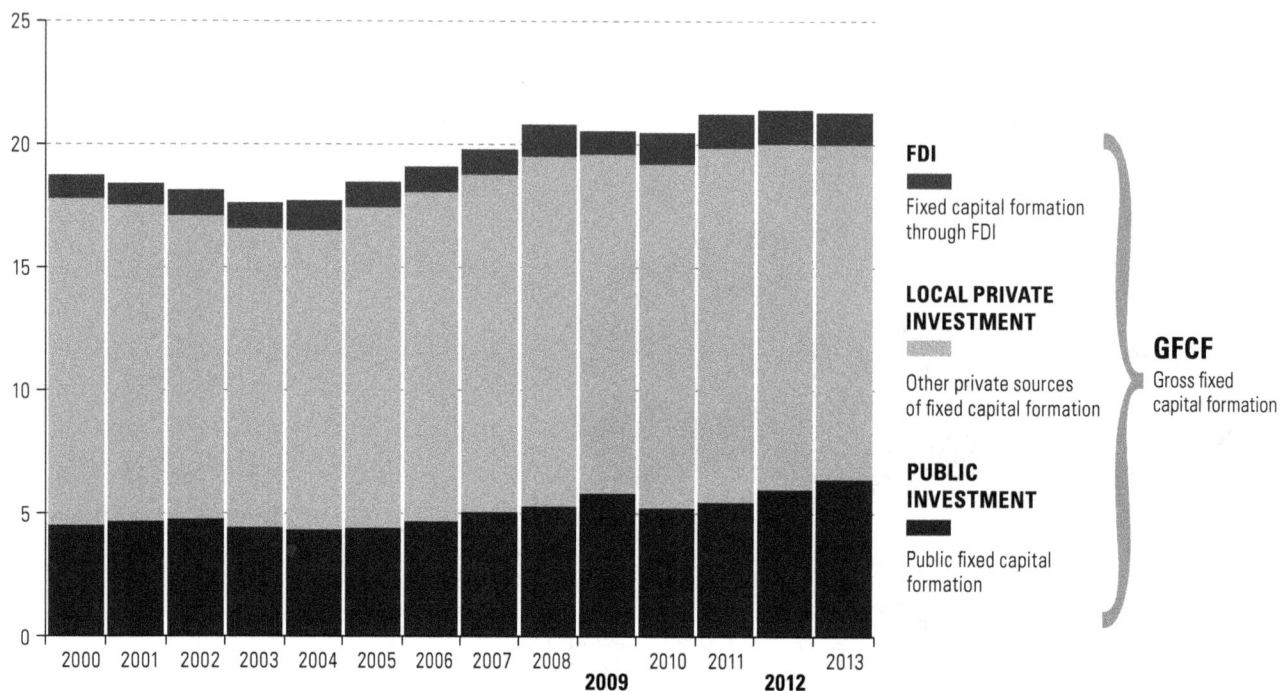

FDI
Fixed capital formation through FDI

LOCAL PRIVATE INVESTMENT
Other private sources of fixed capital formation

PUBLIC INVESTMENT
Public fixed capital formation

GFCF
Gross fixed capital formation

Source: Economic Commission for Latin America and the Caribbean (ECLAC), on the basis of ECLAC, *Economic Survey of Latin America and the Caribbean, 2015* (LC/G.2645-P), Santiago, 2015.
Note: Public investment includes investment by public administrations, and investment by non-financial public enterprises.

Figure III.4
Regions of the world: gross fixed capital formation, average 2009-2013
(Percentages of GDP)

Gross fixed capital formation in Latin America and the Caribbean is low in comparison with other world regions

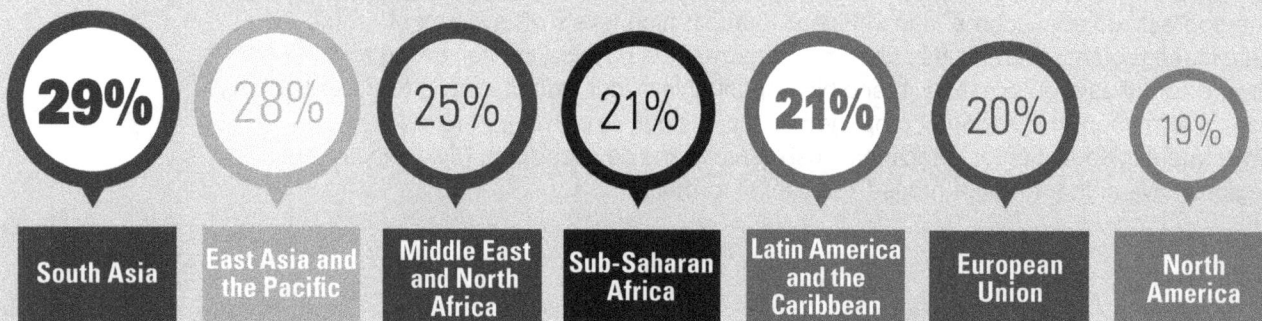

South Asia	East Asia and the Pacific	Middle East and North Africa	Sub-Saharan Africa	Latin America and the Caribbean	European Union	North America
29%	28%	25%	21%	21%	20%	19%

Source: Economic Commission for Latin America and the Caribbean (ECLAC), on the basis of World Bank, World Development Indicators, 2015 [online database] http://data.worldbank.org/data-catalog/world-development-indicators.
Note: The group averages are not weighted.

If one considers investment rates by country income level, countries outside the region display a concave relation (low- and high-income economies have similar rates of fixed capital formation), and upper-middle-income countries display the highest levels (see figure III.5). In Latin America and the Caribbean there is no relationship of that type: the highest rates of gross fixed capital formation correspond to the countries with the highest income levels. Investment levels in the region are below those of the rest of the world in all categories considered in figure III.5, especially in lower-middle and upper-middle-income countries.

Figure III.5
Latin America and the Caribbean and the rest of the world: average rate of gross fixed capital formation by country income group, average 2009-2013
(Percentages of GDP)

Gross fixed capital formation rates are lower for countries in all income brackets in the region than in the rest of the world

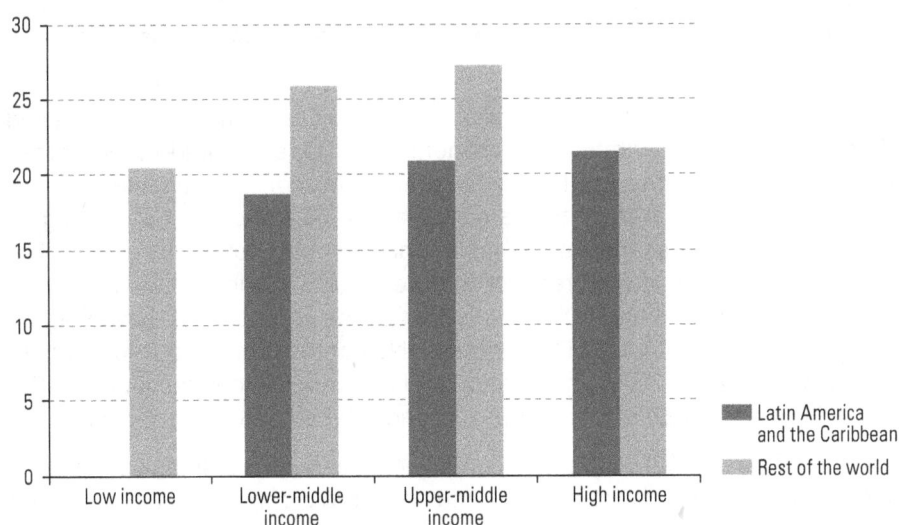

Latin America and the Caribbean

Rest of the world

Source: Economic Commission for Latin America and the Caribbean (ECLAC), on the basis of World Bank, World Development Indicators, 2015 [online database] http://data.worldbank.org/data-catalog/world-development-indicators.
Note: Income groups follow the World Bank classification. The Latin American and Caribbean region has one low-income country, six countries in the lower-middle income group, 17 in the upper-middle income group and 10 high-income countries. The group averages are not weighted. For the region's single low-income economy (Haiti), comparable data are not available.

B. Major shortage of intangible capital in the region

The developed economies of North America and Europe have lower rates of fixed capital formation than those of Latin America and the Caribbean, but productivity levels that are several times higher. The explanation for this can be found in the cumulative stock of physical capital per worker and in the accumulation of intangible capital.[5] At higher levels of development, the ratio between intangible capital and tangible or physical capital increases as economies become more knowledge-based.

An initial measure of intangible capital is investment in education and capacity-building. As the annual investment in this type of capital is hard to measure and it depreciates more slowly than physical capital, most research studies use a measure of the stock of education, frequently estimated by years of schooling among the

---

[5] Apart from its non-physical nature, the definition of intangible capital is hotly debated. This section focuses on human capital and innovation capital.

active population.[6] A second measure is innovation capital, defined as "the value of innovation-related assets that contribute to productivity growth in the economy" (McKinsey, 2013). This type of capital has three components: physical capital, knowledge and human capital.

Following the McKinsey methodology,[7] figure III.6 shows estimations of innovation capital for selected countries in Latin America and the Caribbean and in the Organization for Economic Cooperation and Development (OECD).[8] The highest levels of innovation capital worldwide are in the United States, Sweden and the United Kingdom. The average stock of innovation capital in the region is just 15% of GDP, compared with 34% in OECD countries.[9] In the region, Brazil and Chile have the largest stocks of innovation capital; the former owing to its high level of investment in research and development (R&D), among other elements; and the latter, owing to investments in higher education, which exceed the OECD average (OECD, 2014b). Central American countries have the smallest estimated stocks, particularly Guatemala and El Salvador.

The key factor explaining the low stock of innovation capital in Latin America and the Caribbean is the very low rate of investment in R&D (see figure III.7). Whereas in the OECD member States (excluding Chile and Mexico) that variable explains 39% of an innovation capital stock that is equivalent to 34.4% of GDP, in the region it contributes just 12% of an innovation capital that amounts to 15.2% of GDP. The region is also lagging behind with respect to patents (0% compared with 1%) and intellectual property expenditure (6% versus 7%). Some components, however, are greater in the region than in OECD countries: the contributions made by tertiary education (42% as against 25%), information and communications technology (ICT) infrastructure (27% versus 22%), and higher education abroad (7% compared with 1%).

> The key factor explaining the low stock of innovation capital in Latin America and the Caribbean is the very low rate of investment in R&D.

The paucity of R&D initiatives in the region reflects the relative shortage of research universities, lack of government support and the heavy concentration of private enterprises in low-technology sectors.

In some cases, however, major technological efforts are being made. Brazil, for example, is ranked third in public R&D expenditure on agriculture worldwide, accounting for 4% of the total, following China and India (13% and 7%, respectively). As a result, between 1970 and 2009 productivity in that sector grew by 176% (ahead of China's 136%) (Beintema and others, 2012).

---

[6]   According to this information, Guatemala has the lowest levels of schooling in the region, followed by Haiti and Honduras. At the other extreme, Chile has the highest levels, ahead of Argentina and Panama. The average for Latin American and Caribbean countries is 8 years of schooling, in contrast with 11 years in countries of the Organization for Economic Cooperation and Development (OECD) (excluding the Latin American members, Chile and Mexico).

[7]   Most of the indicators of these components can be calculated using the methods discussed in the debate on measuring intangibles (Corrado, Haltiwanger and Sichel, 2009; Corrado and others, 2012; Edquist, 2009), with some further improvements proposed by McKinsey.

[8]   The main problem in developing an indicator of innovation capital for Latin America and the Caribbean is the relative lack of information, since several of the indicators that were used in the McKinsey report are not available. This problem is overcome by using a comparative method to estimate the ranges of variation of the missing values for countries that do not have any data: by comparing data from countries that do have values with those that do not, it is possible to estimate lower and upper bounds for innovation capital (ECLAC, 2016).

[9]   The OECD averages are unweighted and exclude Chile, Ireland and Mexico. Ireland has a disproportionate level of innovation capital owing to the way it is calculated, since the total is boosted by intellectual property expenses that reflect that country's role in tax management schemes. The same is true to a lesser extent for Luxembourg and the Netherlands.

Figure III.6
Organization for Economic Cooperation and Development (OECD) and Latin America and the Caribbean
(selected countries): innovation capital, 2014
(*Percentages of GDP*)

Stocks of innovation capital are much lower in Latin America and the Caribbean than in the OECD member countries

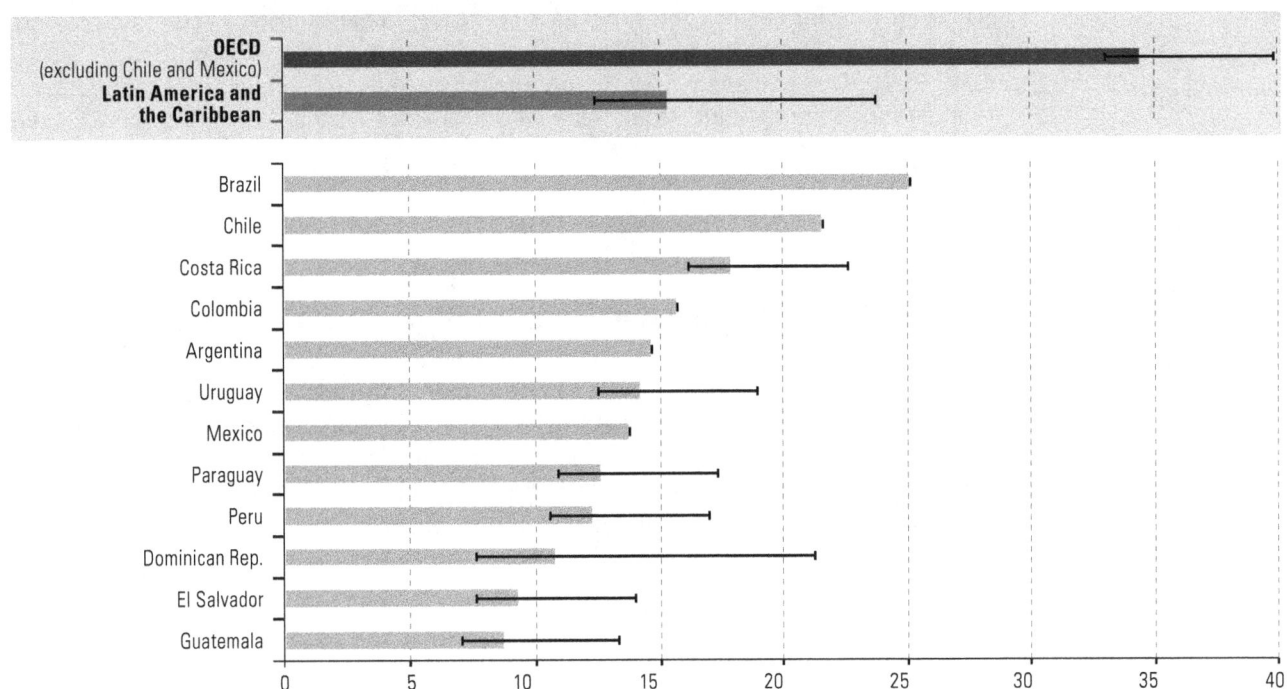

Source: Economic Commission for Latin America and the Caribbean (ECLAC), on the basis of ECLAC, "Innovation capital in Latin America: analyzing the region's competitive strengths in innovative capacity", unpublished, 2016.
Note: The averages for OECD, the Caribbean and the region as a whole are simple averages of all countries for which data are available. The thin lines indicate the lower and upper bounds of the estimation for countries for which information is incomplete.

Figure III.7
Organization for Economic Cooperation and Development (OECD) and Latin America and the Caribbean (selected countries):
distribution of the components of innovation capital, 2014
(*Percentages*)

In relative terms, OECD countries spend much more on research and development and less on tertiary education than Latin America and the Caribbean

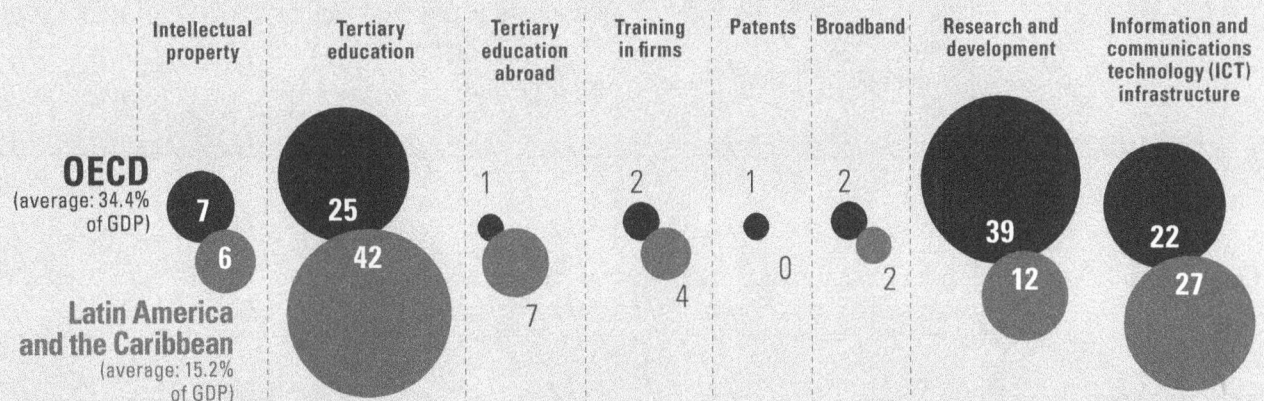

Source: Economic Commission for Latin America and the Caribbean (ECLAC), on the basis of ECLAC, "Innovation capital in Latin America: analyzing the region's competitive strengths in innovative capacity", unpublished, 2016.
Note: The figures for OECD do not include Chile or Mexico.

Altogether, the countries of the region have low levels of both physical and intangible capital. In developed economies, the production structure tends to be more intensive in intangible capital as they move towards more knowledge-intensive sectors. The different path followed by countries in the region has generally led to low levels of productivity. These low productivity levels are partly explained by the structural heterogeneity that manifests itself as very low productivity among the smaller firms. In OECD countries, the smallest enterprises have productivity levels between 60% and 75% of those of large firms, whereas in Latin America and the Caribbean, the equivalent ratio is only 20% to 35%, and the situation is even worse among microenterprises (OECD/ECLAC/CAF, 2014). One explanation for the poor results achieved by small firms in the region is their lack of integration into national or global value chains. In this context, FDI can make a difference.

C. Foreign direct investment for technology and international engagement

Although FDI makes only a small contribution to gross fixed capital formation, transnational enterprises can play an important role in economic development by helping to transform economies through the creation of intangible capital. The positive effects of FDI can be transmitted through technology transfer and skill development, while also encouraging local firms to enter value chains that increase their exposure to the international economy.

Transnational firms can help overcome the technological barriers to entry into new markets, particularly in the case of proprietary technology. For example, when the United States enterprise Intel invested in an assembly plant in Costa Rica, that country had no local ICT industry, and the company's arrival radically transformed the local economy. Although Intel announced a significant downsizing of its activities in the country in 2014, Costa Rica has kept its advanced ICT cluster.

From a broader perspective, it is useful to review the composition of announced FDI projects, according to their technological intensity.[10] On average, between 2003 and 2015, 43% of the value of those projects in the region corresponded to medium-high-technology activities, followed by 33% related to medium-low technology, and 20% corresponding to low technology, leaving just 5% for investments of high technological intensity (see figure III.8).

These proportions have changed over time. Although low- and high-technology projects have remained stable, the share of medium-low technology projects has declined from 50% to 15% over the same period, whereas medium-high technology projects have expanded from 30% to 60%. The reduced share of medium-low technology projects is explained by a slump in extractive projects.

---

[10]   There is no certainty that these project announcements will turn into real investments. Moreover, in some cases the amount is an estimate.

The technology intensity of announced new investments appears to be rising

Figure III.8
Latin America and the Caribbean: technology distribution of announced foreign direct investment (FDI) projects, 2003-2015
(Percentages)

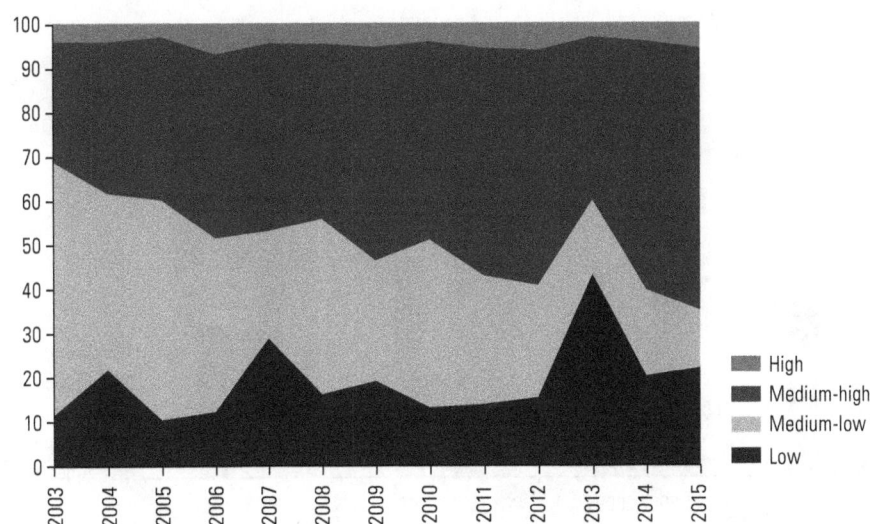

Legend: High, Medium-high, Medium-low, Low

Source: Economic Commission for Latin America and the Caribbean (ECLAC), on the basis of Financial Times, *fDi Markets*.

Medium-high technology activities also experienced major changes. The weight of manufacturing dropped from a peak of 89% in 2005 to 33% in 2013, before recovering slightly to 39% in 2015.[11] The most dynamic sectors were telecommunications, which doubled its share from 15% to 30%, and renewable energies, which grew from around 5% to 25%. In 2015, renewable energy accounted for 33% of the value of all medium-high technology projects. In that year, telecommunications represented 17% and the automotive industry just 6%. These figures reveal a radical change in the composition of announced projects, which has been unfolding for some time.

This change in the technological intensity of newly announced projects could strengthen the transformative impact of FDI inflows: they could have an effect on the technological intensity of all economic activity, especially in smaller countries and those with less diversified production structures. Figure III.9 shows the proportion of the value of announced projects of medium-high technology intensity for five of the region's countries in different periods. The importance of these projects increased in all the economies, except for Colombia. The most rapid change occurred in Chile, where the share rose from 13% in 2004-2006 to 71% in 2013-2015. That result was accentuated by the steep decline in mining projects, which are particularly important in that country.

In 2015, renewable energy accounted for 33% of the value of all medium-high technology projects.

[11]   Vehicle assembly plants account for between 15% and 20% of announced projects.

Figure III.9
Latin America (selected
countries): announced
investment projects of
medium-high technology,
2004-2015
(Percentages)

Announced investments in medium-high technology projects expand the most in Brazil and Chile

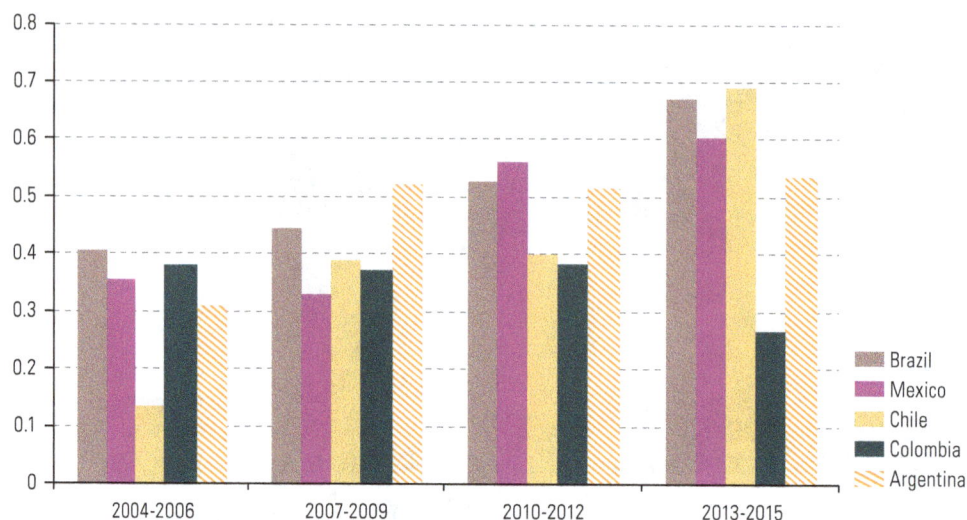

Source: Economic Commission for Latin America and the Caribbean (ECLAC), on the basis of Financial Times, *fDi Markets*.
Note: The figures refer to project announcements. The percentage is calculated on the basis of the (estimated) value of investment projects.

Mexico, followed by Brazil, is the main recipient of investments in high-technology projects, exceeding 10% of the total value in 2003-2015. Feedback effects tend to reinforce this concentration. First, FDI is directed towards places with local capacities; and, second, the fact that high-technology FDI has gone to a country in the past helps to build capacities and attract more of the same.

In the case of R&D investments, although project announcements have waned considerably over the last few years, the global share of Latin America and the Caribbean has increased slightly from 3.4% in 2003-2005 to 4.4% between 2013 and 2015. This is important because evidence from developed countries shows that transnationals invest proportionately less in R&D than domestic firms, because their subsidiaries can access advanced technologies through their parent companies, and they undertake activities that are more distant from R&D efforts (Un and Cuervo-Cazurra, 2008).

Foreign direct investment also has positive impacts on capacity accumulation in recipient countries, although the relationship between the two variables is complex and the direction of causation is debatable.[12] The Mexican city of Puebla, which exemplifies the importance of this relationship is a model of educational spillovers from activities undertaken by the German firm Volkswagen, particularly at its Audi assembly plant. This manufacturing centre uses some of the most advanced technologies available in the market; and, to use them effectively, it created a large-scale training centre where both Audi employees and local suppliers receive training to enable them to work with this technology. This means that it is not only the employees of the firm who benefit from the training, but also the suppliers, who are very numerous in this case. Nonetheless, the effect does not necessarily have to be positive. For example, Rojo, Tumini and Yoguel (2011) report that transnational firms in Argentina tend to absorb available capacities to the detriment of local firms; in other words there is a negative spillover.

---

[12]   Noorbakhsh, Paloni and Youssef (2001) show that an improvement in human capital attracts FDI; Blomstrom and Kokko (2003) analyse the effect of FDI flows on human capital accumulation.

When local workers take on management responsibilities, local management capacity grows. In the case of the hotel sector in the Caribbean, the top executives tend to be recruited internationally and assigned there directly by the company. Nonetheless, below that level, and in certain specialized posts, local workers have the opportunity to develop new management skills in a professional environment.

Local firms can imitate or copy some of the best practices of transnationals (Gorg and Greenaway, 2003). Business process outsourcing (BPO) activities in Barbados are one example where foreign firms have helped to modernize the sector. Similarly, the Government of Belize is seeking to move local firms from BPO to knowledge process outsourcing (KPO), by engaging a foreign firm.

Other than Mexico, the region's countries have weak participation in global value chains, and the region displays little productive integration (ECLAC, 2015b). The proportion of foreign value added contained in a country's gross exports is a measure of its upstream participation, whereas the proportion of domestic value added incorporated in third-party exports represents a measure of downstream participation (Bohn and others, 2015). Figure III.10 shows that participation in global value chains by six Latin American countries was less than that of Asia in 2011, (41% compared with 52%). This is explained by a less intensive use of imported inputs in Latin American exports, in other words fewer backward linkages. Excluding Mexico, the region's global participation index is below 38%.

The participation of the region's countries in global value chains is weak

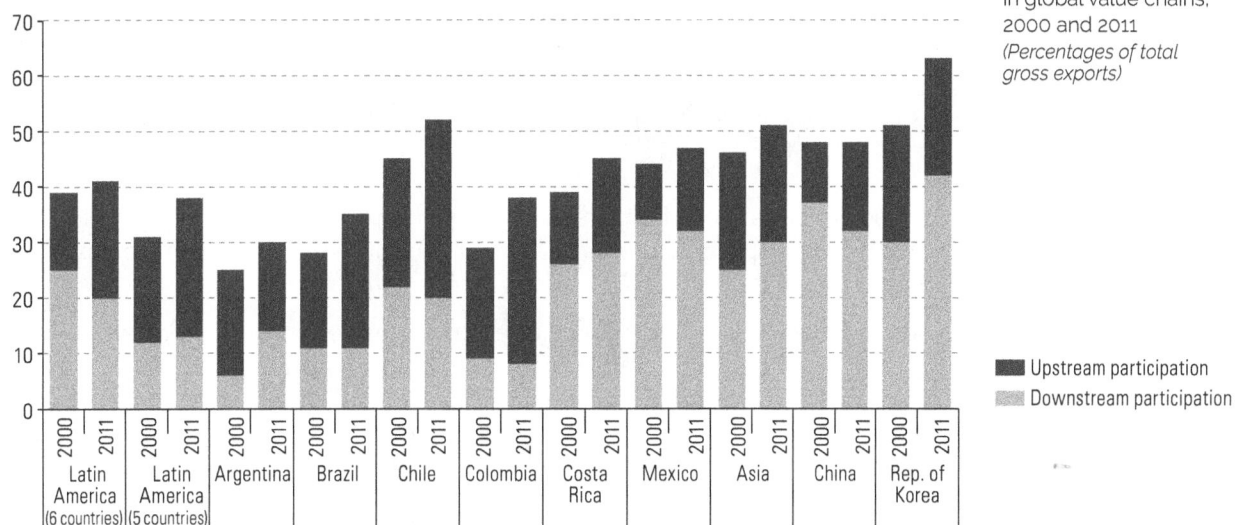

Figure III.10
Selected countries and regions: upstream and downstream participation in global value chains, 2000 and 2011
(Percentages of total gross exports)

Upstream participation
Downstream participation

Source: Economic Commission for Latin America and the Caribbean (ECLAC), on the basis of Organization for Economic Cooperation and Development (OECD)/World Trade Organization (WTO), Trade in Value-Added Database (TiVA).
Note: Latin America (6 countries) corresponds to the aggregate of Argentina, Brazil, Chile, Colombia, Costa Rica and Mexico; Latin America (5 countries) excludes Mexico.

From the standpoint of international connectivity in goods, services, people, finance and data, the region is also poorly connected with the rest of the world; and this entails certain risks in an increasingly integrated global economy, where international networks favour knowledge dissemination and productivity growth. Compared with the world's best connected countries (United States, the Netherlands and Singapore), Latin American and Caribbean countries are lagging far behind. Mexico is the highest ranked (twenty-first), with Brazil (forty-fourth) and Chile (forty-fifth) far behind (see figure III.11).

Figure III.11
Latin America and the Caribbean (24 countries): McKinsey Global Institute (MGI) Connectedness Index, 2016
(Ranking among 139 countries)

The region's economies are not well connected with the rest of the world

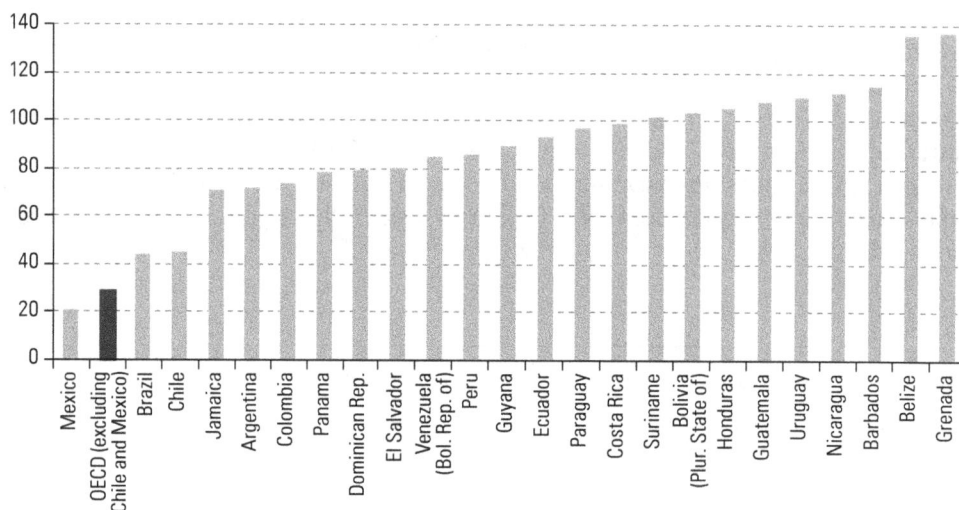

Source: Economic Commission for Latin America and the Caribbean (ECLAC), on the basis of McKinsey & Company, "Digital Globalization: The New Era of Global Flows", 2016 [online] http://www.mckinsey.com/business-functions/mckinsey-digital/our-insights/digital-globalization-the-new-era-of-global-flows.

Attracting investment from transnationals integrated in global value chains can stimulate local suppliers into improving their capacities and joining those chains as autonomous agents.

A major debate is unfolding in the region on the relationship between FDI and participation in international trade (Zhang, 2001; Bengoa and Sánchez-Robles, 2003; Cuadros, Orts and Alguacil, 2004). The conclusions suggest the existence of a strong two-way relation: integration increases FDI flows and these in turn increase trade possibilities. For economies to be able to benefit from their membership of a value chain it is crucial to develop local capacities (Cimoli, Dosi and Stiglitz, 2009). Those capacities mean being able to deliver a given level of quantity and quality, stemming from the economy's sectoral specialization. The lack of those capacities substantially reduces the chances of benefiting from integration. If local firms are unable to meet the demands of transnationals, they will not be able to integrate fully into their chains and the benefits will be reduced.

D. Intangible capital accumulation through foreign direct investment

The above provides a basis for relaunching the debate on how to measure and evaluate the benefits of FDI in the receiving country. An initial approach focuses on issues associated with external financing, from a balance of payments standpoint, and macroeconomic variables such as gross fixed capital formation, exports and employment. This view adopts an aggregate approach and tends to evaluate FDI inflows by size ("the bigger the better").

An alternative or complementary view seeks to evaluate the microeconomic aspects of FDI, which stem from the operations of foreign firms in the host country. In this case, the focus on FDI is replaced by a focus on the activities of transnational enterprises. Here the key concern is their contribution to the local economy in areas such as the emergence of new activities that extend or deepen industrialization, access, transfer and assimilation of technologies, establishment and deepening of production linkages, human resources training and local business development. All of these elements contribute directly to the formation of intangible capital in an economy.

Although there is consensus on the potential benefits of FDI, the difference between the two approaches is how these are actually obtained. Under the first approach, the benefits arise in the form of spillovers from the foreign firms in the local economy, which occur automatically once a certain level of investment has been achieved. The more modern view, shared by ECLAC,[13] is that, although FDI is likely to have positive effects in host countries, they are by no means automatic. It therefore needs to be shown —and not just assumed— that they are positive. A direct implication is that FDI policy should focus less on attaining a critical mass of investments and more on ensuring that these are aligned with the country's productive development objectives. The focus of attention should thus be on FDI quality.

1. Proactive and integrated policies

The different policy approaches that countries can adopt for attracting FDI are distinguished by the degree of government intervention and proactiveness and the degree of integration with other economic development policies. Governments have two main alternatives for attracting FDI.

The first consists of passive policies, which, despite not reflecting a lack of interest in FDI or being synonymous with low investment flows, imply an absence of specific attraction policies. In general, the authorities consider that the comparative advantages or macroeconomic conditions are sufficient, and they see no need to intervene in the process. At most, they confine themselves to defining a legal framework with administrative procedures that regulate FDI, without intervening in firms' decision-making processes. This strategy could suffice to attract investment by firms targeting a country's intrinsic advantages, in other words, market potential or the opportunity to exploit natural resources. This type of policy is not necessarily integrated with productive development policy, and its success is measured essentially by the magnitude of the investment flows. Nonetheless, the global trend is to move towards increasingly sophisticated frameworks, in which it is not only flow size that is important but also the type of investment: in other words, quality investments that contribute to, and are consistent with, the country's development goals.

---

[13]   See ECLAC (2004, chapter I; 2006, chapter II) and Gligo (2007).

When FDI attraction policies are coordinated and integrated with other development policies, the conditions that make a country attractive to investors are enhanced, and the benefits of FDI can be exploited to the full.

The second alternative consists of active policies that recognize the importance of FDI in economic development. In general these entail the creation of a specialized department or agency responsible for promoting the country and engaging with potential investors, with the possibility of establishing incentives. It is also recognized that not all investments are the same, and governments seek those that contribute to national development. In this stage, governments focus on investment projects to enhance efficiency in the production of export-oriented goods and services, so competition between countries is more intense.

When FDI attraction policies are coordinated and integrated with other development policies, the conditions that make a country attractive to investors are enhanced, and the benefits of FDI can be exploited to the full. These integrated policies help the country to achieve its previously defined goals.

Countries that are most successful in attracting FDI and harnessing its benefits are those that have adopted more active and targeted policies (UNCTAD, 2004 and 2005). Where the country's policy objectives coincide with the interests of transnational firms, a virtuous circle can be generated to the benefit of both parties. A maturity path can be traced for FDI policy which, as it becomes more proactive and integrated with other development policies, has a better chance of capturing and harnessing its benefits (see diagram III.1).

Diagram III.1
Foreign direct investment (FDI) policy: maturity and likelihood of success, by proactiveness and integration

The likelihood of capturing FDI benefits increases with more active and integrated policies

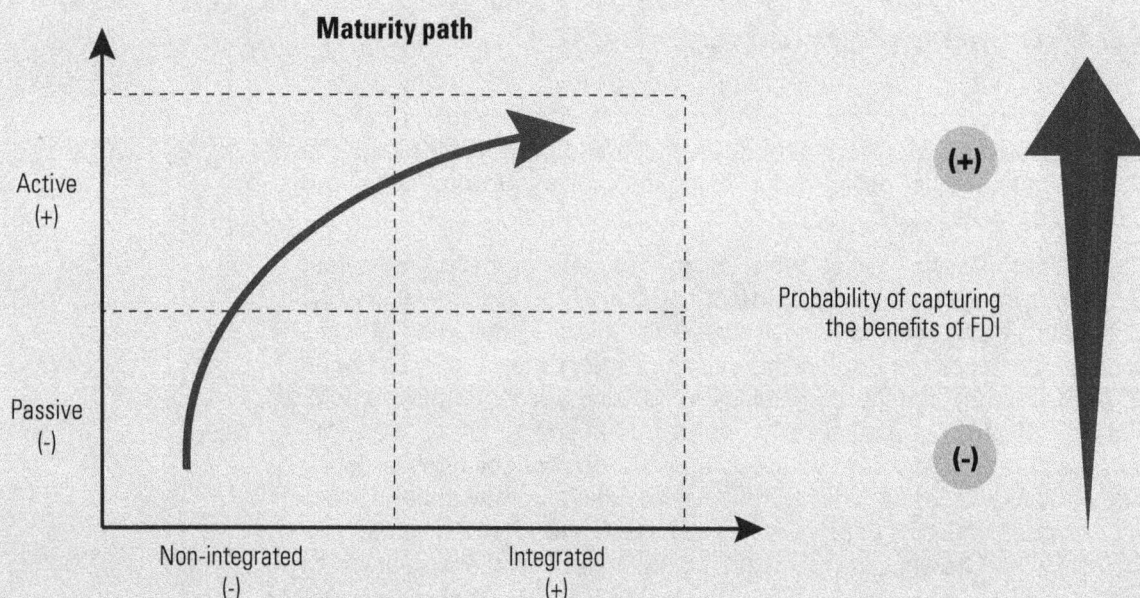

Source: Economic Commission for Latin America and the Caribbean (ECLAC).

2. Horizontal policies: necessary but not sufficient

Policymakers generally agree on the importance of having a pro-investment business climate, which helps not only to attract FDI but also to boost national investment. The investment climate is a combination of the ease of doing business, efforts to attract investment and the costs and benefits associated with business activity. In this connection, policies have often focused on reducing the tax burden for investors, which, although important, is not a decisive factor.

In relation to the business climate, many of the region's countries have a low position in rankings such as the Doing Business Index published by the World Bank. The highest rated countries are Mexico, Chile and Peru, of which only Mexico is in the world's top 40, ranked at number 39. Furthermore, the index shows that only a few countries have improved their relative position in recent years —Costa Rica, El Salvador, Jamaica and Mexico being among them (see figure III.12). World Bank (2013) argues that a 1 percentage point improvement in the Doing Business Index is associated with an increase in FDI of between US$ 250 million and US$ 500 million, without establishing causality.

Figure III.12
Latin America and the Caribbean (32 countries): Doing Business Index, 2016
(Ranking of 189 countries and territories)

Few countries in the Latin America and the Caribbean are known
as good places to do business and the situation is worsening

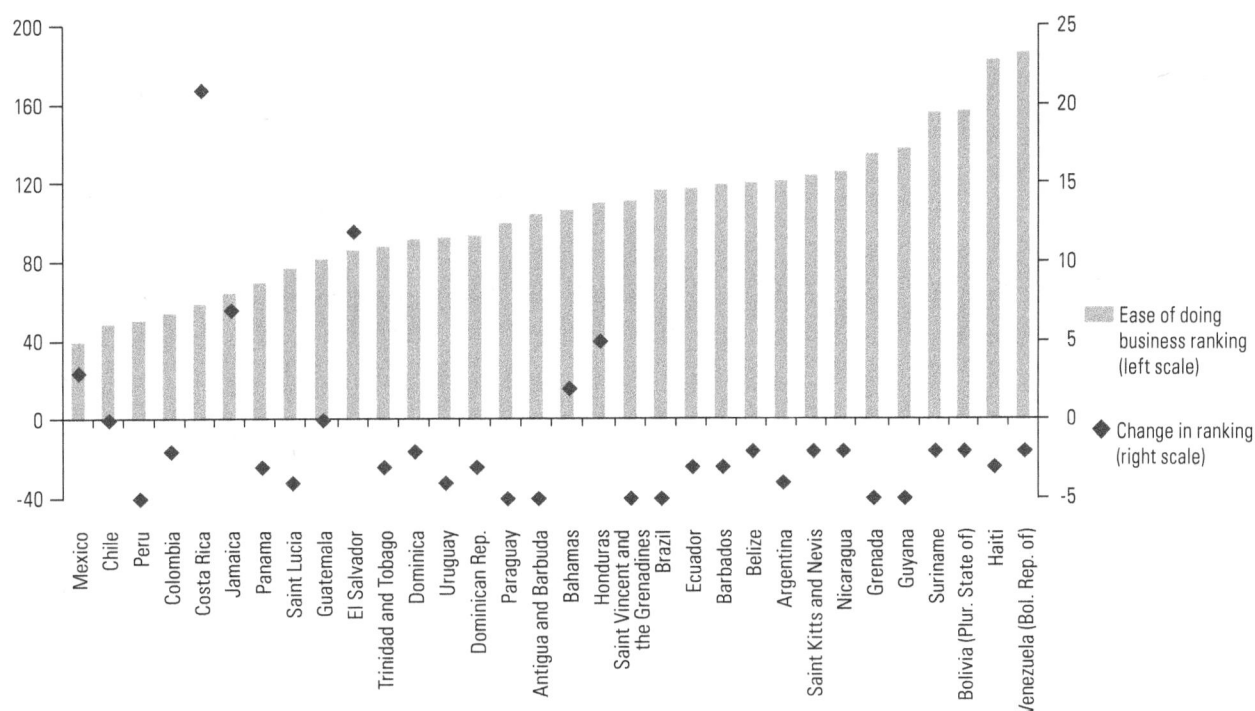

Source: Economic Commission for Latin America and the Caribbean (ECLAC), on the basis of World Bank, *Doing Business 2015: Going Beyond Efficiency*, Washington, D.C., 2014.
Note: The World Bank ranks 189 countries and territories. A change in ranking is measured as the difference between the ranking in 2015 and 2016.

Improving the business climate is an important area of public policies and their implementation by investment promotion agencies, which play a key role in reducing information asymmetries and aligning potential investors with business opportunities in the host country. The degree to which investment promotion agencies can fulfil this function depends largely on national legislation and the financial and human resources available to them. The regional experience provides various lessons. First, they need to be consolidated as a one-stop facility where investors can obtain all information and undertake the corresponding procedures. Second, investment promotion agencies are more effective when they coordinate efforts to promote exports and investments. Third, institutional autonomy and the political support they receive are crucial to their effectiveness. Lastly, it is more efficient to work with international and local investors in areas where they face similar problems, such as developing and integrating into global value chains.

In countries where investment promotion policies are not transparent in terms of the incentives offered, increasing information on norms and practices will reduce subjectivity in granting the incentives, and thus strengthen their legitimacy.

3.   Selectivity and mechanisms for transferring benefits

Diagram III.2
Two spheres of action for capturing and transferring the benefits of foreign direct investment (FDI)

Proactiveness is important in two spheres, at different points in the investment process (see diagram III.2): to capture and transfer the potential benefits of FDI. The first is the targeted promotion of projects at the evaluation stage for potential investors. The second, in the implementation and operation phase of the investments, seeks to generate mechanisms that enable those investments to integrate more effectively in the local economy.

Selective interventions should be made at the initial phase of the investment cycle in order to generate stronger links with the local economy at later stages

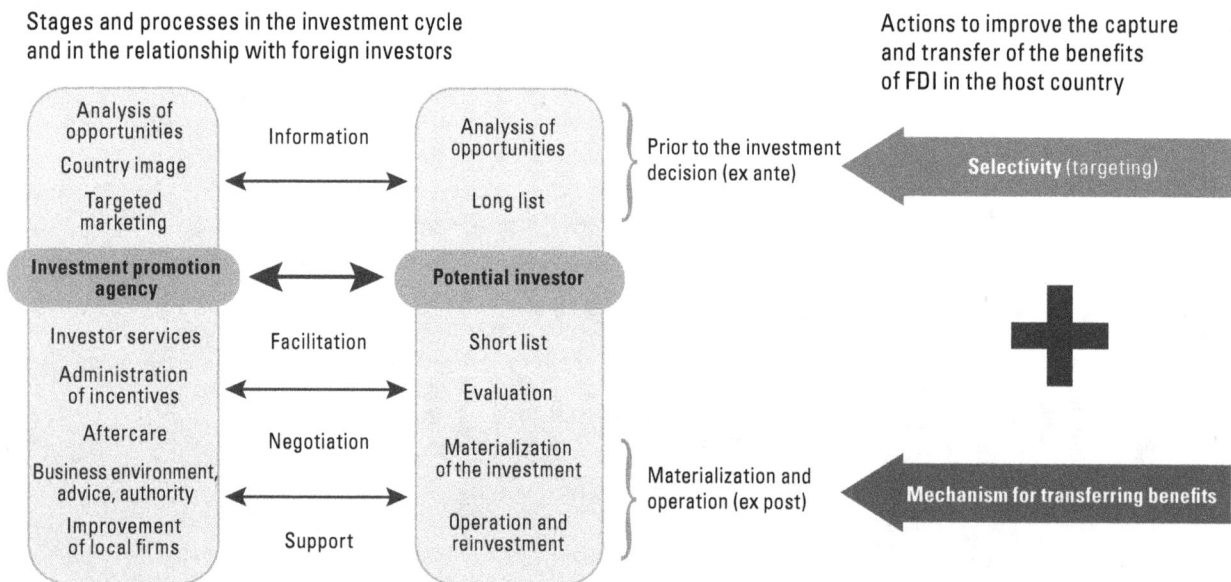

Stages and processes in the investment cycle and in the relationship with foreign investors

Actions to improve the capture and transfer of the benefits of FDI in the host country

Analysis of opportunities
Country image
Targeted marketing

Information

Analysis of opportunities
Long list

Prior to the investment decision (ex ante)

Selectivity (targeting)

Investment promotion agency

Potential investor

Investor services
Administration of incentives
Aftercare
Business environment, advice, authority
Improvement of local firms

Facilitation
Negotiation
Support

Short list
Evaluation
Materialization of the investment
Operation and reinvestment

Materialization and operation (ex post)

Mechanism for transferring benefits

Source: Economic Commission for Latin America and the Caribbean (ECLAC).

The rationale of selectivity is simple. As investments are not all the same, attracting higher quality investments that are consistent with the country's development goals would, in principle, generate greater benefits, as well as being an efficient way to use promotion resources.

Selectivity and targeting are interchangeable terms. They refer to the decision that a country or an investment promotion agency adopts to prioritize or prefer one type of investment over another, according to a specific criterion, to then adopt measures that make it possible to capture the corresponding projects. Targeting, which can use different strategies (see diagram III.3), arises from the confluence of three factors: development policy goals, the country's advantages and investors' requirements.

Diagram III.3
Targeting strategies

The likelihood of attracting investment increases when policy goals, the country's advantages and investors' requirements are aligned

Relationship between advantages, needs and objectives

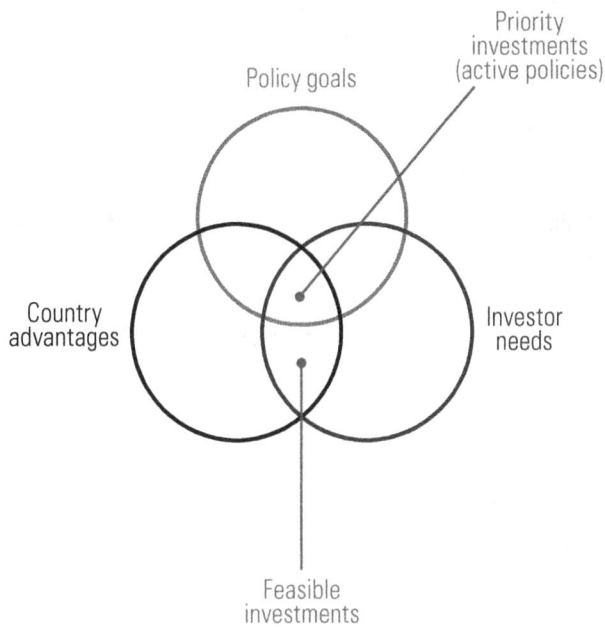

Examples of targeting

Targeting strategy	Examples
By sector	Information technologies, automotive, biotechnology, agribusiness, tourism and others.
By function	Manufacturing, logistics, commercial, research and development, back office and others.
By type of project	Large-scale investment, job creator, technology intensive, export and others.
By type of firm	Fortune 500, well-known brand, successful firms and others.
By geographical zone	Latin America, neighbouring countries, United States, Asia, Japan, Europe and others.

Source: Economic Commission for Latin America and the Caribbean (ECLAC), on the basis of N. Gligo, "Políticas activas para atraer inversión extranjera directa en América Latina y el Caribe", *Desarrollo Productivo series*, No. 175 (LC/L.2667-P), Santiago, ECLAC, 2007.

The intersection of country advantages and investor requirements gives rise to viable projects; but if these do not coincide with the country's policy objectives, there is no reason to implement active policies to attract them. Similarly, policy objectives may not resonate with enterprise requirements, particularly when the country does not have advantages that make it attractive for those investment projects.

Costa Rica's medical instruments export industry, developed almost entirely by foreign firms, is its main non-traditional export sector. This has been one of the three priority sectors defined by the Costa Rican Investment Promotion Agency (CINDE). Beyond this strategic definition, a targeted promotion effort was made to attract a very specific type of firm. CINDE identified that an obstacle for scaling-up towards more sophisticated exports was the lack of sterilization services in the country. Once this problem had been identified, a search was made for international firms to persuade them to set up in the country. This effort bore fruit, firstly with the installation of BeamOne (electron beam sterilization) in 2008, and then with the arrival of Sterigenics International (with ethylene oxide) in 2013, which made it possible for new medical instrument firms to set up business by being able to use those services.

Costa Rica's targeting on the medical instruments industry —and also on business services and microelectronics— stemmed from the advantages revealed by the installation in the country of global firms such as Baxter, Procter & Gamble (shared services) and Intel. In contrast, efforts in Chile to develop the global services cluster sought to diversify the production matrix and analyse its potential advantages. Accordingly, a targeted promotion strategy was defined along with an integrated support programme that included financial incentives and tools to close human resource gaps. This programme was implemented by the Chilean Economic Development Agency (CORFO) between 2000 and 2010. In 2011, the US$ 1 billion export target was surpassed, making the country a major player in terms of investments in global services.

The entry of transnational firms can transform existing industries by increasing competition from new operators or through technological updating. An example in the region is investment in telecommunications, a market in which the entry of foreign competitors with technological advantages enhanced the quality of services and increased competition, with subsequent reductions in charges on voice and data communications.

Acting on a targeted basis requires the development of certain institutional capacities:

- Definition of policy goals: the ideal situation is the existence of a formal and explicit development policy, which can be coordinated with the FDI attraction policy and help to define objectives.

- Identification of the country's advantages: this strategic analysis task should be undertaken by a permanent team with sectoral experience and international connections.

- Knowledge of firms' needs: there should be a fluid relationship with potential investors and those already established in the country, and the capacities needed to evaluate the projects technically.

Although selectivity aims to find and attract investments aligned with specific objectives, it does not resolve the problem of transferring the potential benefits, either from the selected firms or from the remainder of FDI. To achieve that, measures such as improving the capacities and competitiveness of local firms can be adopted, to ensure that their production meets the quality standards and offers the prices needed for foreign firms to become their suppliers. Programmes to create links between local and foreign firms are also needed.

In Costa Rica, for example, a programme has been implemented, which, despite limited scope in terms of the amounts involved, has had positive results in terms of its growth. It originated in the Local Industry Development and Improvement Programme (MIL), promoted by CINDE in the 1990s, and the Programme to Foster Entrepreneurial Linkages (PROFOVE) run by Costa Rica's Foreign Trade Corporation (PROCOMER). It focuses on identifying production processes among firms operating in free zones that offer business opportunities to Costa Rican enterprises (Martínez and Padilla, 2016).

In 2001-2013, export linkages encompassed a total of 1,682 businesses with a value of US$ 69.9 million (see figure III.13). The figures for 2015 show that the linkages in terms of initial purchase orders totalled US$ 9.3 million to October.[14]

Figure III.13
Costa Rica: value of linkages for export, 2001-2014
(Millions of dollars)

The export linkages programme in Costa Rica has shown positive results

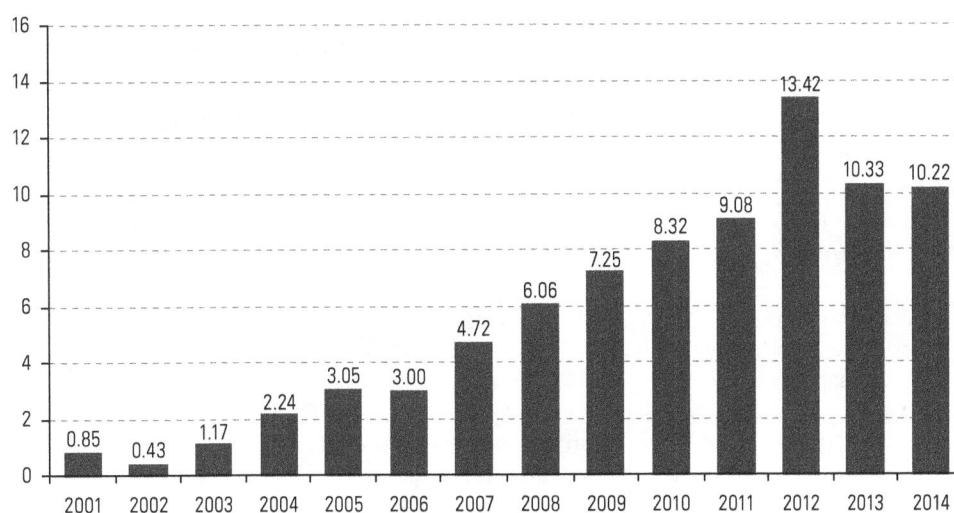

Source: Economic Commission for Latin America and the Caribbean (ECLAC), on the basis of J. M. Martínez and R. Padilla, "Política industrial en Costa Rica", 2016, unpublished.

Costa Rica's experience shows that making the most of the externalities generated by the actions of foreign firms involves three lines of action (CEE, 2014): (i) adopting an institutional framework that articulates and strengthens actors at the strategic, political, technical and executive levels, thereby ensuring smooth implementation of priority strategies in terms of production linkages; (ii) creating a national supplier development programme that combines existing initiatives and new programmes —accessible to linked firms and those seeking to form linkages— in areas where there are gaps; and (iii) setting up an intensive programme to promote suppliers for entrepreneurs and firms that have shown capacity to grow and internationalize rapidly, generating high-quality jobs.

[14] In the last five years, national purchases of goods and services (tradable and non-tradable goods) by firms operating under the tax-free regime grew at an annual average rate of 16%. In 2014, those purchases amounted to US$ 1.573 billion (PROCOMER, 2015).

E.   Conclusions

The quantitative analysis made in the first part of this chapter strengthens the ECLAC argument that the amount of FDI flows is a limited measurement of its potential benefit in the receiving country. The benefits cannot be taken for granted through spillover effects, nor do aggregate statistics adequately reflect certain characteristics of FDI. One third of FDI is directly targeted on gross fixed capital formation; another third on the acquisition of local firms; and the last third on displacing investments and expenditure that would have been undertaken anyway.

This scenario again highlights the need to focus on the quality of FDI, particularly its capacity to contribute to the formation of intangible capital in the local economy. There is consensus on the potential benefits of FDI, but harnessing them is not an automatic process. The transfer and absorption of FDI benefits depends on the characteristics of the investment and the specific features of the recipient country.

The possibility of harnessing these benefits depends on the skill level of the labour force, the competitiveness of the local industry and its capacity to supply foreign firms, and the existence of an associated cluster. Host countries must meet the challenge of capturing these benefits because, in the absence of the necessary conditions, foreign firms could become enclaves within those countries, and only a fraction of their benefits will be transferred to local economies.

Bibliography

Beintema, N. and others (2012), "ASTI global assessment of agricultural R&D spending" [online] http://www19.iadb.org/intal/intalcdi/PE/2013/10811.pdf.

Bengoa, M. and B. Sanchez-Robles (2003), "Foreign direct investment, economic freedom and growth: new evidence from Latin America", *European Journal of Political Economy*, vol. 19, No. 3.

Blomstrom, M. and A. Kokko (2003), "Human capital and inward FDI", *CEPR Working Paper*, No. 167.

Bohn, T. and others (2015), "Integration into global value chains: a guide to data sources and indicators", *OECD Trade Policy Papers*, in press.

CEE (Comisión Interinstitucional de Encadenamientos para la Exportación) (2014), "Propuesta de políticas públicas para el fomento de encadenamientos en Costa Rica", San Jose, unpublished.

Cimoli, M., G. Dosi and J. Stiglitz (2009), *Industrial Policy and Development: The Political Economy of Capabilities Accumulation*, Oxford University.

Corrado, C., J. Haltiwanger and D. Sichel (2009), *Measuring Capital in the New Economy*, University of Chicago Press.

Corrado, C. and others (2012), "Intangible capital and growth in advanced economies: measurement methods and comparative results", *IZA Discussion Paper*, No. 6733 [online] ftp://repec.iza.org/RePEc/Discussionpaper/dp6733.pdf.

Cuadros, A., V. Orts and M. Alguacil (2004), "Openness and growth: re-examining foreign direct investment, trade and output linkages in Latin America", *The Journal of Development Studies*, vol. 40, No. 4.

ECLAC (Economic Commission for Latin America and the Caribbean) (2016), "Innovation capital in Latin America: analyzing the region's competitive strengths in innovative capacity", unpublished.

___(2015a), *Economic Survey of Latin America and the Caribbean, 2015* (LC/G.2645-P), Santiago.

___(2015b), *Latin America and the Caribbean in the World Economy, 2015. The regional trade crisis: assessment and outlook* (LC/G.2650-P), Santiago.

___(2007), *Foreign Direct Investment in Latin America and the Caribbean, 2006* (LC/G.2336-P), Santiago.

___(2006), *Foreign Direct Investment in Latin America and the Caribbean, 2005* (LC/G.2309-P), Santiago.

___(2004), *Foreign Direct Investment in Latin America and the Caribbean, 2003* (LC/G.2226-P), Santiago.

Edquist, H. (2009), "How much does Sweden invest in intangible assets?", *IFN Working Paper*, No. 785 [online] http://papers.ssrn.com/sol3/papers.cfm?abstract_id=1536544.

Gligo, N. (2007), "Políticas activas para atraer inversión extranjera directa en América Latina y el Caribe", *Desarrollo Productivo series*, No. 175 (LC/L.2667-P), Santiago, Economic Commission for Latin America and the Caribbean (ECLAC).

Gorg, H. and D. Greenaway (2003), "Much ado about nothing? Do domestic firms really benefit from foreign direct investment?", *IZA Discussion Paper*, No. 944 [online] http://papers.ssrn.com/sol3/papers.cfm?abstract_id=475044.

Harrison, A.E. and M.S. McMillan (2003), "Does direct foreign investment affect domestic credit constraints?", *Journal of International Economics*, vol. 61, No. 1.

Lautier, M. and F. Moreaub (2012), "Domestic investment and FDI in developing countries: the missing link", *Journal of Economic Development*, vol. 37, No. 3.

Marin, D. and M. Schnitzer (2011), "When is FDI a capital flow?", *European Economic Review*, vol. 55, No. 6.

Martínez, J.M., and R. Padilla (2016), "Política industrial en Costa Rica", unpublished.

McKinsey & Company (2016), "Digital Globalization: The New Era of Global Flows" [online] http://www.mckinsey.com/business-functions/mckinsey-digital/our-insights/digital-globalization-the-new-era-of-global-flows.

___(2013), *Innovation Matters: Reviving the Growth Engine*.

Noorbakhsh, F., A. Paloni and A. Youssef (2001), "Human capital and FDI inflows to developing countries: new empirical evidence", *World Development*, vol. 29, No. 9.

OECD (Organization for Economic Cooperation and Development) (2014a), "FDI in Figures. April 2014", Paris [online] http://www.oecd.org/daf/inv/FDI-in-Figures-April-2014.pdf.

___(2014b), "Chile", *Education at a Glance, 2014* [online] http://www.oecd.org/education/Chile-EAG2014-Country-Note.pdf.

OECD/ECLAC/CAF (Organization for Economic Cooperation and Development/Economic Commission for Latin America and the Caribbean/Development Bank of Latin America) (2014), *Latin American Economic Outlook 2015. Education, Skills and Innovation for Development* (LC/G.2627), Santiago.

OECD/ECLAC/CIAT/IDB (Organization for Economic Cooperation and Development /Economic Commission for Latin America and the Caribbean/Inter-American Center of Tax Administrations/Inter-American Development Bank) (2016), *Revenue Statistics in Latin America and the Caribbean 1990-2014*, Paris [online] http://www.oecd-ilibrary.org/taxation/revenue-statistics-in-latin-america-and-the-caribbean-2016_rev_lat_car-2016-en-fr?mlang=fr.

PROCOMER (Foreign Trade Corporation of Costa Rica) (2015), *Balance de zonas francas: beneficio neto del régimen para Costa Rica 2010-2014*, San José.

PwC/World Bank (2016), *Paying Taxes 2016* [online] http://www.doingbusiness.org/~/media/GIAWB/Doing%20Business/Documents/Special-Reports/Paying-Taxes-2016.pdf.

Rojo, S., L. Tumini and G. Yoguel (2011), "La evolución del empleo en las empresas multinacionales en la Argentina. Desarmando mitos a través de nuevas evidencias", *Multinacionales en la Argentina. Estrategias de empleo, relaciones laborales y cadenas de valor*, M. Novick, H. Palomino and S. Gurrera (eds), Buenos Aires, United Nations Development Programme (PNUD).

Un, C.A. and A. Cuervo-Cazurra (2008), "Do subsidiaries of foreign MNEs invest more in R&D than domestic firms?", *Research Policy*, vol. 37, No. 10.

UNCTAD (United Nations Conference on Trade and Development) (2015), "Cross-Border M&A Database" [online] http://unctad.org/Sections/dite_dir/docs/WIR2015/WIR15_tab09.xls

___(2005), *World Investment Report 2005. Transnational Corporations and the Internationalization of R&D* (UNCTAD/WIR/2005), Geneva.

___(2004), *World Investment Report, 2004. The Shift towards Services* (UNCTAD/WIR/2004), Geneva.

World Bank (2015), World Development Indicators [online database] http://data.worldbank.org/data-catalog/world-development-indicators.

___(2013), *Doing Business 2013: Smarter Regulations for Small and Medium-Size Enterprises*, Washington, D.C. [online] http://www.doingbusiness.org/~/media/GIAWB/Doing%20Business/Documents/Annual-Reports/English/DB13-full-report.pdf.

Zhang, K.H. (2001), "Does foreign direct investment promote economic growth? Evidence from East Asia and Latin America", *Contemporary Economic Policy*, vol. 19, No. 2.

Publicaciones recientes de la CEPAL
ECLAC recent publications

www.cepal.org/publicaciones

Informes periódicos / *Annual reports*

También disponibles para años anteriores / *Issues for previous years also available*

- Estudio Económico de América Latina y el Caribe 2015, 204 p.
  Economic Survey of Latin America and the Caribbean 2015, 196 p.

- La Inversión Extranjera Directa en América Latina y el Caribe 2015, 150 p.
  Foreign Direct Investment in Latin America and the Caribbean 2015, 140 p.

- Anuario Estadístico de América Latina y el Caribe 2015 / *Statistical Yearbook for Latin America and the Caribbean 2015, 235 p.*

- Balance Preliminar de las Economías de América Latina y el Caribe 2015, 104 p.
  Preliminary Overview of the Economies of Latin America and the Caribbean 2015, 98 p.

- Panorama Social de América Latina 2015. Documento informativo, 68 p.
  Social Panorama of Latin America 2015. Briefing paper, 66 p.

- Panorama de la Inserción Internacional de América Latina y el Caribe 2015, 102 p.
  Latin America and the Caribbean in the World Economy 2015, 98 p.

Libros y documentos institucionales / *Institutional books and documents*

- Panorama fiscal de América Latina y el Caribe 2016: las finanzas públicas ante el desafío de conciliar austeridad con crecimiento e igualdad, 2016, 90 p.

- Reflexiones sobre el desarrollo en América Latina y el Caribe: conferencias magistrales 2015, 2016, 74 p.

- Panorama Económico y Social de la Comunidad de Estados Latinoamericanos y Caribeños, 2015, 58 p.
  Economic and Social Panorama of the Community of Latin American and Caribbean States 2015, 56 p.

- Desarrollo social inclusivo: una nueva generación de políticas para superar la pobreza y reducir la desigualdad en América Latina y el Caribe, 2015, 180 p.
  Inclusive social development: The next generation of policies for overcoming poverty and reducing inequality in Latin America and the Caribbean, 2015, 172 p.

- Guía operacional para la implementación y el seguimiento del Consenso de Montevideo sobre Población y Desarrollo, 2015, 146 p.
  Operational guide for implementation and follow-up of the Montevideo Consensus on Population and Development, 2015, 139 p.

- América Latina y el Caribe: una mirada al futuro desde los Objetivos de Desarrollo del Milenio. Informe regional de monitoreo de los Objetivos de Desarrollo del Milenio (ODM) en América Latina y el Caribe, 2015, 88 p.
  Latin America and the Caribbean: Looking ahead after the Millennium Development Goals. Regional monitoring report on the Millennium Development Goals in Latin America and the Caribbean, 2015, 88 p.

- La nueva revolución digital: de la Internet del consumo a la Internet de la producción, 2015, 98 p.
  The new digital revolution: From the consumer Internet to the industrial Internet, 2015, 98 p.

- Globalización, integración y comercio inclusivo en América Latina. Textos seleccionados de la CEPAL (2010-2014), 2015, 326 p.

- El desafío de la sostenibilidad ambiental en América Latina y el Caribe. Textos seleccionados de la CEPAL (2012-2014), 2015, 148 p.

- Pactos para la igualdad: hacia un futuro sostenible, 2014, 340 p.
  Covenants for Equality: Towards a sustainable future, 2014, 330 p.

- Cambio estructural para la igualdad: una visión integrada del desarrollo, 2012, 330 p.
  Structural Change for Equality: An integrated approach to development, 2012, 308 p.

- La hora de la igualdad: brechas por cerrar, caminos por abrir, 2010, 290 p.
  Time for Equality: Closing gaps, opening trails, 2010, 270 p.
  A Hora da Igualdade: Brechas por fechar, caminhos por abrir, 2010, 268 p.

Libros de la CEPAL / *ECLAC books*

138 Estructura productiva y política macroeconómica: enfoques heterodoxos desde América Latina, Alicia Bárcena Ibarra, Antonio Prado, Martín Abeles (eds.), 2015, 282 p.

137 Juventud: realidades y retos para un desarrollo con igualdad, Daniela Trucco, Heidi Ullmann (eds.), 2015, 282 p.

136 Instrumentos de protección social: caminos latinoamericanos hacia la universalización, Simone Cecchini, Fernando Filgueira, Rodrigo Martínez, Cecilia Rossel (eds.), 2015, 510 p.

135 *Rising concentration in Asia-Latin American value chains: Can small firms turn the tide?, Osvaldo Rosales, Keiji Inoue, Nanno Mulder (eds.), 2015, 282 p.*

134 Desigualdad, concentración del ingreso y tributación sobre las altas rentas en América Latina, Juan Pablo Jiménez (ed.), 2015, 172 p.

133 Desigualdad e informalidad: un análisis de cinco experiencias latinoamericanas, Verónica Amarante, Rodrigo Arim (eds.), 2015, 526 p.

132 Neoestructuralismo y corrientes heterodoxas en América Latina y el Caribe a inicios del siglo XXI, Alicia Bárcena, Antonio Prado (eds.), 2014, 452 p.

Copublicaciones / *Co-publications*

- Gobernanza global y desarrollo: nuevos desafíos y prioridades de la cooperación internacional, José Antonio Ocampo (ed.), CEPAL/Siglo Veintiuno, Argentina, 2015, 286 p.

- *Decentralization and Reform in Latin America: Improving Intergovernmental Relations, Giorgio Brosio and Juan Pablo Jiménez (eds.), ECLAC / Edward Elgar Publishing, United Kingdom, 2012, 450 p.*

- Sentido de pertenencia en sociedades fragmentadas: América Latina desde una perspectiva global, Martín Hopenhayn y Ana Sojo (comps.), CEPAL / Siglo Veintiuno, Argentina, 2011, 350 p.

Coediciones / *Co-editions*

- Perspectivas económicas de América Latina 2016: hacia una nueva asociación con China, 2015, 240 p.
  Latin American Economic Outlook 2016: Towards a new Partnership with China, 2015, 220 p.

- Perspectivas de la agricultura y del desarrollo rural en las Américas: una mirada hacia América Latina y el Caribe 2015-2016, CEPAL / FAO / IICA, 2015, 212 p.

Documentos de proyecto / *Project documents*

- Complejos productivos y territorio en la Argentina: aportes para el estudio de la geografía económica del país, 2015, 216 p.

- Las juventudes centroamericanas en contextos de inseguridad y violencia: realidades y retos para su inclusión social, Teresita Escotto Quesada, 2015, 168 p.

- La economía del cambio climático en el Perú, 2014, 152 p.

Cuadernos estadísticos de la CEPAL

42 Resultados del Programa de Comparación Internacional (PCI) de 2011 para América Latina y el Caribe. Solo disponible en CD, 2015.

41 Los cuadros de oferta y utilización, las matrices de insumo-producto y las matrices de empleo. Solo disponible en CD, 2013.

Series de la CEPAL / *ECLAC Series*

Asuntos de Género / Comercio Internacional / Desarrollo Productivo / Desarrollo Territorial / Estudios Estadísticos / Estudios y Perspectivas (Bogotá, Brasilia, Buenos Aires, México, Montevideo) / *Studies and Perspectives* (The Caribbean, Washington) / Financiamiento del Desarrollo/ Gestión Pública / Informes y Estudios Especiales / Macroeconomía del Desarrollo / Manuales / Medio Ambiente y Desarrollo / Población y Desarrollo/ Política Fiscal / Políticas Sociales / Recursos Naturales e Infraestructura / Seminarios y Conferencias.

Revista CEPAL / *CEPAL Review*

La Revista se inició en 1976, con el propósito de contribuir al examen de los problemas del desarrollo socioeconómico de la región.
La *Revista CEPAL* se publica en español e inglés tres veces por año.

CEPAL Review first appeared in 1976, its aim being to make a contribution to the study of the economic and social development problems of the region. CEPAL Review is published in Spanish and English versions three times a year.

Observatorio demográfico / *Demographic Observatory*

Edición bilingüe (español e inglés) que proporciona información estadística actualizada, referente a estimaciones y proyecciones de población de los países de América Latina y el Caribe. Desde 2013 el Observatorio aparece una vez al año.

Bilingual publication (Spanish and English) proving up-to-date estimates and projections of the populations of the Latin American and Caribbean countries. Since 2013, the Observatory appears once a year.

Notas de población

Revista especializada que publica artículos e informes acerca de las investigaciones más recientes sobre la dinámica demográfica en la región. También incluye información sobre actividades científicas y profesionales en el campo de población. La revista se publica desde 1973 y aparece dos veces al año, en junio y diciembre.

Specialized journal which publishes articles and reports on recent studies of demographic dynamics in the region. Also includes information on scientific and professional activities in the field of population. Published since 1973, the journal appears twice a year in June and December.

Las publicaciones de la CEPAL están disponibles en:
ECLAC publications are available at:

www.cepal.org/publicaciones

También se pueden adquirir a través de:
They can also be ordered through:

www.un.org/publications

United Nations Publications
PO Box 960
Herndon, VA 20172
USA

Tel. (1-888)254-4286
Fax (1-800)338-4550
Contacto / *Contact*: publications@un.org
Pedidos / *Orders*: order@un.org